Composers of North America

Series Editors: Sam Dennison, William C. Loring, Margery Lowens, Ezra Schabas

No. 1 *William Wallace Gilchrist,* by Martha Furman Schleifer

No. 2 *Energy and Individuality in the Art of Anna Huntington, Sculptor, and Amy Beach, Composer,* by Myrna G. Eden

No. 3 *Ruth Crawford Seeger: Memoirs, Memories, Music,* by Matilda Gaume

No. 4 *A Musical American Romantic Abroad: Templeton Strong and His Music,* by William C. Loring

RUTH CRAWFORD SEEGER:
Memoirs, Memories, Music

by
MATILDA GAUME

Composers of North America, No. 3

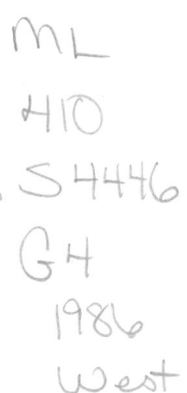

**The Scarecrow Press, Inc.
Metuchen, N.J., & London
1986**

FRONTISPIECE: Ruth Crawford Seeger, ca. 1948

Grateful acknowledgment is hereby made for permission to reprint the following items:

Excerpt from page ix of The American Songbag by Carl Sandburg, copyright 1927 by Harcourt Brace Jovanovich, Inc., renewed 1955 by Carl Sandburg. Reprinted by permission of the publisher.

Excerpt from the April 9, 1931, edition of the Daily News (New York City): "Music in Berlin" by Edward Ansel Mowrer. Copyright 1931 New York Daily News. Reprinted by permission.

Guest register for the MacDowell Colony, Peterborough, New Hampshire, Summer 1929. Reprinted by permission of the MacDowell Colony, Inc.

Transcript of the question-and-answer period following the concert sponsored by the Composers Forum-Laboratory in New York City, April 6, 1938. Reprinted courtesy of the National Archives, Washington, D.C.

Excerpt from book review by B.A.B. [Ben Botkin] of American Folk Songs for Children by Ruth Crawford Seeger in the New York Folklore Quarterly, Spring 1954, pp. 73-4. Reprinted by permission of the New York Folklore Society and the Editor of New York Folklore.

Excerpt from an unsigned music review in the May 25, 1933, issue of Musical America. Reprinted by permission of the publisher.

Excerpts from "A Budding Composer in New York," by Matilda Gaume, to be published in the periodical American Music. Used by permission of the University of Illinois Press.

Excerpt from letter of Nicolas Slonimsky to Ruth Crawford, dated March 16, 1932. Used by permission.

(acknowledgments cont'd on next page)

Library of Congress Cataloging-in-Publication Data

Gaume, Matilda, 1910-
    Ruth Crawford Seeger : memoirs, memories, music.

    (Composers of North America ; no. 3)
    Bibliography: p.
    Discography: p.
    Includes index.
    1. Seeger, Ruth Crawford, 1901-1953. 2. Composers--United States--Biography. I. Title. II. Series.
ML410.S4446G4   1986   780'.92'4 [B]   86-15632
ISBN 0-8108-1917-1

Copyright © 1986 by Matilda Gaume

Manufactured in the United States of America

Excerpt from Virgil Thomson's review in the New York Herald Tribune, March 16, 1949. Used by permission of the author.

Excerpts from Frederick Jacobi's letter to Ruth Crawford Seeger, dated June 18, 1933. Used by permission of Frederick A. Jacobi, Jr.

Excerpts from the interview tapes made for the author by Margaret Valiant, May 29, 1980. Used by permission.

Excerpts from Stella Roberts' letter of January 8, 1972, to the author. Used by permission.

To the Estate of Ruth Crawford Seeger, for permission to use the following materials: Piano Prelude No. 3, Suite for Small Orchestra, Suite No. 2 for Piano and Strings, Loam (from Five Songs to poems of Carl Sandburg), Chant, No. 3, Rissolty, Rossolty, and John Henry (from American Folk Songs for Children); letters, diaries, programs, photographs, newspaper and periodical clippings, autobiographical information, poems, memorabilia, and miscellaneous information, found in the Seeger Collection (SC), Music Division, Library of Congress (Wc); letters from the Seeger Family Collection (SFC); also Ruth's letters to Gerald Reynolds, housed in the New York Public Library, and relevant materials from the Guggenheim Foundation.

To the Crawfords,

Carl and Katherine,

and the Seegers,

Charles, Michael, Peggy,

Barbara, and Penelope

CONTENTS

Foreword ix
Preface xi
Introduction xv

PART I: THE LIFE OF RUTH CRAWFORD SEEGER

1. Background, Early Life, and Training
   (1901-1921) 3
2. The Chicago Years (1921-1924) 19
3. The Chicago Years (1924-1929) 34
4. MacDowell Colony (Summer 1929) and
   New York (1929-1930) 57
5. The European Experience (1930-1931) 73
6. Back in New York (1931-1935) 90
7. Life and Death in Washington, D.C.
   (1935-1953) 104

PART II: THE WORKS OF RUTH CRAWFORD SEEGER

8. Art Music 131
9. Folk Music Activities 173
10. Selected Writings 189

PART III: END PAPERS

Chapter Notes 223
Catalog of Music 236
Additional Folk Music Articles 244
Discography 245
Bibliography 247

Index 255

FOREWORD

This biographical series is designed to focus attention on significant North American composers from colonial times until the present. Few had their works performed frequently during their lifetime; all have suffered from undeserved neglect.

Each volume consists of a substantial essay about the composer and a complete catalog of compositions. The essay deals with the composer's life and works in the context of the artistic thought and musical world of his or her time. Critical comments by contemporaries are included, as are illustrations and musical examples. Some works which merit performance today are singled out for analysis and discussion. The catalog of the composer's output has full publication details, locations of unpublished works and, where necessary, incipits.

We hope that this series will make its readers more conscious and appreciative of our North American musical heritage and serve as a guide to performing musicians seeking works of interest.

Sam Dennison
William C. Loring
Margery M. Lowens
Ezra Schabas

Series Editors

PREFACE

Ruth Crawford Seeger (1901-1953), American composer of distinction, was also a person of outstanding talent in several other areas. A woman of quiet charm and great determination, she was also well versed in the fine art of living. I first became acquainted with her work as a composer during my student days through the pages of Modern Music, every issue of which I eagerly devoured. Some years after the earliest recording of her string quartet (1934), I developed an interest in her music which eventually became the subject of intensive study on my part.

The guiding spirit behind my decision to investigate as thoroughly as possible all aspects of Ruth Crawford Seeger's life, both personal and professional, is an ongoing interest in the vital personality of this woman who developed so dramatically both as a person and as a musician. I have tried to collect all of Ruth's diaries, correspondence, random jottings, and her published and unpublished writings, as well as her music--manuscripts, printed editions, and recordings. Further, I have tried to locate as many living voices from her past as possible. I have also collected and studied the small amount of printed material concerning her available at the present time. All these materials have been meshed with those of a more general historical nature to draw a picture of Ruth Crawford Seeger within the framework of her time.

The story of Ruth Crawford Seeger is here told for anyone interested in the making of an American musician and the fascinating environment of the yesterdays which nurtured her development--the musical avant-garde of the time. Her story presents a refreshing view of a segment of modern music history as seen through the eyes of a young woman from

Middle America. Ruth herself often provided material for this narrative, drawing as it does on her personal, often homey and intimate, thoughts on the musical life of the period. After several chapters relating to her life and times, there follow discussions of her creative activities in the field of music. These are introductory in nature and are not intended to present an in-depth study of either her art or folk music activities. I have tried, however, to convey some of the most important aspects of her compositional style and her treatment of folk materials. I have also endeavored to evaluate her contributions to and her place in the development of an American music. For the convenience of readers of varying interests, I have placed the discussion of the music in separate chapters. The selections from Ruth's writings presented in Chapter 10 offer fascinating and enlightening glimpses of her daily activities and thought patterns.

ACKNOWLEDGMENTS

Many people have contributed to the realization of this book. I would like to express my gratitude to Dr. John Reeves White, who suggested Ruth Crawford Seeger as a topic for my doctoral dissertation, and Dr. Malcolm Brown, who so capably directed its actual writing (a detailed analysis of Ruth's art compositions); both supported my idea of expanding the original study. My editor, Dr. William C. Loring, has made many welcome suggestions and offered needed advice on countless details, all gratefully received. His patience and encouragement have helped tremendously.

For permission to quote from their recollections of Ruth Crawford (Seeger) I owe a special thank-you to Althea Parmenter, a high-school friend of Ruth from Jacksonville, Florida, days; Albert Hirsh, who supplied the photograph of Madame Djane Lavoie Herz, as well as recollections of her as his piano teacher; Vivian Fine, Martha Beck Carragan, Dane Rudhyar, and Alfred Frankenstein, all of whom knew Ruth from her Chicago days until her death; Chuck Miller and Kathy Shimberg, piano students of Ruth in the Washington, D.C., area, and Sidney Robertson Cowell, Alan Lomax, and Peter Seeger, all associated with Ruth during her years of involvement with folk music. I am also grateful to Radiana Pazmor, Alan Stout, Rae Korson, and Grace Welsh, all of whom added their individual reminiscences of Ruth.

Mr. Edward N. Waters, Mr. Don Leavitt, Mr. Wayne Shirley, Mrs. Ann McLean, and others in the Music Division of the Library of Congress have been most cooperative, as has the Guggenheim Foundation, the staff of the New York Public Library, the Manuscript Division, Library of Congress, and the Humboldt (Nevada) County Clerk's Office.

Several colleagues at West Texas State University and other friends helped in various ways: Dr. Joe Nelson, an accomplished composer himself, discussed with me the theoretical and compositional aspects of Ruth's works. Dr. Charmazel Dudt not only lent her critical eye to the reading of the entire manuscript but she also helped to initiate me into the intricacies of Hindu word meanings. Dr. Garrett Welch provided translations from German; my good friend Margaret Harper shared her knowledge of Spanish and Portuguese. Elizabeth Davidson, who became well acquainted with the dramatis personae through hearing step-by-step reports of my research, spent many hours patiently reading and re-reading various drafts of the manuscript. The entire staff of the Cornette Library at West Texas State University has been helpful in more ways than I can enumerate; special mention, however, must be made of the expertise of Miss Patricia Donovan and capable coworkers in the reference and interlibrary loan divisions, Mrs. Faye Hendrickson, microfilm division, and Mrs. Wanda Vanvalkenberg, periodicals. My special thanks go also to Mrs. Martha Morris, head of the Music Library at West Texas State University, who, among other things, has patiently and expertly untangled more audio tapes for me than I care to remember. Two grants from the Organized Research Committee at the university aided tremendously in my acquaintance with and intensive study of Ruth's scores.

Above all, I would like to thank the members of Ruth's family for having supplied invaluable information. Through the courtesy of Ruth's brother and his wife, Carl and Katherine Crawford, as well as the kindness of Barbara Seeger Perfect, I have had access to generous amounts of materials relating largely to Ruth Crawford's youth and young womanhood, as well as to the Graves and Crawford families; even more important were Barbara's and Carl's reminiscences of their mother and sister. The executors of the estate of Ruth Crawford Seeger have graciously permitted me the use of materials in the possession of or under the jurisdiction of the Seeger family, as well as materials now contained in the Seeger

Collection, Music Division, Library of Congress. Unless otherwise indicated, the photographs are used courtesy of the Crawford and Seeger families. Michael and Penny have added their recollections of growing up in the Seeger household and their valuable insights into Ruth's personality and character; Peggy has recounted extensive memories of her mother, which helped immeasurably to fill out the picture of Ruth as, to borrow Carl Sandburg's words, "a rare mother." Charles Seeger has also supplied a summary of Ruth Crawford's study with him and of her musical development from 1929 onward. He has also furnished extensive printed materials concerning Ruth's works and professional activities. His information concerning himself and his own family helped to build a background for their lives together. Perhaps most important are his reminiscences of Ruth contained in his letters to me and in in our extensive conversations which both of us enjoyed thoroughly. He was indispensable!

M.G.

INTRODUCTION

The history of twentieth-century American music can no longer be written without including at least two, and perhaps more, members of the Seeger family. Their names are known in both art and folk music circles--as scholars, composers, and performers. Undoubtedly, Ruth Crawford Seeger is one of the most outstanding figures in this musically prominent family. Born Ruth Crawford, married to Charles Seeger, she is today held in high regard by all who know her and her accomplishments.

Ruth Crawford was a true child of the twentieth century. Born when it was still emerging from the dying Romanticism of the nineteenth, she spent her early years in an atmosphere of traditional values, disturbed only by her brother Carl's involvement in the terrible conflict that was WWI. As the country changed its pace and began to enjoy such new inventions as the phonograph, the radio, and the motor car in the early twenties, Ruth started her ventures into the wider world when she went from Florida to the big city of Chicago. Here she found herself once more in a rather conservative atmosphere provided by the American Conservatory of Music, a bastion of old-world musical values. By the late 1920s, however, her perspective began to broaden to include the new and the experimental that was taking place, especially in the field of music. While she was not often to be personally affected by major events and seldom recorded her reactions to them, her destiny was nonetheless shaped by several of them. The Jazz Age and the Prohibition Era did not noticeably touch her; the Great Depression did. Communism did color her thinking as did the social reforms of the New Deal. During this period "the people" became important and the cultivation of folk arts flourished. Political panaceas for economic trouble were provided by Communism which grasped the opportunity to infiltrate the thinking of our intellectual leaders, and unions became strong and powerful.

All this was changed with the bombing of Pearl Harbor on December 7, 1941, when the country was united in a common cause against the enemy of Fascism and military spending propelled the country back to prosperity. And once again Americans fought--this time in a global conflict. The years of WWII saw Ruth struggling for the financial survival of her family, saw her caught up in the grassroots movement with her involvement in the folk music renaissance, while the years of the Korean War and the big Red scare--the closing years of her life--brought a mixture of distress and success. She died very young, but not before her accomplishments assured her a niche of her own in the history of our country's culture.

Ruth Crawford Seeger is now considered one of the important American modernists, belonging to the generation of composers who formed the advance guard of the 1920s, including Cowell, Varèse, Riegger, Ruggles, George Antheil, Adolph Weiss, and Aaron Copland. Rather frequent performances of her works were heard in the late twenties and the thirties, many of which, however, received something less than a musically perceptive reading. Some critics, to be sure, wrote favorable reviews, notably Marion Bauer and Nicolas Slonimsky; others failed to comprehend what the composer was trying to impart in her music. From the late thirties until her death, Ruth also earned the admiration and gratitude of her peers for her scholarly folk song transcriptions and arrangements as well as almost immediate critical acclaim for her several books of folk songs for children. During the late sixties, Ruth Crawford Seeger was rediscovered by a new generation, and from the seventies on her works received good public performances, good recordings, and favorable press comments. Doubtless, the new interest in women's place in our society, both past and present, facilitated recognition of Ruth's very real accomplishments. She proved that an unknown and a woman could write inspired, worthwhile, even valuable music and contribute minor masterpieces to music's repertoire.

Ruth was not only a child of her times; in retrospect, she was almost a spokeswoman for them. In fact, she was an avant-garde kind of person much of her life, though again, she doubtless did not think of herself as such. In her own

Introduction xvii

mind, she was just Ruth Crawford, an ordinary person, seeking the things ordinary people wanted. But--and perhaps she did not ever fully realize this--she was also an extraordinary person in many ways--in her sensitivity, her introspection, her philosophical bent, her intellectual interests, her social consciousness, her consuming interest in the experimental, all tempered by her sober, balanced, outlook on life. As a young person, Ruth had characterized herself as a bundle of contradictions--and so she remained. She was a fascinating combination of the dreamer and the doer, the old and the new, the conservative and the radical. Ruth's willingness to grasp every opportunity for self-improvement and to adapt herself to whatever situations she faced, her talent in overcoming any handicaps related to her sex, and her accomplishments as a composer, author, transcriber and arranger, and teacher, mark her as a woman of unusual stature.

Ruth Crawford Seeger contributed a solid core of durable musical ideas which have helped to enrich America's cultural legacy. She provides a good example of what Eric Salzman aptly referred to as the "tradition of the new in American music."[1]

PART I:

THE LIFE OF RUTH CRAWFORD SEEGER

Chapter One

BACKGROUND, EARLY LIFE, AND TRAINING
(1901-1921)

"What is the soul? When it leaves the body we do not see it. And where is God? Everywhere? But what is he? Why can't I know all these things? Because thou shouldst then know as much as God. Yes, true. But how--how I want to know it all."
(Ruth Crawford, diary entry, January 6, 1918)

Ruth Crawford, the sixteen-year-old author of the quotation above, early displayed an unquenchable intellectual curiosity and an uncommonly strong zest for life's adventures. Destined to achieve recognition as an outstanding American composer, her first ambition was to become a writer, a "poetess" --one which she pursued throughout her high-school days and continued to nurse in one way or another during most of her life. Stories and poems flowed from her pen, although daily events were often more engrossing than any story she might write. She was also an inveterate letter writer and keeper of diaries. Family, social, and business correspondence provided innumerable occasions to record the outward events of her life; her diaries and other less formal writings gave her opportunities to record her thoughts and philosophical musings.

Circumstances, however, led her to pursue a career in music. Starting in her late teens, her musical talent provided her with an opportunity to earn much-needed money as a piano teacher. Piano teaching continued through most of her days to provide Ruth with adequate financial resources to allow her to develop her musical talents in other directions.

Only in approximately her last decade did she have occasion to combine literary and musical interests. This occurred when she prepared the introductory and explanatory materials for several books in the field of folk music.

Despite all the words Ruth put to paper, she left very few written references to relatives other than members of her immediate family. Her brother, Carl, was the keeper of the family records. Through him we learn that Ruth's paternal grandfather, Thomas Crawford, was born in Monroe, then Virginia, now West Virginia, on April 27, 1827. His wife was born Eliza Porter, in Kanawha County, August 13, 1831. Grandfather Crawford was reputed to be a very prosperous farmer near Fairfield, West Virginia. On his modest farm, possibly 200 acres, he raised such products as corn, lettuce, and potatoes. Grandmother Crawford was quite a religious person, though without the dedication that developed in Ruth's father. Ruth's acquaintance with the elder Crawfords could not have been very extensive since her own father died when she was thirteen and, after his death, there was not much visiting back and forth between granddaughter and grandparents.

Of the several children (five boys and three girls) born to Thomas and Eliza Porter Crawford, Ruth's father, Clark, was the oldest, born June 11, 1854. Clark later told his son, Carl, that he felt a call to the ministry as he sat in front of the fireplace one evening playing cards. Clark was the only one of the eight children to become thus associated with the church; the others were involved largely with mining and railroading activities.

By the time he was twenty-two, Clark Crawford was a licensed traveling minister of the Methodist Episcopal Church. He then put himself through two small colleges and later attended Ohio Wesleyan and Drew Theological Seminary. Excerpts from several resolutions passed by church committees indicate his wide and popular acceptance by the congregations he served. These included such places as Morgantown, West Virginia, Providence, Rhode Island, and subsequently Pasadena, California.

Ruth's maternal grandparents were the Reverend William Plummer Graves and his wife, Mary Unity Fletcher Graves. Reverend Graves was born in Elizabethtown, New York on

Background, Early Life, and Training 5

November 4, 1819, where he spent his early years on his father's farm. He taught school until he was twenty-one at which time he decided to enter the ministry. In preparation for his new vocation, he entered the Troy Conference Academy at West Poultney, Vermont, where he later became a teacher as well as a student.

Mary Unity Fletcher was born in Shelburne, Vermont, on December 22, 1819. She obtained her early education in the public schools of Shelburne and later taught there. Mary studied further at the Troy Conference Academy, where she met her future husband. Their marriage took place on October 4, 1847, in the bride's home near Shelburne Falls.

Reverend Graves's pastoral assignments brought him from Vermont across the midwest and eventually to Pasadena, California, where he retired in 1893. It was during his pastorate in Victoria, Illinois, that Ruth's mother, Clara Alletta, fifth in a family of four girls and two boys, was born on December 9, 1859. She attended public schools in several small towns in Illinois and later went to Northwestern University in Evanston, Illinois. Like her mother and father, Clara taught school for several years. She later went to Colorado from Illinois with one of her brothers where she became "one of those first female stenographers." She thus earned money to buy a pump organ and later a Sohmer piano which daughter Ruth eventually used for piano practice.[1] It is significant too, in the light of Ruth's own family life, that her mother played the piano each evening as a signal that it was time for Ruth to go upstairs to bed.[2]

When the Graves decided to retire, Clara went with them to California, and the family became members of the First Methodist Church in Pasadena where Clark Crawford was at the time serving as minister. Subsequently, Clark Crawford and Clara Alletta Graves were married. Little detail of Clara's meeting, acquaintance with, and courtship by Clark Crawford has been recorded, but Carl recalls his mother's description of their first encounter. As Clara, who was a beautiful young woman, walked down the aisle of the church one Sunday morning, her glance met the glance of the young minister. Apparently it was love at first sight on his part; whether Clara responded immediately in like manner we do not know; that she ultimately responded positively is evidenced by the fact that their wedding took place on January 17, 1895.

Mr. and Mrs. Clark Crawford, wedding photograph (January 1895, Pasadena, California)

Clark and Clara Crawford had two children, a boy and a girl. Carl, the son, was born in 1895 while the couple still lived in Pasadena. From Pasadena they moved to East Liverpool, Ohio, and it was here that Ruth Porter Crawford was born on July 3, 1901. In a pattern familiar to parsonage life, the Crawford family moved often. At the father's death, they had also lived in Akron, Ohio; St. Louis, Missouri; Muncie and Bluffton, Indiana; and finally Jacksonville, Florida, where the family moved in 1912.[3]

Ruth's parents could be considered as upper middle class, both socially and economically. They were both well educated and, since her father was a minister, they were accorded a prominent place in the communities where they lived. To judge from the homes in which Ruth was raised, with their cheerful gardens and family pets (cats were Ruth's special

Background, Early Life, and Training

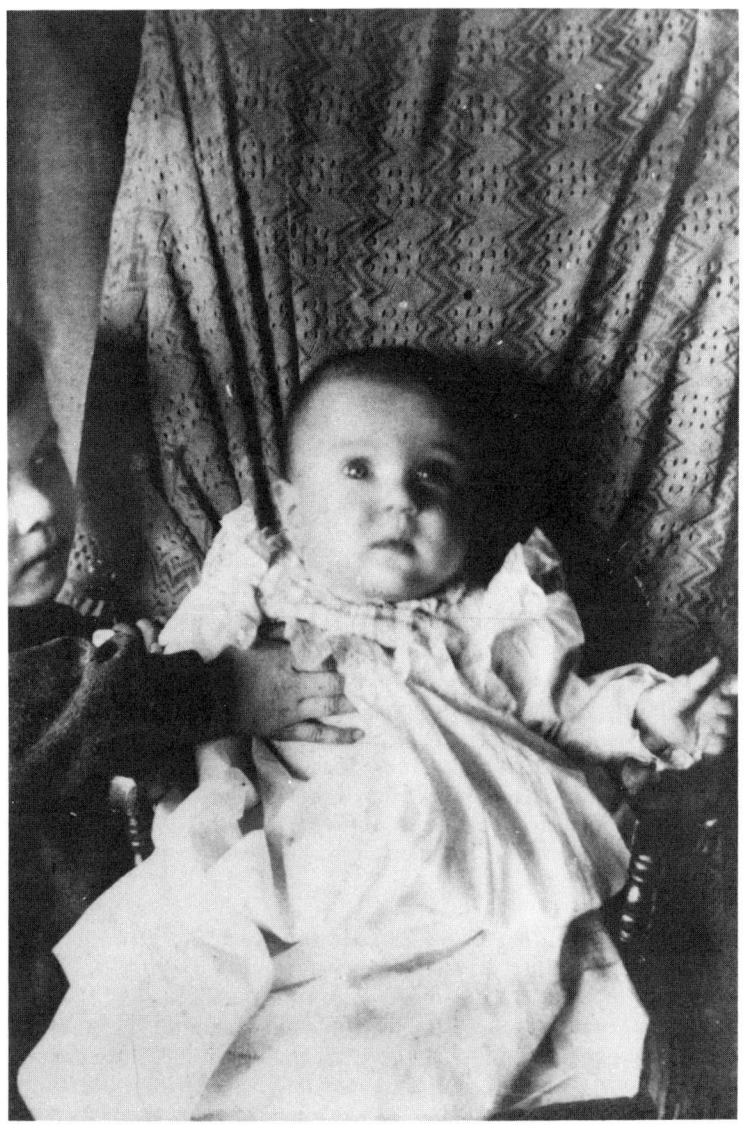

Ruth Porter Crawford (Carl at her side), at age five months (East Liverpool, Ohio)

favorites), they seemed also to enjoy a degree of economic security and, though not affluent, they were at least comfortably situated. Ruth inherited her mother's good looks and her personality. Family photographs show Ruth to be a beautiful baby, a good-looking if somewhat plain teenager, and a very pretty young woman. She possessed her mother's devotion to a cause, her love of the arts, and her determination to achieve her goals against the odds. From her father she received a studious disposition, an interest in things intellectual, and his concern for the welfare of people in general.

Ruth's own recollections of her early years give a vivid picture of this period of her life. In Muncie she enjoyed playing the usual childhood games and attending the Sunday School picnics, while she merely endured the ordeal of getting dressed in her finery for Sunday School classes. As special treats, she enjoyed chocolate sodas and chewing gum, that "forbidden thing." When she was six, her mother gave her her first darning lesson and--far more exciting--took her to her first piano lesson.[4]

From Ruth's ninth year on, Mr. Crawford started to suffer failing health and by the fall of 1912, he began receiving treatment at the Mayo Clinic in Rochester, Minnesota, preliminary to a prostate operation. The summer after the family moved to Jacksonville, Reverend Crawford returned to Mayo's for the removal of his right kidney; his death occurred the following year. Ruth was not allowed many years in which to know her father, but as a young girl, she was aware of his interest in people, his cheerfulness, and his studiousness.[5]

With Mr. Crawford's death, the economic situation changed somewhat, and Mrs. Crawford was faced with the prospect of supporting her two children and herself. Clara Crawford was not one to allow adversity to alter her course of action very long, so she rented a large three-story house in downtown Jacksonville and operated this as a rooming house. She was thus able to keep a home for the children and to provide them with the necessities, and even a few niceties, of life. She was a good mother, a good homemaker, and a determined woman who worked long and hard to achieve her goals. In these and other respects, she provided Ruth with a model for her own family relationships.

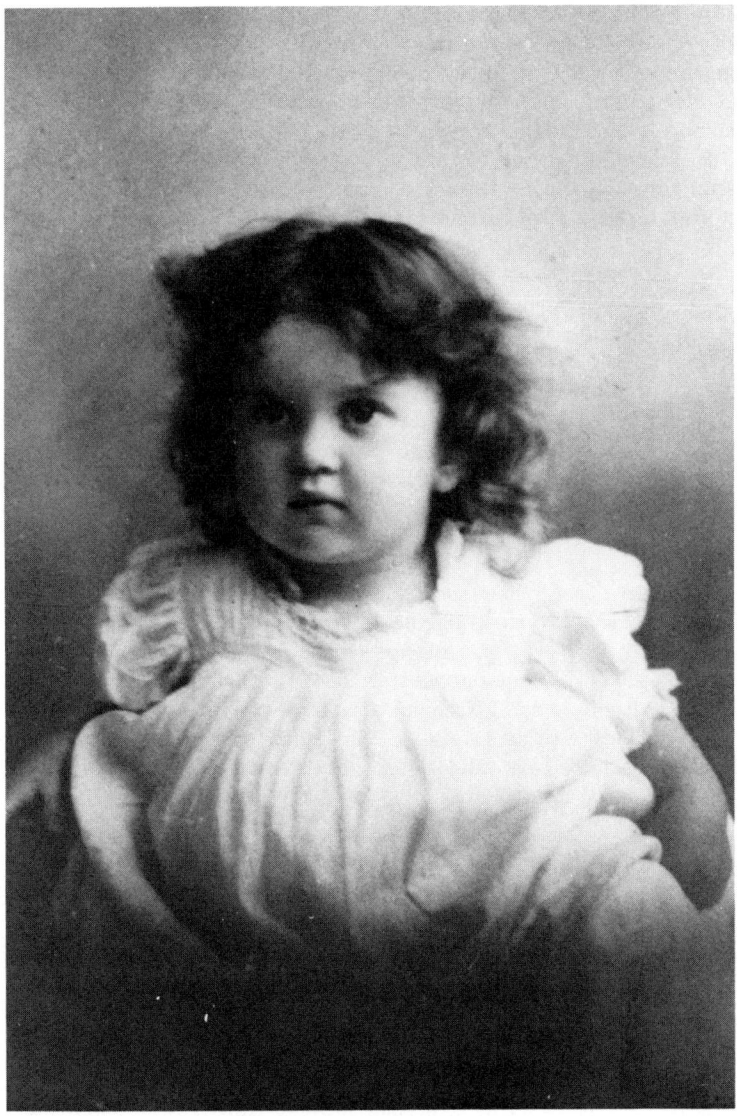

Ruth Porter Crawford at age two

By the time Ruth entered Duvall High School in Jacksonville as a freshman in the fall of 1914, she had become a serious and introspective person. Even as a young girl she demanded much of herself and strove earnestly to improve her attitudes and habits. Her tirades against herself are relentless in their analysis and exposition of her weaknesses. Her frank admission of her tendency to become impatient and annoyed with small things is interesting in light of later comments to this same effect made by her family.

> Oh dear me! I wish I liked myself better! Faulty temper, lack of will power, increasing irritability in trifles, listlessness, neglect of duty as to sewing, lack of system in my work, bent to putting off unpleasant tasks: are these faults not enough to make a person dislike herself. You are so pleasant and smiling in company, Ruth--the very picture of amiability and good will. But when by yourself, the very smallest thing irritates you.... Can't you mend your ways?[6]

Her strong sense of social consciousness and her feeling for humanity in general, coupled with a close affinity with nature, were part of her personality from her very tender years. Most impressive of all, perhaps, was her ability to detach herself from petty, everyday trifles, and to view herself as one small soul in a sea of humanity, assessing herself with remarkable insight and objectivity in relation to the world in general.

Although Ruth's brother, Carl, was the socialite in the family and liked the girls and parties and fun, Ruth was not unaware of these things. They had a place in her life, albeit not the same place they had for Carl. She liked boys, but was not sure just how to create situations which would involve her with those in whom she was interested. One of Ruth's earliest romances was with a boy named Kenneth Huffaker, who apparently was only mildly interested in the serious young scholar-musician. One evening after orchestra practice (Ruth was at the time playing piano in a small group of amateur musicians who rehearsed weekly) Kenneth asked if he might walk home with her. She was elated and excited and "had a grand time, save for one thing, which spoils the whole evening for me almost; my hat was on crooked!!!"[7] Carl, who was conscious of the differences in personality

Ruth with her mother and father (Muncie, Indiana, 1907)

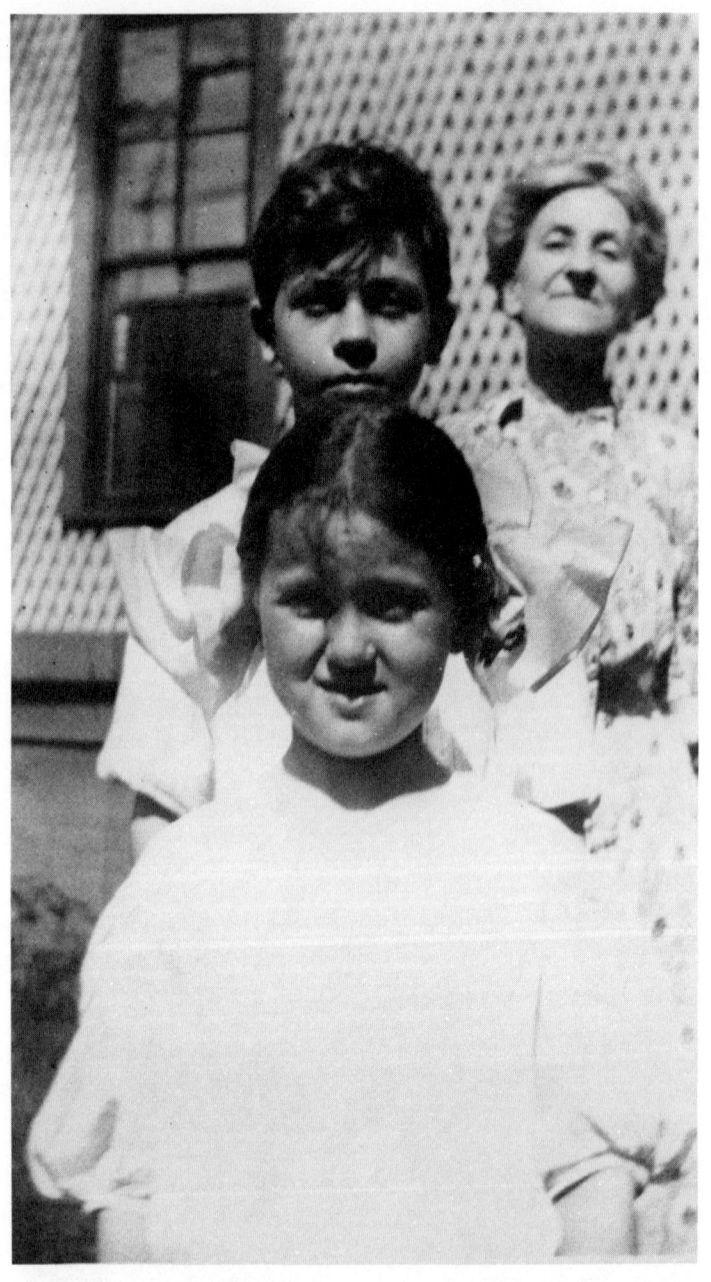

Ruth and Carl with Aunt Libby, their mother's oldest sister (Muncie, 1909)

Background, Early Life, and Training

between him and his sister, gave Ruth some advice which she valued enough to consider seriously:

> Yes, Ruth, if you want to be popular with the boys, you've got to get some pep! Be vivacious and lively and a good sport. Meet people every chance you get, make acquaintances with girls who know all about such things.... You've got to be interesting, so interesting that they'll <u>want</u> to come to see you.[8]

There is no indication that Ruth ever felt repressed or deprived in her early years. She was a happy, if sober, child and enjoyed the love and attention of her parents and brother. Luckily for posterity, her introspective nature, her self-searching, aided by her ability and willingness to confide in her diary, caused Ruth to commit to paper comments which provide valuable insights into her thought patterns.

"Today the world seems entirely different from yesterday." October 1, 1917, was indeed an eventful day for Ruth. She entered her senior year in Duvall High School, enrolling in five courses--French, Latin, English literature, psychology, and How to Study, even though she felt that her eyes were not strong enough to study so many subjects.[9] This is the first indication of an eye weakness which remained with Ruth throughout her life. No explanation was ever offered as to exactly what her eye trouble might have been; further, no photograph ever shows Ruth wearing eyeglasses. Ruth felt that by the time she was a senior she had made strides in her battle with her earlier feelings of inferiority. She had been shy and uncommunicative and felt she was unattractive--ugly even--but she had now decided she was as good as anyone else and would not put herself down any more. She had changed her outlook on life and she liked the changed person she felt herself to be.

During her senior year, Ruth served as class historian and directed the senior class play. She also maintained her interest in writing, submitting poems and articles to <u>The Oracle</u>, the school paper, which she had served as a staff member throughout her high-school career. "Knowledge is power" is the very appropriate motto which appeared with her senior class picture.[10]

Ruth Crawford at age fourteen (Jacksonville, Florida)

Background, Early Life, and Training					15

Not long after the family settled in Jacksonville, Ruth had resumed her piano study, had become deeply interested in it, and had started practicing intensively. Perhaps her most influential piano teacher in Jacksonville was Miss Bertha Foster, who operated her own school of music. Madame Valborg Collett, another of Ruth's teachers at Miss Foster's school, whom Ruth described as "a beloved but much-feared Leipsic-trained Norwegian teacher,"[11] inspired Ruth to add an even more serious note to her practicing. Ruth's later application for a Guggenheim fellowship states that she also studied with Beryl Rubenstein for six weeks in Jacksonville in 1919. A further word about Bertha Foster--although she was the only "hometown" piano teacher Ruth studied with for an extended time and thus lacked the glamour of a foreign name and foreign ways, Miss Foster was apparently a person with great strength of character, strong convictions, and a woman of action. Ruth seemed to assume that Miss Foster belonged in the same hierarchy as her own family. In addition, Miss Foster had studied music abroad as well as in the United States so had something more than a provincial outlook to pass on to her talented students. She apparently took an active role in the musical activities of Jacksonville. She not only had a well-qualified faculty at her School of Musical Art, but under her sponsorship, the school launched a concert series for several seasons in the late teens and early twenties and maintained a correspondent with the Chicago-based Musical Leader, who reported musical activities in Jacksonville. One such correspondent, "W.M.," wrote of a "lecture recital by Mrs. Edward MacDowell who comes here March 31 under the auspices of Miss Bertha Foster, director of the School of Musical Art."[12] It is quite likely that Ruth had her first of several contacts with Mrs. MacDowell at this time. Ruth herself mentions hearing such visiting artists as Grainger, Paderewski, and Hoffman.

At the beginning of her senior year, Miss Foster offered Ruth a teaching position at the School of Musical Art for the year following her graduation which pleased Ruth and her mother very much, as they both hoped Ruth would somehow be able to develop and use her musical talent further.[13] At his time, Ruth also changed piano teachers from Miss Foster to Madame Collett, who made a strong impression on her. Probably Madame Collett gave Ruth her first contact with a foreign accent and manners, which both fascinated and awed the young student. Ruth's first lesson with Madame was pleasant enough, but the second was a rather traumatic experience, and Ruth was not

sure she wanted to assume the responsible practicing which
Madame indicated she expected. After writing a detailed
description of the lesson, Ruth admitted that she had come
from this experience feeling dejected and exhausted.[14] It
is not easy to assess the quality of piano instruction Ruth
received at the School of Musical Art, particularly from
Madame Collett. Ruth later felt that perhaps Madame Collett's
emphasis on striving for perfection might have caused her
natural self-consciousness to become more pronounced.[15]
Further, the fact that she sought help from both osteopathic
and electrical treatments for tense, cramped muscles during
this time would indicate that Ruth did not feel physically
free in her approach to the keyboard.[16] As we shall see,
muscular tension in her arms was to plague Ruth throughout
her piano playing career. However, Madame Collett did give
Ruth an added impetus to serious piano study and helped her
practice habits, particularly in the area of planned and con-
sistent fingering.

Ruth had started teaching piano the summer before her
last year in high school and had felt quite elated that she
was able to earn even a small amount of money (between
$7.00 and $8.00 a month) as it made her feel a little more
worthwhile.[17] The summer after her graduation Ruth also
took lessons in teacher training in preparation for her new
position as assistant at the School of Musical Art scheduled
to start in September. And for the next three years, she
continued to both give and take piano lessons. Her teachers
at the school urged her to save her money and go to New
York or Chicago and study with Godowsky or Harold Bauer.[18]
During this time, Ruth also took a few harmony lessons
which she thoroughly enjoyed--presumably with Bertha Foster, who taught harmony at the school--and made several
attempts at writing musical compositions, including <u>Elf Dance</u>,
Variations, and <u>Whirligig</u>. So far as is known, none of these
early works survives--Ruth does mention them, however, later
on in her letters to her mother from Chicago. Ruth long remembered her teachers at the School of Musical Art, especially Miss Foster, who later earned the admiration of one of
Ruth's most particular critics, her husband, Charles Seeger.

The family financial situation was gradually changing
again. Carl was now old enough to support himself, and
Ruth was partially self-supporting. Mrs. Crawford no longer
felt it was necessary to operate the rooming house, which she

Background, Early Life, and Training 17

had done since her husband's death, and she and Ruth were now settled in a comfortable bungalow in Jacksonville. The future seemed secure enough--teaching piano was a satisfying if not a highly lucrative occupation for a talented young pianist and prospects in Jacksonville were promising. This might have been the end of Ruth Crawford's story if a small amount of money had not been made available to Ruth--enough to send her away to study music for one year.[19] One can only speculate regarding the source of this windfall. It is not likely that her colleagues at the School of Musical Art were involved. Had they been, there would doubtless have been some notice of such an honor in the local newspapers. Nor would Carl have yet been in a position to support his sister financially, although many times in later years, he sent her either money or gifts. It is possible that someone in her father's family might have been her benefactor--there was an uncle who was reputed to have had much money and a cousin, Nellie Hastings, who sent her money while she was in Europe and whom, in fact, Ruth visited in Europe when Nellie made a trip there in 1931.[20]

Also, one can only speculate why Ruth chose Chicago rather than New York for further music study. A Chicago magazine was regularly reporting on musical events in Jacksonville, Ruth's mother had studied at Northwestern University in the Chicago suburb of Evanston and was thus familiar with the area--all or none of which may have influenced her decision.

The oft-made comment that it is remarkable that a person coming from such a limited background should accomplish what Ruth did and develop so dramatically fails to take into consideration that this person of many talents was also extremely sensitive to her situation and responded more deeply and more quickly than might be expected. An unusual group of people--mostly women--surrounded Ruth and provided sound guidance for the development of her talents. Opportunities for musical experiences in Jacksonville were limited, yes, but the right people--people with vision--can be as influential in Jacksonville as in Chicago or New York. Both her teachers and her parents were above average in intelligence. Her mother, who guided her alone from age thirteen, was a forward-looking, perceptive person who was completely wrapped up in her daughter and the development of her talents. Miss Foster, her mentor in matters musical, shared Mrs. Crawford's

interest in Ruth. She, too, was forward-looking, and she
helped to implant in Ruth's mind the spark that kindled her
interest in further music study. It is to Ruth's credit that
she was able to derive from these people concepts which
helped her rise above the ordinary. So Ruth took her first
step into the unknown. We can imagine that she did so with
the same sense of adventure and zeal which she exhibited
throughout her life as new opportunities were opened up to
her.

   This rather shy girl, somewhat unsure of herself socially and admittedly highly sensitive and self-conscious, was
nonetheless strongly motivated to cultivate her interests and
break the confines of a provincial city, her hometown of
Jacksonville, Florida. She had a kind of intuitive feeling
which led her, all her life, to push beyond her present condition and to discover whatever new adventures might be
awaiting her.

Chapter Two

THE CHICAGO YEARS
(1921-1924)

"I think and think--Am I doing wrong to stay up here? To whom is my duty greater--my mother or what talent I possess?" (Ruth Crawford, in a letter to her mother, February 9, 1923)

During the decade of the twenties, Chicago enjoyed a reputation as an important musical center, boasting superior accomplishments in the orchestral, operatic, recital, and educational fields. The Chicago opera productions had been compared favorably not only with those of New York's Metropolitan, but with those of any in the entire world. Its roster of singers was so outstanding that the Met begged the Chicago company to share with it some of its great names.[1] Frederick Stock, who conducted the Chicago Symphony Orchestra from 1905 until his death in 1942, performed works by the then leading "modern" composers. In 1921-22, the season of Ruth Crawford's arrival in Chicago, concert-goers heard works by Debussy, Ravel, Goossens, Vaughan Williams, Stravinsky, Schoenberg, and the Americans John Alden Carpenter and Leo Sowerby. As the decade progressed, world famous musicians visited Chicago, including Prokofiev, Ravel, Casella, d'Indy, and Richard Strauss in the early years; later in the decade, such artists as Wanda Landowska, Ravel, Bartók, Rudhyar, and Honegger appeared before the Chicago public. There were numerous recitals and concert life flourished. A comparison of musical activities in New York and Chicago shows that most of the artists appearing on New York stages made their way to Chicago where Arthur Judson, the New York impresario, had as his local manager one Siegfried Herz, whose wife proved to be not only an outstanding piano teacher but an important social asset in entertaining visiting celebrities and introducing them to interested Chicagoans. Booked for Chicago appearances during Ruth's first year at the American Conservatory were, among others, Wilhelm Bachaus, Joseph Lhevinne, Josef Hoffman, Artur Schnabel, Artur Rubinstein, Sergei Rachmaninoff, Leopold Godowsky, Percy Grainger, Jascha Heifetz, Pavlova, Galli-Curci, Chaliapin, Richard Strauss, and the Flonzaley String Quartet. Chicago also boasted its own music magazine, <u>The Musical Leader</u>, at this time under the editorship of Florence Ffrench, which emphasized musical activities in the Midwest, but which also reported on musical activities in New York, with Marion Bauer as its Eastern correspondent. Some foreign news items also appeared. During the 1920s such bastions of the avant-garde as the ISCM (International Society for Contemporary Music) and Pro Musica moved into the Chicago area, and Chicago musicians figured in the activities of the New York-based League of Composers, Henry Cowell's New Music Society, and the Copland-Sessions concerts. And, important for the discussion at hand, the music schools and conservatories were flourishing.

When Ruth Crawford came to Chicago then, in the fall of 1921, she moved into a musical environment notable for its increasing excellence and outstanding names. When she left Chicago in the summer of 1929, she was already acquainted with several strands of modern European and American avant-garde musical activity. The intervening years in her life were very important in shaping her future as a composer.

In 1921, the faculty of the American Conservatory, where she had decided to enroll, included many highly respected, competent, and widely known names, and Ruth was fortunate to count several of these among her teachers: Heniot Levy, Polish-born composer and pianist, who studied composition with Max Bruch and concertized widely in Europe before coming to the conservatory as a piano teacher in 1900; Louise Robyn, a native of Chicago, who was not only a successful piano teacher but an outstanding authority in the field of piano pedagogy; John Palmer, another native Chicagoan, who enjoyed a local reputation as a successful teacher of theory and composition; and Adolf Weidig, whose reputation as a violinist and orchestra conductor was equalled by his accomplishments as a teacher of theory and composition. A native of Hamburg, Weidig studied violin there and later became a pupil of Hugo Riemann in theory and Rheinberger in composition. He came to Chicago in 1892 as a violinist with

The Chicago Years (1921-1924)

the Chicago Symphony and in 1898 joined the faculty of the American Conservatory where he taught until his death in 1931. Although Weidig's own compositions were conservative in style, he was sympathetic to his students' interests in more adventurous idioms and styles and was able to guide them effectively in their efforts.[2] High praise has been heaped on his teaching abilities both by his former students and the Chicago press. Weidig demanded two things of his students--serious talent and serious work--given these two, he was ready to help students in any and all ways he could. The annual composition recital given by members of his class was considered to be an important musical event of the season in Chicago.

Ruth Crawford brought to this exciting new milieu, adequate training in piano, a smattering of theory, her native intellectual curiosity, her analytical mind, and her musical talent, which prepared her to make the most of the opportunities which were now open to her. She accepted the challenge her new situation offered and plunged immediately into the sea of musical adventures which surrounded her. Heniot Levy, her new piano teacher who was also well and favorably known in the Chicago area as a prominent performing artist, and her introduction to the Chicago Symphony Orchestra concerts both impressed Ruth deeply. Her limited musical experiences, prior to this time, had not included that monumentous occasion for a musician--initiation into the marvels of a symphony orchestra.[3] Further musical joys would unfold with the passage of time.

Ruth went to the conservatory with the idea of pursuing advanced study in music and of receiving training as a pianist. She did not state specific goals, but her mother and her teachers believed she should be given a chance for further musical education and Ruth herself was ambitious and anxious to improve her skills and learn as much as she could. Once at the conservatory, her first goal seems to have been completion of the course of study for the associate teacher's certificate.

Levy apparently thought Ruth had serious musical talent, and he felt that she could fulfill the requirements for the certificate, which included two years of harmony, even though she had come to Chicago with the money and the intention of remaining only one year. This meant, then, that she would have to take the second year of harmony along with the first. In November, Ruth started her study of second-year harmony by taking private lessons with Palmer. "He has his students write all their own melodies for harmonization, which you well know will please me."[4] From her very first semester at the conservatory, Ruth showed unusual interest in harmony courses which only too often are of minor concern to the performance-oriented student. Ruth was obviously pleased, even intrigued, with the musical activities at the conservatory:

> I am still as happy as ever and wondering how I can ever exist away from all these wonderful sources of knowledge. I believe Miss Robyn--tho Mr. Weidig comes in a close second--has opened my eyes more than anyone else to the immense store of knowledge which I do not possess.... I have decided that I shall never marry a man who will not promise to live in Chicago, so that I can start every one of my thirty-five children in Miss Robyn's class.[5]

Ruth was completely absorbed in her new musical surroundings and thoroughly enjoyed drenching herself in each experience. She continued to attend the Chicago Symphony concerts and to develop further her interest in orchestra instruments, particularly strings, which had been continuous since her high-school days, when she played in amateur instrumental groups and violin accompaniments for her brother and some friends. She soon started attending piano recitals too, hearing such artists as Jan Chiapusso, Godowsky,[6] Huberman, and Elly Ney.[7] She also told her mother of hearing some of Scriabin's piano music as well as one of his symphonies.[8]

During Ruth's first winter in Chicago, she lived at the YWCA, as did several other girls attending the conservatory. She was willing and able to keep her financial costs at a minimum and to make every minute count. For $1.00, she rented practice time from one of the girls who had a piano so she could practice late at night. Furthermore, she kept exact account of her expenses.[9] An interesting comment on the economic scene stated that apples were down to ten cents a pound which made them only three cents apiece. "Good ones, too."[10]

Carl continued to be closely interested in his sister's welfare. His concern for her well-being is evident throughout

her conservatory years as he warned her to be careful about
the kind of girl friends she made. He complimented her on
her pleasant relationships with her teachers, and advised her
not to carry her economizing so far that she jeopardized her
ability to do her best work. He knew that she had to scrimp
and save to make ends meet. Carl often sent his sister money
for a new dress or perhaps some jewelry. He also sent her
money on a monthly basis.[11] Ruth looked around for some
kind of job where she could earn much-needed funds, and by
November she had found an opportunity to usher, at first at
some of the downtown concerts and later at several Loop
theaters.[12] She was elated at the chance to hear and see
worthwhile events and make money at the same time. She
worried a bit at first about what her father might have
thought about her presence in a theater, but her mother re-
assured her that it was all right for her to be there--she
even urged her to go to the theater.[13] In fact, Mrs. Crawford often encouraged Ruth to widen her experiences and to
make the most of her talents and of any opportunities that
came her way.

Mrs. Crawford had not been in a position to indulge
in purely social activities during Ruth's childhood, and this
fact doubtless influenced Ruth in her own later attitudes
toward such. This example, coupled with Ruth's serious and
industrious nature, caused her to forego the social events to
which she had been invited at Christmas time in order to
visit such places as the Art Institute and the Field Museum.
The operatic world was also a new experience for Ruth, and
she absorbed all she could from the performances she was
able to attend. "Thursday is opera night for me.... I
take the scores to follow when I can."[14] Sponge-like, she
absorbed the new cultural opportunities her situation offered
her, although very quickly her innate good taste showed in
her ability to be selective in her choice of entertainments and
perceptive in her criticisms and judgments of them.

After the Christmas holidays were over and school work
started again, Ruth plunged once more into her harmony
lessons with Palmer and Weidig, both of whom felt that Ruth
showed considerable originality in her class exercises. When
Weidig gave the harmony class an assignment to bring a composition, Ruth brought her little Elf Dance, a piece she had
written several years previously in Jacksonville. Weidig
thought it showed distinct talent and was interested to know
where Ruth had received her early education.[15]

Clara Graves Crawford, Ruth's mother, at her home in Jacksonville, Florida (early 1920s)

The Chicago Years (1921-1924)

Ruth's musical development continued to expand during the spring as did her awareness of her own capabilities. "Did I tell you Miss Robyn discovered that I have absolute pitch? I am so happy. Since then I have been listening to traffic cop whistles, the screech of brakes, and the squeak of doors. Ours squeaks in C sharp!"[16] This observation is particularly interesting in light of her later comment that certain sounds in the third movement of her string quartet were inspired by noises emanating from a New Year's Eve celebration.

Health problems began to bother Ruth during the early months of 1922. Her eyes, which had troubled her since high-school days, continued to do so. She bought McFadden's "Strengthening the Eyes," and after strenuous pursuit of the exercises recommended in this publication, her eyes began to improve, at least for the time being.[17] In addition, during the spring Ruth began to experience considerable difficulty with tense muscles in her arms. These muscular difficulties were doubtless the same type Ruth mentioned in her 1918 diary where she indicated that she was getting occasional treatments from an osteopath.[18] Ruth wrote her mother:

> I cannot practise! My left arm has gone on strike. I have kept thinking that with my letting up on practising--with the rest it would thus be getting, it would be all right. But for the past week I have done this: got in only two hours Friday, an hour Saturday, (etc.).... It even hurts my neck to write. I have been utilizing my time copying notes, and I find I may not even be able to do that....[19]

Although Ruth tried to pace her practicing and other uses of her arm, she continued to experience painful sensations when she used it for any length of time and became genuinely concerned about it. "Just a few lines tonight, for I must save my arm. I took an electric treatment Saturday, but it made me worse instead of better." Late in the spring, Ruth began taking a series of treatments from a Mrs. Shostac, who she felt had successfully diagnosed her trouble. "It is in my neck muscles and in my placement of weight."[20] Ruth had obviously not yet learned the knack of avoiding undesirable muscular tension in her arms by using weight only rather than weight combined with unnecessary force.

Ruth Crawford (Chicago, ca. 1921)

The Chicago Years (1921-1924)   27

As the end of the school year approached, Levy asked whether Ruth would be returning in the fall. When she explained that she wanted very much to return but would have to earn her own way, he told her of a prospective piano teaching position on the south side of Chicago for which he had been asked to recommend a teacher. Ruth was interested in and accepted Levy's offer, so apparently it was agreed between Ruth and her mother that she should plan to return to Chicago for a second year.[21]

Ruth began to turn her thoughts toward home and family, and to make her plans for the summer. She wanted to review all of second year harmony by herself and to continue practicing as much as her tense muscles would permit. "Then of course, I shall have to do some sewing, though there is really not so very much I need in the way of clothes."[22] Clothes for herself always came in last on any want list Ruth ever made. We can imagine that her enthusiasm for her first year in the big city spilled over to her old friends and family at home where she must have enjoyed the respite from being cramped in one room and eating all her meals in a common dining room.

Ruth's first year in Chicago had broadened her musical vision and given her a new perspective on the field of music study. She had devoured eagerly every chance she had to learn and quickly adjusted to the enriched environment in which she found herself. Theoretical studies, doubtless influenced somewhat by the troubles Ruth experienced with tense muscles, were already vying with her piano practice for a share of her time and energy. The world of opera and the theatre, as well as of the symphony orchestra, fascinated her. Recitals by world-famous artists further enriched her life. Ruth was very happy in the midst of all these new experiences, and she knew there was no turning back for her now--she was eager to meet the challenge which she would face on her return to Chicago in the fall.

However, she resolved to try to be sensible about her practicing and to take it easy until she saw how her arms would respond to strenuous use. She was able to follow out her plans of the previous spring to find piano pupils to help support herself. After canvassing some neighborhoods, she found several prospects and finally obtained "the enormous sum of six pupils. They are dear youngsters; I always love the children--but dread their mothers! You never know what the latter expect. They may take it for granted that their progeny will also be prodigies and be playing Liszts rhapsodies in a few weeks."[23]

To supplement her meager income from piano teaching, Ruth returned to her job as usher. Neither of these work situations had a great measure of stability and she was often hard-pressed to pay for living expenses. She was more than willing, however, to endure this kind of Spartan existence to get an education.

Ruth had learned to practice mentally, since she was still unable to spend a great deal of time at the piano because of her tense muscles. Much of this kind of practicing Ruth did on the street cars where she figured she spent about eight hours a week. "I find that going over them mentally [the compositions she was studying], note for note not only fixes them in my memory, but actually improves them technically."[24]

Ruth was afraid to study piano with Levy again as his ambitions for her advancement tended to cause him to forget her difficulties with tense muscles. She thought of studying with Louise Robyn first for a few weeks since Robyn apparently was aware of Ruth's problem with muscular tension. She realized that Ruth must go slowly and that she needed help in learning how to relax. When Ruth decided that, at least for the time being, she could not continue to study piano with Levy, she became discouraged and began to wonder what she was in school for. "Would I not better have taken Mama's usually best advice and stayed at home?" But the answer was persistent; her theoretical work, which was assuming increasing importance to her, made all her efforts to gain a musical education worthwhile. Ruth felt that this aspect alone justified her remaining in Chicago.[25]

In late November, Ruth made her decision to study piano with Robyn. Robyn, who had taught her the previous year as instructor in the piano methods class, had come to know and admire Ruth's work, to appreciate her talent, and as a result had become interested in Ruth's problem with her tense muscles. When Ruth told Robyn that her arm was not so good, she replied that she would like to experiment on her without it being any cost to Ruth. She wanted to see if she could cure her arms at the piano and told Ruth it would be of help to her in her work. Would Ruth be willing? Ruth was willing.[26]

Ruth's theoretical studies continued to give her both pleasure and satisfaction. Weidig complimented her highly on her counterpoint exercises concerning one of which he told her, "Miss Crawford, that is one of the best pieces of work that has ever been handed to me. The voice leading, the choice of chords--everything--is perfect."[27]

Her mother had told her repeatedly that talent was not enough; that on the long haul, it was hard work that counted, and Ruth was beginning to realize the truth of this statement as well as to comprehend the basic elements of successful composition:

> I have to work so hard for what effects I get, and when I do get them, they come as if by accident. My wondering as to what makes a great composer's works great has brought me to the realization that it is not only the themes--the melodies that are important; of much more consequence is the development of the ideas, the interweaving of the melodies, the background which creates the atmosphere. Every new composition which I attempt brings me more worshipful, more humble, more awed, at the feet of the great masters.[28]

Ruth was not yet enrolled in a composition class per se, but Weidig in his theory courses introduced composition every two weeks. This gave Ruth opportunities to try her hand at writing music which would receive critical attention from a teacher. She obviously relished these chances and made the most of them. Such experiences, coupled with the trouble Ruth continued to suffer with tense arm muscles, doubtless caused her interest in writing music gradually to dominate her musical activities; references to piano study and performance occur less and less.

After a class presentation of her compositional efforts, a work for violin and piano Weidig commented:

> That you have something to say goes without saying, but you have difficulty in finding the means.

> There are idioms here and there. Your time is so
> idiomatic.... Next year, with private lessons, will
> be the true testing time. Your ideas are refined and
> modernistic; whether they are spontaneous or studied
> will be discovered then.[29]

Mrs. Crawford, likewise, believed strongly in her daughter's talents and felt that Ruth should put forth her best efforts to make a name for herself in music. An occasional letter from her clarified her position as to what might be best for Ruth's future.

> You certainly give very interesting accounts of
> your encounters with "Adolf." I sure do think there
> is no doubt of his interest in your ability and there
> is no reason why he should not be sincere. He has
> nothing to gain by deceiving. There is no reason
> why you should not have discovered in yourself a
> talent for some phase of music. Your mother loved
> it and tried to impart a love for it in you and you
> have taken at least a lesson a week since you were
> six years old. Why should you not have absorbed
> enough to begin to give it out? Just take for granted
> that you ought to and stop worrying about it. What
> man has done (Schumann) woman can do (Crawford).
> What will your stage name be?[30]

Mrs. Crawford was far in advance of her time. Both inclination and circumstances had placed her in a position of assuming equality with men in the matter of making a living and raising a family. Although Ruth developed some of her mother's confidence and daring and had eventually to help financially in the raising of her own family, she was not so positive as Mrs. Crawford in her estimate of her musical abilities.

By late March, Weidig had apparently formed his judgment of Ruth's talent. In a long letter to her mother, Ruth recounted his comments about her potentialities. During a conversation with Ruth and a friend, Weidig had spoken of one of his former students. Then he said: "There is another girl I shall never forget. She is a very gifted girl--she is going to do big things in composition, and besides she is a very fine pianist."[31]

The Chicago Years (1921-1924)

And still Ruth had doubts--perhaps Weidig was wrong! She feared the burden of responsibility for developing her talents and the possibility of failure in much the same way she had dreaded the responsible practicing she had had to undertake when she started her piano study with Madame Collett back in Jacksonville. She also realized that Weidig had deliberately advised her of his confidence in her capabilities to make her feel responsible for the development of her talents. This would seem to be a climactic point in Ruth's decision to become a composer as she had long been awaiting this pronouncement from her respected and admired mentor whose judgment she trusted. Weidig further emphasized his confidence in Ruth's capabilities when he told Robyn that Ruth would take part in his composition program the following year. "She's really ready this year," he said.[32]

Thus Ruth began to consider the problems, largely financial, of returning to Chicago for a third year. She thought that having had to work during her second year had not been a handicap to her musical development. By this time, Ruth had also begun to consider the possibilities open to her as a composer. She felt that she could add a little to her teaching income through publication of songs and children's teaching pieces, both of which should have sale value.

Ruth finally began to share some of her mother's and her teachers' confidence in her talents, to push her doubts to the back of her mind, and to adopt a positive attitude toward her potentialities. During her second year, she had developed her interest in writing for chamber music groups and her idiomatic approach to rhythm, both characteristic of Ruth's later compositional efforts. She felt, however, that she needed more definite knowledge of the different classical forms used in instrumental music and the development techniques they presupposed, although she never evinced any real affinity for either.

Ruth also began to exchange her wide-eyed wonder at all the musical joys Chicago had brought her for a more mature outlook and an acceptance of her future as a musician of one kind or another. Weidig's strong conviction that Ruth's talent for composition should be developed and Robyn's personal interest in Ruth's physical problems at the piano were in large measure responsible for her progress during this year in Chicago. Robyn went out of her way to supply Ruth with little extras such as giving her the scores to take with her to the opera and the symphony. And Weidig kept trying to build up Ruth's confidence in her talent and at the same time advise her of her strengths and weaknesses as a potential composer.

After receiving her graduate diploma in spring 1923, Ruth spent the summer with her mother in Florida. She had often expressed the wish that her mother join her in Chicago, so in the fall they went back together and shared an apartment until Mrs. Crawford's death in 1928. Their limited financial resources were supplemented by Ruth's income from piano teaching and her continued job as usher.

Ruth resumed her piano study with Robyn, as well as normal training instruction. Her theoretical studies with Weidig continued, and included private composition lessons--a goal Ruth had looked forward to almost from her entry into the conservatory. Weidig continued to be pleased with her progress:

> Weidig, I think I told you, gave her unlimited praise over a composition at her last lesson. She has a violin and piano duet ready for this week's lesson that she herself is "daffy" over. It will remain to be seen how the great Adolf will grade it. He is a violinist, you know, and Ruth's violin parts may not be scientifically true....[33]

Ruth continued to seize every opportunity to widen her musical experiences; she still attended the symphony concerts in Orchestra Hall, and for a short period of time presumably played in the percussion section of an unnamed orchestra.[34] Her arms were improved and she was able to practice more than previously and apparently was making good progress.

As Weidig had forecast the previous year, he chose Ruth to appear on his annual composition recital in Kimball Hall (May 31, 1924). She played one of her most ambitious works up to this time, <u>Kaleidoscopic Changes on an Original Theme</u>, ending with a fugue. This work, as well as several other fruits of her compositional efforts during these early years, remain in manuscript, the earliest dated 1922, the latest, 1924.

The Chicago Years (1921-1924)

It obviously did not take Mrs. Crawford long to assess Ruth's situation in Chicago and to understand why Ruth wanted and needed to continue to develop her, now conceded, unusual musical talents. By the time Ruth received her bachelor's degree on June 18, 1924, Mrs. Crawford had formulated her own ideas and plans for Ruth for the following year. She wanted her daughter to continue her study of both piano and composition:

> This next year she must have the best teacher to be found--perhaps it will not be in the American Conservatory. And too, she should continue her composition with Weidig, and take the Masters Degree.[35]

These three years had been a time of revelation in Ruth's life and a time when her chief responsibilities were to stretch her mind, widen her experiences, and improve her talents. Socially, Ruth was still tied to her family, her teachers, and the girl friends she met in her classes at the conservatory. Her life revolved around her work and the Chicago musical scene, which left little time (or interest) for other activities. These would come later, but in the meantime she was completely absorbed in her beloved music and happily anticipated a future filled with music making.

Chapter Three

THE CHICAGO YEARS
(1924-1929)

"I felt more powerfully than ever today what poems people are; not the part of them that speaks, but the mysterious, intricate network of thoughts and feelings which remain unexpressed." (Ruth Crawford, Diary entry, October 28, 1927)

With the close of the school year, May 1924, another chapter in Ruth's life ended. She and her mother continued their intimate and fruitful relationship, despite the inevitable change in their respective views of life brought about largely by Ruth's experiences during the next years which caused her to expand her social outlook, as well as her musical and intellectual perspectives.

Ruth continued as a student at the American Conservatory, working on and receiving her master's degree in composition, <u>summa cum laude</u>, in 1927. From 1927 to 1929, she was awarded a Juilliard scholarship for the study of composition and orchestration with Adolf Weidig.[1] These awards were extension scholarships granted by the Juilliard committee to students outside of New York.[2]

Although Ruth was still studying with Weidig, his earlier strong influence seems to have slacked off. Perhaps Weidig did not feel comfortable with Ruth's music with its strong emphasis on dissonance. Stella Roberts, longtime teacher and fellow student of Ruth's at the conservatory, recalls vividly the unusual character of Ruth's compositions.

The Chicago Years (1924-1929)

She too studied composition with Weidig and remembers him as "somewhat baffled by the newness of her [Ruth's] idiom."³ Nevertheless, Weidig had great respect for Ruth and her talent and always encouraged her to do her best. Perhaps Ruth sensed the growing disparity of their ideas, although she always held Weidig in great esteem and freely acknowledged her indebtedness to him, as the following excerpt shows:

> Sprinkling sevenths and ninths plentifully and insistently, and observing or breaking the solemn rules of harmony with equal regularity, I was guided with great understanding during the next years by Adolf Weidig of the American Conservatory in Chicago, who seems to me to have had an unusual balance between necessary discipline and necessary allowance for individuality.⁴

Ruth also continued teaching piano at the conservatory (as well as privately and at Elmhurst College in the Chicago suburbs). Too, she kept up her study of piano, but not at the conservatory. Through a new teacher, Madame Djane Lavoie Herz, who taught privately in Chicago, a new dimension was added to Ruth's life. Her circle of friends and acquaintances began to widen considerably and soon included people who were influential both musically and intellectually far outside the walls of academe in which she had been sheltered for much of her life.

Only two of Ruth's works bear dedications--one is her Piano Prelude No. 6 which has the following inscription: "With deep love and gratitude, To Djane, My Inspiration." Djane Lavoie Herz was a French Canadian who went to England at age sixteen where she studied piano at the Royal Academy. She later studied in Paris after which she became a pupil of Arthur Schnabel in Berlin. There she met the famous Russian composer and mystic, Alexander Scriabin and later became his pupil for two years when he lived in Brussels and, not surprisingly, she became a devotee of the man and his works. An accident to her hand in the late teens caused her to forego a concert career, after which she started teaching piano.⁵

Madame Herz came to Chicago probably around 1919-20 with her husband, Siegfried, who had been a concert manager

in Canada.⁶ In Chicago he became associated with the
Arthur Judson management which situation afforded him opportunities to know many of the top artists of the day.
This cannot but have affected his wife's position--it also
doubtless had some influence on the outlook of her various
piano students. Madame Herz had no institutional affiliations,
but preferred to teach privately and quietly at home. Her
personal friends included musical celebrities often passing
through Chicago, and society folk who were important musically. Her approach to piano teaching has been described
as being somewhat informal--"students are permitted to listen
to all lessons, and they may ask questions; there is no following of the clock and after lessons they discuss music,
books or other interesting subjects."⁷

Herz's piano studio on Grand Boulevard (later Bellevue
Place), which was also the Herzes' home,⁸ was often the scene
of musical soirees where the famous and the talented mingled
and had occasion to discuss current musical trends and ideas.
Names of prominent musicians known to have been present at
these soirees include Henry Cowell who visited Chicago during
the 1920s to play and probably talk about his current compositions. In 1924 he introduced Chicagoans to his unusual
keyboard techniques, and in the spring of 1928, he assisted
Georgia Kober, well-known Chicago musician and president of
the Sherwood School of Music, in a recital which featured his
works.⁹ Also attending were Dane Rudhyar, French-American
composer and friend of the Herzes for many years, Edgard
Varèse, even then a radical experimentalist in the use of
sound, and Adolph Weiss, bassoonist and student of Weidig,
who in 1925 went to Europe to study with Schoenberg. Ruth
actively participated in Madame Herz's musical soirees and
doubtless on occasion played some of her own piano works.¹⁰

Ruth had become a piano pupil of Madame Herz in the
fall of 1924 after receiving her Bachelor of Music degree from
the American Conservatory in the spring, and she continued
her study and association with Herz until she left for New
York in the fall of 1929, via the MacDowell Colony. How Ruth
became acquainted with and a student of Madame Herz is not
known, but she was obviously the kind of teacher Mrs. Crawford had in mind when she said that Ruth must have the best
possible piano teacher. Although Madame Herz did not participate in the advertising which most teachers and performers
inserted in the music magazines, she came to prominence in

Ruth Crawford, a sketch from life by Carl Bohnen (Chicago, ca. 1926)

the city in 1923 when her pupil, Gitta Gradova, made a somewhat sensational New York debut and was accorded lavish praise by the critics.[11] Probably Mrs. Crawford became aware of Herz's abilities as a teacher through the local press.

Ruth's association with Madame Herz soon developed into a warm personal relationship which played a large part in Ruth's social and intellectual, as well as her musical, development. Those who knew Madame Herz recall her as a very strong person. A former pupil observed that "Madame Herz was an authoritative and arresting personality. She was 100% alive and throbbed with energy. She was an overwhelming personality ... rather short, with a very erect posture, a body with catlike energy and flexibility."[12] Another student remembers that "she was very attractive, very dynamic, and she tended toward the flamboyant ... she was definitely a colorful, vibrant person ... she was what you would call charismatic ... and somewhat exotic.... In her studio there were Buddhist statues--I think this was part of the Scriabin influence."[13]

It must have been an exhilarating experience for a young and talented person like Ruth to be associated with such a person as Madame Herz and to be included in and accepted by such select gatherings as those at the Herz studio. Ruth reacted positively to her new musical stimuli. She felt that these experiences were quite valuable in helping her find new paths for her musical imagination to explore.

> Contact in 1925 with Djane Lavoie Herz, with whom I studied piano, and with Dane Rudhyar, and later with Henry Cowell, established a definite turning-point in my work, and enabled me to see far along the way toward which in my numerous student compositions I had been groping. I discovered Scriabine [sic] at this time; the music of Schoenberg and Hindemith I did not hear until later; Stravinsky's "Sacre" and "l'Oiseau de Feu" came to me about this time.[14]

Ruth also reacted negatively at times to her new environment and experiences. Although she had the greatest love and respect for Madame Herz (as well as friendship with her husband and their son, Tristan), she often felt reserved and a bit uncomfortable around her teacher; she felt she really had nothing of value to contribute to the group of people who gathered at the Herz home:

The Chicago Years (1924-1929) 39

> I seem to have no originality when I am there;
> no ability to get out of my coat of steel. I have an
> exaggerated feeling of inferiority when I am with
> Madame Herz or Gradova.[15]

Ruth's long-standing bouts with feelings of inferiority were expressed throughout her life, although these were generally accompanied by firm resolutions to concentrate on her positive qualities while working to overcome the more negative aspects of her personality. She berated herself for her lack of knowledge in areas outside of music, felt that she needed to develop her vocabulary, and made plans to do so systematically by adding five to ten words daily to it. Even as a high-school student, Ruth had read serious literature extensively, and in Chicago she continued to expand her background in literature and philosophy. Madame Herz used to tell her "be positive--never negative"--to which her reaction was "but you must have fundamentals to be positive about."[16]

Madame Herz was her friend and confidante--she was also Ruth's piano teacher. Did Ruth possibly harbor ideas of reaching professional performance standards in piano? Probably not--Ruth herself never expressed her desire to reach such a goal. She had, as many students do, grown up with musical training--desiring it, loving it, but not questioning her motive for pursuing it. By the time it became necessary for decisions concerning her musical future, she had come to feel that composing was of primary interest to her. Nonetheless, she continued to develop her pianistic skills to the best of her ability simply because anything she thought worth her while to do, was worth her best efforts. Her piano training at the conservatory, directed as it was by skilled teachers, never enabled her to overcome the muscular tenseness in her arms to the point where she could play freely and without physical discomfort. Nor did Herz's, although Madame's approach to teaching piano "stressed relaxation of wrist especially--the relaxed weight ... she stressed equally the technical aspects that permitted control over the dynamic effects, the brilliance of passage work, the control of pianissimo...."[17] Too, Ruth was so deeply impressed with Gradova's technique and artistry that she doubtless felt she fell far short of professional goals.

Gradually, the strong influence which Mrs. Crawford had exerted over her daughter came to be supplanted by the ideas and ideals inspired by these new Chicago experiences and acquaintances. This seems to be true also of the early strong impact of the teachers at the conservatory. Ruth was obviously groping to find ways to reconcile two different lifestyles--the old, rooted in her upbringing and her conservatory training, and the new, represented by the more worldlywise one she encountered <u>chez</u> Herz.

Ruth often referred to herself as a child and to her behavior as childish. However, she continuously sought guiding principles that she could accept as her own. She assiduously discussed and analyzed basic philosophical ideas with her close friends, but was slow to accept any of these as fundamental to her own personal relationship to the world. She was not sure, in these years, when she was no longer guided by the lifestyle of a conservative conservatory student, what her convictions really were, or whether she was ready to embrace any particular philosophy wholeheartedly. She related her philosophical musings to her childhood affinity for cats:

> I recall tonight how I used to envy cats and long to be one, so that I should have no responsibilities, no pains of ignorance, no knowledge expected of me, no sieges of depression. Who knows what thoughts cats feel between their purring spells?[18]

Ruth was drawn not only to Madame Herz, who seemed strong and confident, but also to Dane Rudhyar, whose interest in mysticism held a fascination for her. Rudhyar was a young, handsome, and unattached man when Ruth first met him in Chicago and it is quite possible that he held a personal, romantic attraction for her. These natural feelings were probably accentuated in part by new ideas and ways of living and in part by Mrs. Crawford's apparent distrust of what she felt was too much sophistication on the part of Ruth's new acquaintances. Mrs. Crawford communicated these feelings to Ruth who reacted as a typical member of the next generation.[19]

Rudhyar, whose artistic and philosophical leanings relate to the work of the Russian composer, Scriabin, first met Madame Herz in the fall of 1917 in New York, and they became close friends, sharing a mutual interest in the Russian master. Early in 1925, Rudhyar visited the Herzes, staying as a guest in their Chicago apartment for about three months. During this time, Ruth and Rudhyar became good friends, and

The Chicago Years (1924-1929)

he played Ruth some of his own compositions.[20] Through both Madame Herz and Rudhyar, Ruth came to have a wider acquaintance with Scriabin's music, some of which she had heard as early as 1922. Further exposure to his works fascinated and influenced her throughout the decade of the twenties. Paul Rosenfeld's essay on Scriabin produced an effect on her "deeper than almost anything I have ever read."[21] This essay, which stressed the importance of Scriabin as a composer for the piano, describes the composer's work in rather flowery language and, at the same time, relates it to Scriabin's interest in theosophy and mysticism. Rosenfeld's discussion of Scriabin could not fail to impress the romantic side of Ruth's nature which was much in evidence at the time.

When Rudhyar made a return visit to Chicago in the fall of 1928, Ruth renewed her friendship with him and became better acquainted with his musical and philosophical ideas which continued to fascinate her.[22] She was quite impressed with a lecture she heard him deliver for the Chicago chapter of Pro Musica in which he emphasized the need for knowing musics other than European.[23] It is doubtful that Rudhyar ever realized the strong impact he made on this impressionable and sensitive young woman, particularly through his interest in theosophy, in Scriabin, and in non-Western music.

Ruth met Rudhyar again in the fall of 1929, probably in New York. At this time, he was instrumental in helping her get a Guggenheim grant. Rudhyar spoke on Ruth's behalf to Henry Allen Moe, director of the J. S. Guggenheim Memorial Foundation, who held definite reservations about the musical worth of women composers. At Rudhyar's insistence, however, he agreed to give Ruth consideration.[24] She submitted her application, dated November 14, 1929, and was awarded the grant in the amount of $2500, effective the following year, 1930-1931.

Again through Madame Herz Ruth came to know Henry Cowell, whose acquaintance proved to be one of the most fortunate of her life. They soon became and long remained the staunchest of friends. Cowell gave Ruth the courage and the opportunity to be experimental, even though she was not interested in following his particular innovations. Cowell also introduced her to a new world of music activities through his New Music Society of California and related publishing projects. Cowell, who actively promoted performances of new music, arranged for the publication of some of her compositions. Her Piano Preludes, Nos. 6-9, appeared in the New Music edition in 1928, one of Cowell's most important brain children. New Music, which proved to be one of the most important musical ventures of the first half of the twentieth century in the United States, consisted solely of scores of the chiefly American advance guard--works which Cowell felt had merit, but which had little chance for commercial publication. Several other of Ruth's scores would first see the light of day in New Music.

It can be conjectured that Ruth's memberships (as a board member) in the New Music Society of California, and New Music Quarterly Recordings, organized by Cowell, and in the Pan American Association of Composers, organized in 1928 for promoting music of the Americas, the North American section of which was directed by Cowell--all listed on her Guggenheim application--resulted from her friendship with this gifted American composer and innovator. Association with these groups assured Ruth of an entree into what proved to be important American music circles. Further, by the time Ruth met Henry Cowell, he had long since formulated the ideas for--indeed, written one of his most talked of and widely quoted works--New Musical Resources. Doubtless, Ruth had heard him discuss at least some of the ideas in this important book.[25] Cowell was a step on Ruth's way to another and wider musical arena. He championed her cause, he believed in her, he went out of his way to see that opportunities were opened to her. And he would continue in one way or another to figure in many of the important events in Ruth's life.

During the twenties, when it was still likely that neighbors might also be friends, one of her neighbors did, in fact, become acquainted with Ruth and remained a friend throughout her life. This friend, Alfred Frankenstein, was an amateur clarinetist whom Ruth occasionally accompanied on the piano. He also gave Ruth practical suggestions on writing for the clarinet.[26] Frankenstein's professional interests led him to journalistic writing, and he went on to become one of the country's leading music and art reviewers. His major professional assignment took him to California where he served many years as music and art critic on the San Francisco

The Chicago Years (1924-1929)   43

Chronicle. Although a few years younger than Ruth, Frankenstein was admittedly smitten with her and often escorted her to Madame Herz's musical soirees. In the early twenties, recordings of modern music were very hard to get, and Ruth used to come and listen to his records. On returning from a trip to Europe in the mid-twenties, Frankenstein brought back recordings of works by Stravinsky, Hindemith, Milhaud, and a few others, and Ruth found them highly interesting.

Frankenstein also introduced Ruth to Carl Sandburg, who would become another one of her long-time friends. Around the year 1926, Frankenstein was working with Sandburg trying to write down the music for the tunes in The American Songbag. Although Sandburg's songbook was originally planned to contain words and tunes only, the publishers decided it would sell better if piano accompaniments were included. Several people, including Ruth, shared in the preparation of these. Frankenstein felt that this was a very important factor in turning Ruth's attention toward folksong,[27] and Ruth herself acknowledged Sandburg's influence when she told him, referring to the imminent publication of her American Folk Songs for Children, "after all, you started me off on all this."[28]

At that time the Sandburgs lived in the Chicago suburb of Elmhurst where Ruth, in the same year (1926), started teaching piano at Elmhurst College. It happened that the Sandburgs needed a piano teacher for their children. Frankenstein recommended Ruth and she got the job. Mr. and Mrs. Sandburg and their children were drawn to Ruth and she to them, and her acquaintance with them soon turned into a warm, personal friendship with the family.[29] Sandburg referred to Ruth as "a Chicago gal who for years was a sort of added informal unadopted daughter at our house."[30] On occasion Sandburg entertained them all by his singing of folk songs:

> And one evening after a siege of wood chopping on the windblown, chilling lake front and a boisterous, laughter-swept dinner with the two buoyant children, he sat there in the lamplight, singing song after song, simply, sometimes wildly, sometimes mournfully; his understanding voice winding in and out among the irregular nuances and accompanied by stray chords on the guitar. His youngster sitting

opposite with sleep-heavy eyes glued on his face, now and then crooning in drowsily on a song she knew.[31]

Ruth was rather strongly influenced by Sandburg's style of writing poetry as well as his subject matter, and she frequently used his poems in her vocal compositions, giving them sympathetic musical settings. Her own interest in poetry and writing, somewhat moribund during her busy conservatory student years, was keenly invigorated by her acquaintance with Sandburg. She also became fascinated by his outlook on life, especially his feeling for the city of Chicago and his interest in folk music. They further shared a common admiration for the poetry of Walt Whitman. Another facet of Sandburg's work that Ruth would later take up was his activity in writing books for children. Sandburg continued his interest in Ruth and in December 1929 wrote a letter of recommendation for her when she applied for a Guggenheim grant, stressing her character, personality, musical talents, originality, and worthiness to receive such an honor.[32] In later years, when Ruth and Charles Seeger were deeply involved in folk music research, Sandburg again championed her efforts. In retrospect, Charles Seeger acknowledged that Sandburg had planted the seed of Ruth's interest in folksong which only much later developed into intensive research and study in this field.[33]

Possibly identifiable with her friendship and deep admiration for Carl Sandburg, Ruth came to feel a close personal relationship to the city of Chicago, especially the sights and sounds of the traffic, and she felt an endless fascination with street cars and buses. Street cars had their own personalities, and they seemed to provide Ruth with a time and a place for dreaming and ruminating not allowed to her otherwise, as she was quite busy with her studying and teaching activities. On one occasion she asked herself, "What is it I am in love with when I walk or go bus riding?"[34] She does not answer her question here. Another time, after what she called "a bad day, with no thoughts," she tried "my beloved bus ride as a tonic, with no results."[35] A further reference--"Buses and street cars suit my artistic sense more than

---

[Opposite:] Carl Sandburg and Ruth Crawford at the Dunes, Lake Michigan (ca. 1928)

the IC. The latter is too efficient, too fine, too light and
one arrives too quickly. The other two are productive of
thought."[36] One final comment: "Again today, I am impressed by the interesting drama involved by a ride on the
street car. How many life currents thrown together; how
much the limousine addict misses!"[37] The street cars and
buses seemed to rival Ruth's diaries in providing an occasion
for meditation.

Although Ruth's diaries and poetry reflect the influence
of such American writers and poets as Sandburg, Whitman,
and Thoreau, whose works she knew and admired greatly, her
knowledge of literature and of the history of ideas was far-
ranging. Culled from the pages of her Chicago diaries,
titles of works familiar to her include such diverse items as
Plato's Phaedrus, Goethe, Eckermann's Conversations (her
mother's last birthday gift to her), William James, the
Bhagavad Gita, Galsworthy's White Monkey, Schumann's
Letters, Maeterlinck's book on flowers, Flaubert, H. G.
Wells, Anatole France, G. B. Shaw, and many others. Ruth's
mother had developed her own interest in literature, music,
and art to the limited extent which the circumstances of her
life allowed her, so it is not surprising that these areas of
intellectual endeavor should appeal to Ruth also. It is interesting and enlightening to compare her interest in the solid
fare mentioned above with her evident enjoyment in reading
stories in the Pictorial Review, which she relished even as
she felt she should be ashamed of herself.[38] Ruth's own attempts at short-story writing, which she indulged in period-
ically, tended toward this kind of story.

Ruth's intellectual and academic interests in Chicago
were probably wider than they would seem at first glance.
In addition to her extensive and varied literary interests,
already mentioned, she took several courses at the University of Chicago in 1923 according to her Guggenheim application. She also attended what she referred to as the Nietzsche
class during the winter of 1927-1928. This group, which met
in private homes to discuss philosophical ideas, included such
people as Max Otto, Clarence Darrow, and Ben Hecht, as well
as several University of Chicago professors and Djane and
Siegfried Herz.[39] Ruth responded deeply to the intellectual
stimulation afforded her by association with this group.

During the years Ruth and her mother spent together

The Chicago Years (1924-1929)

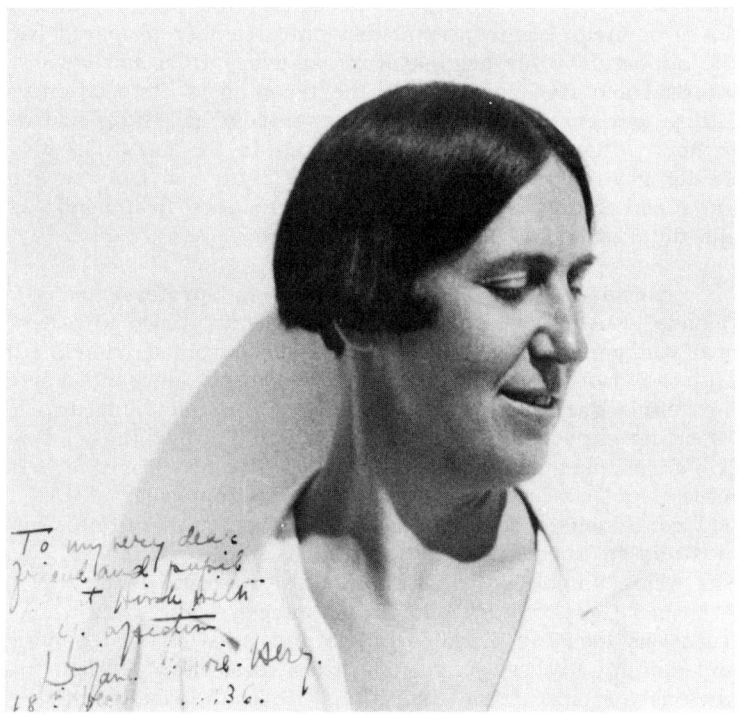

Djane Lavoie Herz (1936)   [photo courtesy of Albert Hirsh]

in Chicago, Ruth was quite busy studying, composing, and teaching. Besides teaching at the conservatory and at Elmhurst College, Ruth taught theory and composition, probably privately. She was understandably impressed with the talent of one of her students--a thirteen-year-old girl named Vivian Fine.[40] Fine first became acquainted with Ruth when they were both piano students of Djane Lavoie Herz. Herz thought that Fine, an unusually talented young girl, needed more in-depth music study than piano alone could provide so she suggested that Ruth teach her theory, which served in those days as a prelude to the study of composition. Fine remembers Ruth vividly and feels that her work in theory and composition with Ruth was decisive in pointing her on the road to her (very successful) composing career. Ruth's ap-

proach to teaching Fine paralleled rather closely the training
Ruth received from Weidig at the conservatory, i.e., liberal
doses of strict, conventional harmonic training tempered with
the opportunity for original work at every turn and a very
informal and free approach to the teaching of composition, allowing and encouraging Fine to experiment as Weidig had done
to her. When Ruth went to New York in the fall of 1929,
Weidig gave Fine the scholarship that Ruth had had, so she
knew and understood his teaching techniques first hand, as
she did Ruth's.[41]

Besides her circle of intellectual and professional
friends, Ruth also kept up an active acquaintance with several younger people, some of whom she remained friends with
after her mother's death. She enjoyed many an early morning tennis game, occasional games of chess and billiards,
swimming expeditions, and long talks in the evenings. One
friend, in particular, may be noted--Alice Lee Burrows. Her
name first occurred in Ruth's diaries in September of 1927
and continued to be mentioned at least through Ruth's year
of study in Europe and her return to New York in 1931.
She was a singer and a member of the dramatic faculty at the
American Conservatory and taught play-writing there when
Ruth was teaching piano.[42] Ruth and Alice enjoyed playing
and singing Brahms songs in informal sessions.[43] Alice was
obviously a close friend in whom Ruth confided and with whom
she corresponded over a period of years. Several of Ruth's
preserved letters to Alice (1929-1930) contain some of her most
disarming, entertaining, and informative observations on the
New York musical scene.[44]

Another friend whose name occurs in the Chicago diaries, Martha Beck (now Carragan), was a graduate student
and piano teacher at the American Conservatory during
Ruth's last years there. They were not intimate as Alice
and Ruth appear to have been, but casual friends who enjoyed each other's company and had stimulating conversations
regarding music. This was their common bond. Martha and
Ruth were the only Chicago recipients of the Juilliard Extension scholarships in composition that were awarded for the
1927-1928 academic year. They kept up their friendship with
intermittent visits until Ruth's death.[45]

And what contact did Ruth have with her brother between 1924 and her mother's death in August 1928? Carl

The Chicago Years (1924-1929) 49

married in 1926, and although he kept in touch with his
mother and Ruth, little of their correspondence remains. In
February of 1928, Mrs. Crawford became ill and submitted
to surgery in May. The abdominal swelling which she suffered was diagnosed as terminal cancer, and the doctors
gave her approximately three months to live. On receiving
word of his mother's illness, Carl and his wife and their
two babies, then living in Charleston, West Virginia, joined
Ruth and Mrs. Crawford in Chicago where they all rented a
house on Constance Avenue, and they all shared in the care
of the invalid.[46] During the final weeks of Mrs. Crawford's
illness, Ruth pondered much on her relationship with her
mother and, as she watched her life ebb away to the point
where they could never again communicate with each other,
she began to realize how much she loved her, how close they
had been, and "how inextricably woven into my life she
is."[47] Ruth's detailed account of her mother's illness and
death is a remarkable and touching and revealing monument
to their relationship.

Mrs. Crawford had been an unfailing bulwark during
Ruth's early efforts to make her way as a professional musician and had encouraged her in her ambitions. She had
spent her life doing what she could to give Ruth a chance to
develop her talents. Years later, Ruth was to exhibit this
same selfless devotion to her own family with infinite patience
and understanding. Clara Graves also had a sense of adventure, exemplified in her sojourn at age sixteen, to Colorado
from Illinois with her younger brother where she taught
school and later became a stenographer. In like manner,
Ruth eagerly faced new experiences, accepting those which
passed her scrutiny as being worthy of her time and attention. Written references to her mother after her death are
few, but the indelible stamp was there; her mother's sense of
adventure, coupled with her sense of devotion never deserted
Ruth, even though they did not see eye to eye on other issues. As Ruth's pattern of living grew more sophisticated,
she and her mother tended to drift apart in such matters as
religion and social concerns. Mrs. Crawford's ambivalence
toward Djane Lavoie Herz--maybe even jealousy of Ruth's new
friends--and her complete distrust of Rudhyar whom Ruth
had met through Madame Herz, were probably factors in their
changing mother-daughter relationship. Mr. Crawford had
been a model of conservatism, which affected Mrs. Crawford
more decidedly than it could have Ruth, since she was very

young when her father died. Though she loved and respected her mother, and in spite of her habit of referring to herself as a child, Ruth was determined to become her own person. In later years, she must often have reflected on the many similarities in their lives.

Regarding the current music scene during her years in Chicago, Ruth left few written comments--there are sporadic references to Goossens, Ravel, Prokofiev, Krenek, Rieti, Honegger, Hindemith, Poulenc. However, it is obvious that she was aware of, understood, and was interested in new ideas, trends, and developments in twentieth-century music. Too, she had knowledge of and personal contact with several important American composers and most of the organizations involved in the performance of new and experimental music which gained some prominence after World War I. That she knew of the activities of such groups as the League of Composers and the International Society for Contemporary Music is evident from the fact that these groups performed her violin and piano sonata. The ISCM, organized in the early 1920s, was dedicated to the spread of knowledge concerning new music with a decidedly international flavor. It is one of the oldest and best established groups interested in furthering the cause of new music, with chapters in all the major music capitals. According to Ruth's Guggenheim application, she was a member of the ISCM which had a Chicago chapter during her years there. This group performed her sonata on its initial concert, February 5, 1928, along with works by Milhaud, Stravinsky, Castelnuovo-Tedesco, and Louis Gruenberg, which is some indication that Chicago musicians recognized Ruth Crawford as worthy to be given a hearing alongside her more illustrious peers.[48] The previous year, the New York-based League of Composers had included this same sonata on a program featuring six young American composers. In addition to Ruth's, works by Randall Thompson, Evelyn Berckman, Marc Blitzstein, Theodore Chanler, and Aaron Copland were performed.[49]

Besides the above-mentioned groups, Ruth was associated with at least two others. She served on the board of the Pro Musica Society, fathered by the French pianist, E. Robert Schmitz, which promoted performances of contemporary music. During the 1928-1929 season, Pro Musica's Chicago chapter sponsored the appearance of Ravel, Bartók, Honegger, Respighi, and Rudhyar in lectures and recitals, and Ruth

The Chicago Years (1924-1929)   51

doubtless heard at least some of these. The Copland-Sessions Concerts, a cooperative project started in 1928 (until 1931) which planned to give performance exposure to both European and American new works, presented works by Ruth Crawford when Richard Buhlig played some of her piano preludes on a program May 6, 1928, in New York City.[50] In addition to these activities, Ruth's talent received recognition in another direction. Her composition, The Adventures of Tom Thumb (1925) for piano and narrator, won first prize in the national composition contest conducted by the Sigma Alpha Iota sorority.[51]

Aaron Copland was beginning his ascent to prominence both as a champion and promoter of his fellow Americans and as a composer in his own right; Edgard Varèse, a native of France, had come permanently to this country (1915) and was writing some of his important, highly innovative scores (Ameriques, Offrandes, Hyperprism, Octandre, Intégrales, Arcana). Henry Cowell, with his unusual treatment of conventional instruments and George Antheil with his use of unconventional music makers, were perhaps our most experimental native composers, and jazz was making its way as an important expressive American musical voice. Critical reviews of the "new music" were often colored by a lack of familiarity with the individual scores and the idiom used, and by a lack of understanding and sympathy with the aims of the composer. Most of the professional critics tended to be conservative and practically all of them denounced jazz outright, although Olin Downes, then critic (1924-1955) of The New York Times, eventually conceded that both jazz and the "new music" were here to stay. Although Ruth assiduously pursued all these developments in art music, her interest in jazz remained peripheral. She made no mention of it, but she did later in Washington, D.C. ask one of her talented students, a boy with a real flair for jazz, to teach her how to play. She soon abandoned the project, however, as she had no talent (or instinct) for that kind of music.[52]

After Ruth received her bachelor's degree from the conservatory she made no specific references to her study of composition or to her piano study--lessons, technique, repertoire--and only a few to her piano teaching--this, despite the fact that musical activities formed the core of Ruth's existence. She did make, however, several statements about her efforts at composition and her difficulties in practicing the piano. She deplored her lack of time for both, her troubles in working out her compositional ideas, her continued inability to use her arms for protracted periods and the weakened condition of her eyes. On one particularly irritable day, Ruth commented: "My wretchedness comes from the returning to my eyes of last year's pulling racking strain which makes practice or composing hard."[53]

Ruth nevertheless continued her efforts to compose. Approximately two dozen manuscripts remain to prove that she tried her hand at composing; however, some of these works were written during her early student days. These include works for piano solo, piano and violin, songs, and some other items. Those dated before 1924 show immaturity, lack of direction, and naivete, but they also reveal talent, imagination, and harmonic daring. Some are doubtless class assignments; some are personal experiments since she wrote quite a number of works before she began her private study with Weidig. Those dated 1924 and later include several compositions of unquestioned value: Five Preludes for Piano (1924-25), The Adventures of Tom Thumb, already mentioned, Four Preludes for Piano (1927-28), Violin and Piano Sonata (1925-26), Suite for Small Orchestra (1926), Suite for Winds and Piano (1927, revised 1929), and Suite No. 2 for Strings and Piano (1929). After Ruth began to consider the possibilities open to her, were she to try to earn her living as a composer, she wrote several teaching pieces. She apparently made no effort to have them published commercially although she herself published one of these in 1926, We Dance Together. Ruth never mentioned popular music; however, she tried her hand at writing pop tunes, for two of which manuscripts remain. These--Lolipop a Papa and an untitled song--both appeared under the pseudonym, Fred Karlan. She soon realized though, that she would not compose for the mass market; that her talents lay in a much more intellectual approach to composition.

Ruth's years in Chicago molded her future both as a person and as a composer. Her somewhat puritan upbringing had provided a solid foundation on which she was able to build a changed set of values while retaining strong character traits which remained basic throughout her life. Her sense of responsibility, her loyalty and devotion to her family and friends and her empathy with people in general, children in particular, with nature and with the intellectual and creative

WE DANCE TOGETHER

RVTH P. CRAWFORD

A piano solo for elementary grades, composed and published by Ruth Crawford Seeger in 1926.

side of life, were all a part of her heritage from her early
years. The outward circumstances of her personal life
changed often and drastically throughout her years in Chicago as her personal experiences became more worldly.
She stretched her mind through continuous acquaintance
with literary and musical masterpieces, she entered a new
social milieu, and became acquainted with new philosophical
concepts and social concerns.

    Her independent mind revealed itself strongly in her
changing attitude toward herself and her position as a woman.
She gradually came to realize that she not only was dissatisfied with herself, but that she actually wanted and longed
to be someone else.[54] The pull between her mother and her
new circles of friends increased; her mother also became more
and more perplexed by Ruth's style of writing as it began to
sound less conventional and more dissonant and rhythmically
complex. Further, Ruth began to consider that her position
as a woman in a man's world put her at a disadvantage. Although in general, she accepted the status of women in the
man's world prevalent during her lifetime, on occasion she
expressed her disapproval of it rather forcibly:

> I also vent my spleen today on the fact of being
> a woman, or rather on the fact that beastly men, not
> satisfied with their own freedom, encroach on that of
> women and produce in them a kind of necessitous
> fear which binds them about. For instance, what is
> more mysterious and delightful than to walk at night,
> especially on deserted and ill-lighted streets, when
> the few windows peek at one delightfully but do not
> intrude on one's aloneness--when shadows are deep
> and silent and the occasional whirrings of cars make
> swift crescendos and diminuendos on the night's symphony? Or to work one's way around the world, a
> poet-tramp, stoker, bell-boy, deck-hand--finding,
> probing into the essence of the roots of living; or a
> recluse for a few years, like Thoreau, building a hut
> off in the deep woods, feeling in his pulse a great
> freedom. Women have gained great independence, but
> men have that which women will never have.[55]

    Ruth saw herself as a bundle of contradictions. She was

The Chicago Years (1924-1929)

... spontaneous with Mildred, Aurelia and the girls. With Madame Herz and her friends I am stiff, uneasy, hesitant; with pupils, lively, a bit overbearing, loudly pleasant; with Gordon, sweet--often apologetic, jocular; with Mr. Hattstaedt, humble, almost a phony. But I am improving here--conciliatory, submissive; with mother--dictatorial, high-handed, ungracious, irritable.[56]

Hers was a sensitive, thoughtful approach to the facts of her existence. She was a serious person with deep feelings which she transmitted to those around her. Although she was somewhat shy, she had developed the knack of making her way with those who interested her. Though things went wrong, as happens to everyone, she was seldom depressed or despondent--nor was she a Pollyanna. She possessed poise and equanimity, and she radiated genuine good will toward all she knew. Ruth matured late sexually--her warm friendship with Alice, her devotion to Weidig and Louise Robyn and to a lesser degree to all of her high school and college teachers, and her adoration of Madame Herz filled her life with meaningful relationships.

Ruth's musical growth during the Chicago years was nothing short of phenomenal. She changed from a talented and ambitious young music student to a promising and budding composer. She had met and made friends with many outstanding musicians interested in contemporary music and had made important contacts with several of the groups devoted to its performance. She had also begun to realize the wider world of music that lay open to her beyond the confines of the windy city. Ruth had already proved that she could support herself through teaching while pursuing her desire to become a composer and, although her financial resources were limited, her ambition was not. Ruth had also come to understand the relative positions of Chicago and New York as they related to the development of contemporary musical idioms that interested her most and as they related to the amount of musical activities and opportunities in general. This was quite possibly a factor in her decision to go to New York in 1929. All we know from Ruth herself about her decision to leave Chicago and try her fortunes elsewhere is contained in two short statements. On December 9, 1928, she commented: "With Buhlig all day. MacDowell called me."[57] In a later resume of her activities, Ruth wrote: "Then a scholarship at the MacDowell Colony came along simultaneously with an offer of a year's stay in the home of a New York patron of modern music. Again I gambled, for there was no capital anywhere, and came east."[58] However, her plans for the winter in New York were aided and abetted by the unflagging zeal and personal interest of one Henry Cowell who arranged for her to have a room in the New York apartment of his friend, Mrs. Blanche Walton, well known as a supporter of struggling young artists, and to study composition with his long-time friend and former teacher, Charles Seeger, of the Institute of Musical Art.[59]

In 1921 Ruth had stated her intention to marry and raise her thirty-five children in Chicago; however, by 1927 "She had decided not to marry, but to concentrate on her career."[60] She really wanted both a family and a career, and though she eventually had both, the pull between the two was never to be completely resolved.

Chapter Four

MACDOWELL COLONY (SUMMER 1929) AND
NEW YORK (1929-1930)

"Only God and my creditors know how poor I am.
I wish my creditors were like God. He takes
his pay too, but he does it gradually, and you
don't realize it until the peanut bag is empty.
Then he blows into it and claps it between his
two hands, and throws away a bag that isn't
any good any more because it has a hole in it.
All the time he is putting peanuts into new bags,
and taking them out of old bags, and there is a
regular stock exchange of peanuts. But he isn't
the kind of creditor who sends you a bill."
(Ruth Crawford, diary jottings, February 27,
1930)

Before going on to New York in the fall of 1929, Ruth spent the summer at the MacDowell Colony in Peterborough, New Hampshire. Although she kept a diary during this period, she did not indicate in any way either how she happened to become interested in this opportunity or who might have helped her obtain the scholarship. It is possible that Blanche Walton, who was to be her patron in New York City, might have instigated these proceedings. Mrs. Walton, an accomplished pianist herself, had been one of the last pupils of Edward MacDowell and knew what such an opportunity could mean to an aspiring young musician. The fact that Ruth received the scholarship at the MacDowell Colony at the same time she was offered the hospitality of Mrs. Walton's home for the coming winter strengthens this speculation. The summer provided Ruth with occasion (her first) to test both her complete personal and musical independence.

Ruth was assigned her own cabin in the pines and was enthralled to be in the midst of nature's beauty. The prospect for her composing was bright and promising, and she was greatly pleased. She quickly and happily adjusted to the routine of the colony which at that time was still personally supervised by Mrs. MacDowell. The colonists, consisting of representatives from all the arts, ate breakfast and dinner together; after dinner, entertainment of some sort, ranging from such activities as recitals to poetry reading, croquet, and stimulating conversation, was available. From 8:30 a.m. to 5:30 p.m., all colonists enjoyed absolute privacy for creative work, with lunch being brought to each cabin door.

Literary people formed the majority of that summer's colonists (1929), and once again Ruth's writing interests were stirred. She soon made many friends and enjoyed their company and conversation immensely. She often mentioned Thornton Wilder, a Mr. Dahlberg and a Jules Bois, who brought her gifts and bits of news from Djane Lavoie Herz. One young writer became a special friend and provided Ruth with a summer romance which she eventually took quite seriously. In fact, she and her friend went so far as to discuss the hazards to her career if she married. Ruth apparently felt there would be a conflict of interests were she to marry and try to pursue a career as a composer at the same time. Also, Ruth's New York plans, which were already worked out in some detail, still held considerable allure for her and she did not really want to relinquish them. So she left the colony with her head winning over her heart.

The musicians were expected to play at a weekly musicale given in the Regina Watkins Hall, a central meeting place for the colony. On these occasions Ruth performed her own compositions. Carl Buchman, another composer, whom Ruth later identified as a pupil of Bernard Wagenaar, and she enjoyed many stimulating hours together, talking of music and composing. Ruth still liked to play tennis and was quite pleased to beat both her friend, Gene, and Charles Haubiel one lucky afternoon.[1]

Ruth's composing activities at the colony consisted of several songs she wrote to poems of Carl Sandburg, three of which, <u>Joy</u>, <u>Sunsets</u>, and <u>Loam</u>, she mentioned in her diary. She seemed to experience difficulty in getting herself oriented to composing in what she called an "environment which was romantic to the point of being unhealthy."² And too, she was for the first time without a teacher of any kind to guide and encourage her either to practice piano or to compose. She berated herself roundly for her seeming lack of initiative, as well as inspiration:

> A wild, mournful day. Work on my songs all morning with no zest, finally crying hard; no inspiration. No will to write, no desire, no vision, no facility. I ask myself why under God's heaven, I am a composer. I say damn, I ask what I am good for. I am not brilliant along any line, I do nothing easily. Have I anything to say? Why write when I have nothing to say? I am sterile, dry. The song I am trying to write is called "Joy."³

Alice's name reappeared, especially during the latter part of the summer when Ruth poured out her feelings in letters to her old friend. A line from one of these is particularly noteworthy since it introduced a motif which appeared throughout most of Ruth's life: "Poor dear Alice, your child is troublesome, a wandering child who does not know her own wants."⁴ Interestingly, Ruth's frequent references to herself as a child are often counterbalanced by her motherly feelings toward other people. Neither of these two aspects of her personality, which persisted throughout her life, ever completely dominated the other, although she harbored feelings of inadequacy to the end.

Near the end of Ruth's summer at the colony, she met and became friends with Marion Bauer:

> Marion Bauer--she has freed me--I am writing again. She asks me to lunch on Tuesday; after lunch she plays some of her preludes... One thing I learned from this beautiful afternoon with Marion Bauer was that I had been forgetting that craftsmanship was also art. I have not been composing and have felt tense, partly because I relied on inspiration only. I was not willing to work things out; I felt that inspiration, emotion within, but when it started to come out, my attitude was so negative that the poor thought crept back into darkness from fear. Discipline. We talked on discipline a few nights ago--necessary--ear-training--hearing away from the

piano. Lie on your couch and hear and study Bach chorales. Make yourself hear; also improvise, not wildly, but making your self hear the next chord. Courage, Marion Bauer tells me--work. You have a great talent. You must go ahead. I do not mean that you must not marry, but you must not drop your work.[5]

Bauer, who evidently thought very highly of her accomplishments and potentialities, continued her interest in Ruth's development long after the summer at the colony. In her book on twentieth-century music, she commented on Ruth's "interesting experimental work in dissonant counterpoint and dissonant rhythm combinations." Bauer made one further interesting and perceptive remark when she said:

> Although distinctly in a cerebral state, her warm emotional nature threatens to break through and when it does, we may expect splendid things from this highly individual thinker and student.[6]

When Bauer wrote these words, she was acquainted with two of Ruth's most important works, the Three Songs on poems of Carl Sandburg for voice, piano, oboe, and percussion, and her String Quartet. Two thoughts in the quotation above are especially apt descriptions of Ruth. "Her warm emotional nature" and "this highly individual thinker" show that Bauer knew her well enough to sense these very strong points in Ruth's personality.

Ruth was obviously dissatisfied with her lack of progress in musical composition and uncertain about her personal life and her romantic feelings. She suffered moods of deep depression and seemed unable to sort out her true feelings toward the problems facing her. Once again, cats, her favorites since childhood, provided her with interesting speculations:

> Rain outside. My mood is gloomier than a London fog. I cannot write. Am I soaked with cocaine that I am so numb? I desire nothing--Nirvana, perhaps. Or to be a cat and have no responsibilities. A cat doesn't get discouraged about her voice on the back fence at midnight. A cat doesn't wonder if her next litter is going to be worthy of her productive genius;

a spontaneous howling; a few weeks later, spontaneous kittens, and life is good.[7]

Although Ruth's musical output during the summer was small, there were personal compensations. She needed this time free from financial worry, for rest from exhausting work and worry during her mother's long last illness; she needed a change of pace, a change of scenery, the stimulation of new faces and minds; she needed to assess her past and consider her future, and to enjoy the utter luxury of a beautiful natural setting in which to fall in and out of love. She apparently pleased Mrs. MacDowell with her deportment and accomplishments since the following winter in New York, Mrs. MacDowell invited her to return the next summer. Ruth was interested and hoped that she and Charles Seeger, by that time her composition teacher, might both be able to go to Peterborough and work together on the writing of a book on dissonant counterpoint. Ruth did not return to the colony as it appeared that Mrs. MacDowell did not approve of the idea of the collaboration on the ground that Charles and Ruth were not married, since this venture would mean that the two of them would spend all day working together, presumably in one or the other of their assigned cabin-studios.[8]

Ruth's transition from the not inconsiderable musical world of Chicago to that of New York was not so abrupt and radical a change as might at first appear. Not too long after Ruth's removal to New York, Madame Herz made her home there, and both Rudhyar and Buhlig were in the city during Ruth's first winter there. New York was also home for Marion Bauer, who had served for several years as Eastern correspondent of the Chicago-based <u>Musical Leader</u>. She had also appeared in Chicago as lecture-recitalist on modern music, and Ruth had become personally acquainted with her at the MacDowell Colony. Several of her friends-to-be in New York were already familiar to her by reputation: Ashley Pettis, champion of American music, Jeanne de Mare, who later made the French translation of Ruth's Three Songs for the New Music Edition, and Mina Hager, a singer, who later performed some of Ruth's songs. Eventually both Vivian Fine and Martha Beck Carragan reentered Ruth's circle of friends in the New York area. And we have already seen that Ruth's works had been given a New York hearing and had been received, for the most part, not unfavorably by the New York press. Groups such as the New York chapter of

Pro Musica and the League of Composers continued to give her music a hearing. And although concert life in New York expanded considerably on Chicago's offerings, the same artists and ensembles performed in both places.

However, there was an almost esoteric quality to the situation in which Ruth found herself when she came to New York. The actually quite small group which revolved around Mrs. Walton, her new patroness, represented only a fringe of musical and cultural activity in New York. Most of the repertoire of recital artists, ensembles, symphony orchestras and opera companies remained strongly conventional and conservative. In Chicago, Ruth had faced reality far more than she would during the coming winter. There she had had to work long hours to make a living, she had faced heavy family responsibilities in the care of her mother through several months of her final illness, and she had worked hard at her studies. Her contact with the everyday world was continuous and her connection with the artistic and intellectual community was something added on--a kind of bonus, which, of course, appealed to her immensely.

A fascinating new kind of living, with a strong touch of glamour for a young girl from Florida, became her way of life when she went to New York. No more daily problems of earning a living or struggling for the niceties of life. Mrs. Walton's patronage assured her not only of superior living conditions and congenial companionship, but also an entree into the musical and intellectual circles which interested her most. In addition, her social contacts widened immensely to include many people she doubtless would not have met by herself. Mrs. Walton, a well-to-do widow as well as a musical amateur, had since the early 1920s championed the cause of many worthy composers interested in the modern music of the day. Notable among the musicians she befriended were Carl Ruggles, Edgard Varèse, Adolph Weiss, Bela Bartók (who made his headquarters with her on his first trip to America), and Henry Cowell.[9] Mrs. Walton's drawing room became a center for the presentation of their works and a meeting place for many other notables--performers, critics, musicologists, dancers--and members of New York society who were interested in and followers of current trends in the arts. Ruth was most fortunate in being placed in the midst of such a stimulating environment, a heady experience indeed, but a challenge she met head on.

MacDowell Colony and New York

The question as to why Ruth was accepted wholeheartedly into this highly select group of people can best be explained on the basis of her personality and her talent. Ruth was unassuming but interested and intelligent, she was kind but curious, she had an unusual blend of child-like qualities and maturity, she was a lady of some refinement but she assumed an easy equality with men in intellectual and musical matters. She was interested in people such as she met and they were interested in her. Her acknowledged talent for musical composition crowned her social and intellectual gifts with a strong appeal to the people who became her associates--and soon--her friends in New York. Henry Cowell's interest in her music and her potentialities assured Ruth of introduction to the circle of his not inconsiderable influence, and she soon proved that his confidence in her was well founded. Through his varied activities, Cowell had contact with all the prominent avant-garde composers of the time, including not only Ruggles, Rudhyar, Riegger, and Seeger, but also Charles Ives, Aaron Copland, Virgil Thomson, and Roger Sessions.

Cowell not only acted as prime mover in arranging for Ruth to live in Mrs. Walton's home; he also lent his persuasive skills to seeing that Mrs. Walton asked Charles Seeger to teach Ruth Crawford composition during this winter.[10] Seeger was also a good friend of Mrs. Walton, having met her through Cowell and having been a guest of her home along with Cowell, Carl Ruggles, Richard Buhlig, and Dane Rudhyar. Seeger, distinguished American teacher and musicologist, whose approach to teaching composition centered around his concepts of dissonant counterpoint and dissonant rhythm, was at this time a member of the advance guard in "modern music" circles. When Cowell showed Seeger some of Ruth's compositions, he criticized them severely, saying why bother about women composers, about whose capabilities in this field he had freely and often expressed his skepticism. Seeger felt that the compositions Cowell showed him relied too much on Scriabinian harmony. Cowell, not to be put down, replied that although he knew Seeger's criticism was just, Ruth had possibilities. Seeger finally agreed to accept Ruth as his pupil with certain stipulations:

> Miss Crawford will pledge herself to take six lessons at such and such a fee which was to be paid by Mrs. Walton in advance. After that we can make a

new arrangement. If she wishes to study with somebody else she's at liberty to do so, but she must promise to take those six lessons.

Seeger's description of the first lessons he gave to Ruth has likewise been recounted by him:

> Mrs. Walton prepared the first lesson as skilfully as she could and arranged that it would take place in her living room where she had a new Steinway, at five o'clock one afternoon. The lesson was to last for an hour or two then there was to be supper served for the three of us. I came and was introduced to Miss Crawford and the doors were duly closed on the living room and the lesson began.
> ...The first lesson with Ruth was spent mostly on my critique of European and American composition up to the year 1930 and my criticism of her work as being too diffuse, having too much reliance on Scriabinian harmony, and advising that she should start off first in making single melodic lines that would be dissonated in accord with my theory that the sooner you could dissonate a melodic line the better ... when the knock on the door signalled supper being ready, it was disregarded. Finally, the knock became more and more insistent and we gave over and by that time the conversation was throwing sparks and we were having a wonderful time. And as I remember the supper afterwards was marvelous.
> The lessons went on for the required six and at the end we made the arrangement that Ruth would have as many lessons as she and I should decide upon and I would earn my living from other pupils and that there would be no charge.[11]

Seeger's skepticism about Ruth's capabilities and talents vanished once the lessons started, and the two of them soon discovered that they shared similar views about what they wanted in so-called "modern music." Ruth, who felt this rapport quite strongly, acknowledged that her study with Seeger provided a vital turning point in her musical development:

> [He] shared with me his conception of the aspects

and as yet untried possibilities, both in form and
content, of a new music, and his views as to various
means of bringing some organic coordination out of
the too often superabundance of materials in use at
present. As a result of this study, my work began
at last to take a "handleable" shape, to present itself
in some sort of intelligible continuity.[12]

Ruth soon proved to be an extremely apt pupil, but
one who also insisted on putting her own quirk, her own individual touch into the working out of an assignment. As a
help in learning compositional techniques, Seeger and Ruth
also spent much time in analyzing both classical and contemporary works--from Beethoven to Brahms to Schoenberg--for
motivic and thematic treatment, dissecting the material and
often metamorphosing it into an entirely new composition.

Although Ruth had heard the earlier compositions of
Schoenberg in Chicago ("Henry wouldn't have let her go all
through the twenties without at least seeing and playing the
Opus 11 and Opus 19"),[13] she had not studied the twelve-
tone works. When Seeger introduced the Suite for Piano,
Op. 25 and the Quintet for Winds, Op. 26 to Ruth, she was
completely fascinated by them. She evidently felt a natural
affinity for the highly organized type of composition these
both exemplified.

Ruth's compositions during her first winter in New
York reflect her attempts to incorporate Seeger's ideas into
the Suite for Five Wind Instruments and Piano as she prepared the revised edition of this 1927 score, and to utilize
them in her first essays in dissonant counterpoint and the
manipulation of a single, but dissonated melodic line[14] (three
of her four Diaphonic Suites for small chamber music groups
and the Piano Study in Mixed Accents). In her powerful
and imaginative setting of Carl Sandburg's poem <u>Rat Riddles</u>,
she combined all her technical skills with highly individual
touches to produce one of her most complex and artistic
works to date. Even though several of Ruth's compositions
from her tutelage with Weidig show many traits of her mature
style, such as a liking for dissonance, a tendency toward
tightly organized works, and a general avoidance of conventional compositional techniques, her year with Seeger emphasized a positive approach to new ways of working which utilized her talents and tendencies to a remarkable degree.

The winter also gave Ruth opportunities for performance of some of her compositions from the Chicago years. One such occasion took place around the middle of January 1930, when Mrs. Walton held a musicale in her spacious apartment for a very select group of people. The program consisted solely of Ruth's works. Heard that evening were the revised version of the Suite for Five Wind Instruments and Piano, performed by the Pan American Ensemble, some of the Piano Preludes which Ruth played herself, Five Songs (Sandburg texts), sung by Radiana Pazmor, an old friend of Henry Cowell from their childhood in San Francisco, with the composer at the piano, and Suite No. 2 for Strings and Piano, played by the New World String Quartet, with Colin McPhee at the piano. As Ruth herself described the affair:

> The reception. Our reception. Blanche's and mine. Dear beautiful Blanche. Rare and beautiful. Exquisite, understanding. Idealism. Devotion to a cause. I told her once that one of my dear friends had asked me to thank her for being so kind to me. "Tell her I'm doing it for Art," Blanche replied. Then with a twinkle in her eye. And she added, "And if you don't write good music, then I'm wasting my time!" We both liked that, and laughed delighted. She has a soaring quality. And an elfin sense of wit. And a frankness and directness that refresh.
> There were over a hundred and twenty people here at the reception. Blanche scornfully corrected my underestimate of seventy. Since we ordered eighty-four chairs, and can seat over thirty in our own, and people were standing in the halls, I think she is right.
> Winthrop Tryon, critic of the <u>Christian Science Monitor</u>, said he hadn't enjoyed an evening so much in years. He told several people that. And he really is a sincere person! Also he told Blanche that he knew no one who could draw the distinguished audience together that Blanche drew here. Marion said the same. Said she thought I couldn't appreciate what a group of people were gathered here. The entire group of dancers interested in modern art, were here. I won't name them, except for Martha Graham who is remarkable. Leon Theremin, whose instrument you remember hearing. Shy, quiet, and Blanche and I fall in love with him. And have

him a week later to dinner and a concert. Paul
Rosenfeld, former critic of the World. He seemed
enthusiastic. Observers said he looked as tho he
were enjoying himself.
    I'm just repeating myself, for I think I've told
you all this before. There is not much else to tell.
Gruenberg was here, also, and Alfred Kreymbourg.
And the whole evening went off so well that it was
an anticlimax, since the preliminary rehearsals had
been belated and hectic. The reception cost Blanche
between three and four hundred dollars. I was so
afraid she was going to be ashamed of me and my music, that I was in agony. Became terribly depressed
in the midst of finishing the quintette. And so
therefore, the anticlimax.[15]

    Ruth's compositions were performed on other occasions
also. The Five Songs was sung for the League of Composers
by Radiana Pazmor and the Suite for Strings and Piano was
performed for the New York Pro Musica Society. Pazmor
also sang the first performance of Rat Riddles for the Pan
American Association. It is evident that Ruth's music was
being given a hearing in New York City and that she was
building on the reputation she had started to attain before
she came east.

    In addition to Mrs. Walton's patronage, Ruth still enjoyed the thoughtfulness and generosity of Marion Bauer,
who continued her interest in Ruth's incipient career and
who personally provided Ruth with tickets and invitations to
musical events of importance. Together, these two good
friends insured the young musician's exposure to the best
that New York City had to offer, including attendance at a
symphony concert conducted by Toscanini where she sat as a
guest in Toscanini's box and met the famous conductor after
the concert. She also met Mrs. Sprague Coolidge, well-known
patroness of music; Carlos Salzedo, accomplished composer
but perhaps best known as a harpist and champion of modern
music, Harold Bauer and Ernest Hutcheson, pianists, Mary
Howe and Lazare Saminsky, composers, and Hans Barth, widely known for his interest in quarter-tone music, especially the
quarter-tone piano which he helped to perfect.[16] Ruth was
also present at a private hearing of Juan Carrillo's music consisting of quarter- eighth- and sixteenth-tone compositions,
both vocal and instrumental.[17] Although the concept of frac-

tional tones goes back to antiquity, their cultivated use in modern times stems from the last decade of the nineteenth century. Carrillo was a Mexican-American composer whose experiments with tones smaller than a half remain among the most important of the twentieth century, and Ruth was fortunate to be exposed to such ideas during her year in New York.

Mrs. Walton's home was not only a center of musical activity but also a social gathering place for many of the avant-garde musicians of the day. Henry Cowell and Carl Ruggles visited often, as did Charles Seeger who was a close friend of both Henry and Carl. Ruth gained valuable insights into the character of these people which she noted with great candor and amazing attention to detail. Her description of Charles Seeger is of particular interest, in view of later developments. These are her words:

> Charlie is tall, aristocratic, ultra-refined, a bit cold. Ara describes him as five feet of ice and ten feet of books. He is handsome and wears a correct moustache, correct glasses and an encyclopedic air. He is fifteen [sic] years younger than Carl Ruggles and a father to him.[18]

Ruth continued her friendship with Henry Cowell, who at that time was teaching at the New School for Social Research. He took her to some of his lectures through which she learned of new vocal experiments in Europe, in which composers used percussive-vocal effects. She also learned of a poet "who makes poetry of vocal syllables and sounds, in musical forms."[19] As in the past, Cowell proved to be an important source of new musical ideas which Ruth quickly absorbed, e.g., she was to experiment with meaningless syllables in her three chants for chorus.

She attended rehearsals of the ISCM and heard experimental compositions there. She was particularly interested in a work by the American composer, Wallingford Riegger, scored for ten strings, in which he experimented with the effects to be obtained "by throwing one range of the same instrument against the other."[20]

Ruth's growing self-assurance and quick-wittedness in the musically sophisticated company in which she found herself shine clearly through the following delightful conversation which took place when she encountered Winthrop Tryon at a musicale:

> "Do you know you are different from other composers?" he asks.
> I am interested and curious. I beg to know how I am different from other composers.
> "Because you don't look at me asking the question with your eyes, 'Well, how do you like my compositions?' You don't care what people think of your compositions, do you?"
> I smile, and reply with emphasis, "I care what <u>some</u> people think of my compositions."[21]

During the winter, Ruth also kept up one other activity--that of story writing. While in residence at the MacDowell Colony the previous summer, she had met and made friends with probably more writers than she did musicians. At Peterborough, Marion Bauer had been instrumental in introducing Ruth to Edna Yost who later interceded for Ruth when Ruth sent the manuscripts for some of her stories to various publishers. The publishers expressed interest in her work, but not to the point of publication. Ruth never really gave up her girlhood ambition to become a writer or the long-held idea that she might be able to supplement her income as a teacher and composer of music by her writing activities. As things eventually worked out, she did become well-known for her writing, albeit not the writing of stories. She refined her writing style most successfully in the essays she provided as introductions to her books of folk songs.

Ruth was acutely aware of her financial poverty, but she was even more aware of the richness of her experiences, and of the kindnesses of the many friends she was able to make largely through the hospitality of Blanche Walton, whose home had become a haven of joy, inspiration, and understanding for her. Not only did Ruth endear herself to Mrs. Walton, but also to many of the people she met through her, particularly her new composition teacher. At the end of the spring season, Seeger planned to go up as usual to his father and mother's place at Patterson, N.Y., to take care of his three boys, Charles, John, and Peter (by his first wife, Constance, from whom he had been living apart for

Ruth Crawford (Westport, Connecticut, ca. 1929)

quite a while). Since neither Seeger nor Ruth liked the idea of stopping the lessons, he arranged to have Ruth live at a farmer's house nearby so that she could continue her work with him. A month later, Seeger and the boys moved to Westport, Ct., and Ruth lived a few miles away with Mrs. Walton. The lessons, now on a daily basis, took the "form of dictation of the resume of a book that was to be published and dedicated to Ruth called <u>Tradition and Experiment in Twentieth Century Music</u>."[22]

It was during this summer that Ruth became acquainted with Charles, John, and Peter Seeger. They remained friends with Ruth as long as she lived, although the two older boys, Charles and John, were practically grown by this time and soon gone from home. Peter, who was only eleven or twelve, developed a warm friendship with Ruth and eventually with Charles and Ruth's children. Peter's lifelong rapport with his father was soon extended to Ruth. As he said, "I got along with Ruth wonderfully. I liked her a lot ... we enjoyed each other's company and I think my father was probably very happy about this because I was very close to my father...."[23]

As the summer drew to a close, Ruth began to make plans to spend the following year in Europe as recipient of the Guggenheim Foundation fellowship awarded her for study in composition. She made arrangements to leave in August from Quebec, Canada. Charles and Ruth made the trip to Quebec by car, stopping overnight with his old friends, Charlotte and Carl Ruggles in Arlington, Vermont. But this is Charles Seeger's story and he told it better than anyone else could:

> That evening standing on a bridge overlooking the river in Arlington we suddenly realized that we were in love with each other and the prospect of parting in four days made the rest of the trip agonizingly--I don't know what word to use--I can't say enjoyable--but intense! I even had the thought that I would get on the ship and go over with her, but I had the feeling it would be the best thing for her to be off on her own for a while and get a little perspective on the nine months work with me and form her own impressions of musical Europe.[24]

Ruth and Charles's interest in each other had been gradually growing probably from as early as February. This is hard to substantiate except by reading between the lines. The apparent suddenness of their realization of the situation was doubtless preceded by much unspoken thought and feeling on the part of both.

Thus ended a brilliant and exciting year for one who appeared to be taking giant steps, not only in her career as a composer, but also in her development as a person. Although short, this period in Ruth's life was one of the richest and most rewarding thus far. She had successfully met the challenge offered by one of the most important cities musically, New York City; she had immersed herself in its musical activities and had been accepted unconditionally by the distinguished company in which she found herself, regardless of her sex. She adapted quickly to the more sophisticated outlook of her peers, though she never lost her native ability to assess others as well as herself in a dispassionate manner regardless of their place of origin. It is hard to exaggerate the richness of Ruth's experiences during this year and the extent of her exposure to all the important trends in contemporary music, to say nothing of the tremendous expansion in Ruth's social outlook, taking in stride the association with many great and near-great names, all of which gave momentum to her ever-present efforts to combat her lack of self confidence and to develop her self both personally and musically.

She had also gained a modest amount of recognition as a composer, had won a Guggenheim Foundation fellowship, and had found not only a composition teacher who was able to draw her out musically, but also a man who was destined to be hers for life.

Chapter Five

THE EUROPEAN EXPERIENCE
(1930-1931)

"I begin to feel that this year should have been just as it is ... in my own personal development ... facing myself alone in reaction to varying situations has and will have given me more of a balance within...." (Ruth Crawford, letter to Charles Seeger, Berlin, January 29, 1931)

The following article appeared in an unidentified newspaper under the dateline of June 30, 1930, and was entitled "Chicago Girl Sails for Foreign Study":

> The first woman to win a Guggenheim fellowship in musical composition sailed this week for a year of European study from Quebec aboard the Canadian Pacific Liner Empress of Scotland. Miss Ruth Crawford, though still in her early twenties, has already composed a quintet for strings and piano, a quintet for wind instruments and piano, a violin sonata and a collection of songs and piano pieces. All of her chamber music has been performed in New York and has won high praise from critics. Miss Crawford studied in Chicago under Adolf Weidig and in New York under Charles L. Seeger and Mme. Djane Lavoie. She will divide her time in Europe by making successive visits to Berlin, Paris, and Budapest where she will continue her studies under noted masters and will perfect certain compositions in larger forms which she now has in manuscript.

This article contains several errors: Ruth sailed in August rather than June 1930; she was twenty-nine years old, not in her early twenties; and she studied with Madame Djane Lavoie Herz in Chicago rather than in New York.

Ruth's formal application for a Guggenheim Foundation fellowship listed the following aims:

> To write one major work of the general magnitude of a symphony, for full orchestra, and various minor works for smaller combinations.
> Also to continue my studies in orchestration and composition, in Paris and Berlin.

Before leaving New York, Ruth prepared for her study by writing to selected composers and by asking other people to write letters of introduction for her so that she could meet and discuss her music with these composers and exchange ideas with them. She did not rule out the possibility of study with specific teachers; neither did she commit herself to a definite course of action, since she knew she was most comfortable in an informal situation where she could feel free to take advantage of whatever opportunities came her way. Ruth felt rather strongly that she needed to discover what she really wanted and to digest her study of the previous winter with Seeger before being presented with additional compositional ideas. She also began to realize the validity of, and to share in, Seeger's estimate of her musical development that she was already a mature composer and perfectly able to work independently. Most important of all, she understood the value of, and looked forward to, having unlimited time at her disposal for her own composing.

When Ruth left New York to begin her European study, her works had already received notable performances in both Chicago and New York. She had displayed outstanding talent for avant-garde musical ideas and had been accepted and encouraged by established musicians active in this area, and with a minimum of sexual discrimination. Ruth possessed not only unusual compositional talent, she was also very knowledgeable concerning new developments both in Europe and in the United States. During her year in New York, she had become personally acquainted with new musical currents as represented by the experimental ideas of Henry Cowell, Edgard Varèse, Carl Ruggles, Wallingford Riegger, Carlos

Chavez, and others in the United States and Latin America. Further, when she arrived in Berlin in the fall of 1930, she was completely familiar with the musical aesthetics of Schoenberg and Hindemith, both of whom were active in that city during her winter there. She likewise knew the works of Stravinsky, Prokofiev, Ravel, Honegger, Milhaud, Berg, Bartók, Hauer, and others prominent in European music circles of the time. Ruth was thus, at least theoretically, familiar with most of the concepts and ideologies current at that time on both sides of the Atlantic.

Although her keen intellectual gifts allowed her to evaluate and appreciate the new developments in music, she nonetheless brought with her to Europe limited experience in practical personal confrontation with the people behind the ideas. No teacher went with her, no close friend, no family. She had to rely completely on her own ingenuity and personal resources to make the contacts and enjoy the experiences awaiting her. Ruth genuinely enjoyed meeting people who interested her, and she looked forward to this activity. She soon began to realize the implications of what she already knew: There were many new approaches to the treatment of the fundamentals of music and to the efforts to extend and eventually annihilate tonality, the supremacy of harmony, and fixed forms; in the same way, she understood the current efforts to elevate melody and rhythm to positions of first importance. From the tone of the quotation that stands at the head of this chapter, Ruth also realized she was maturing rapidly as a person.

There was one thing, however, that Ruth had not counted on as she made her plans for this momentous period in her life. Her new-found love for Charles Seeger would soon be making drastic changes in her previously held attitudes toward her life and, coincidentally, her music. This new personal element disturbed her previous doubt-free ideas as to what goals she wished to pursue. Love, marriage, and a family had always been in her plans for the future, but these had not intruded seriously on her thoughts of becoming a composer. She had not allowed for the devastating effect that new experience would have on her thoughts, words, and actions. Thus her lack of commitment to a specific course of action in Europe was made further pronounced by her efforts to sort out her feelings, to analyze, understand, and cement her relationship with Charles Seeger.

Ruth arrived in London in late August and set out immediately to explore, as much as time permitted, that fascinating city. Her stay there also included a visit with Kenneth Curwen of the Curwen Publishing Company. "On to Curwen's. Kenneth Curwen and his assistant welcomed me; we talk of Carl Ruggles, modern music, Charlie, and spend a very interesting hour. They look long at my songs, but give little hope for printing."[1]

On her way from London to Berlin where Ruth had decided to live during her first months abroad, she visited a number of places including Cologne, Antwerp, Bonn, Frankfurt, Nuremburg, Munich, Liege, Brussels, Rothenburg, and Leipzig. In Liege, she attended some concerts of the Eighth International Society for Contemporary Music Festival. She also met there Yves Tinayre and his wife who subsequently became good friends of hers in Paris; Raymond Petit, French music critic who reviewed modern music for both French and American publications; J. B. Trend, known for his books on Spanish music; and Harry Kling, associated with the Chester Publishing Company, London.[2]

Once in Berlin she soon found a suitable place to live—a room large enough to contain a piano and work area as well as pleasant and adequate living accommodations. Here she immediately set about her composing activities on which she concentrated during her long stay in the city. Work on three chants, Ruth's only contribution to choral literature, originally set for women's chorus, claimed her attention shortly after she was settled. These occupied her time during October and November although she had done some work on the first one before she left New York. Ruth eventually mailed all three to Gerald Reynolds, conductor of the Women's University Glee Club in New York, who apparently expected to perform them as a group. A fourth chant never got past the planning stage. She often referred to the set as the "Reynolds Chants."[3] On his Town Hall program of May 7, 1931, Reynolds included only the chant titled <u>To an Angel</u> (No. 2). Ruth also worked on the first and second movements of her string quartet in Berlin, the last two movements of which she had pretty well finished before she went abroad. She also brought to Europe the Diaphonic Suites which she had commenced in New York with Charles Seeger the previous winter and on which she did further work in Berlin.

The European Experience

Interspersed with her composing activities were Ruth's attendance at "new music" concerts and personal contacts with composers and other musicians. Imre Weisshaus, known as Paul Arma after World War II, and his wife, Virginia, whom she had met the previous winter in New York, were back in Europe, and they became probably Ruth's closest personal friends on the continent. Weisshaus, a composer and a native of Budapest, had studied with Bartók for three years and was familiar with the European musical scene. He was able to help Ruth meet composers of new music and probably helped her arrange for the performance of one of her suites by the Novembergruppe, a performing group apparently associated with the International Society for Contemporary Music, in Berlin. Ruth was doubtless present when this group played her Diaphonic Suite for cello and viola (No. 4) on April 8, 1931[4]--the only performance of her works given in Europe during her sojourn there. As her friendship with Weisshaus developed, she was provided with a firsthand opportunity to observe his work. She noticed that various ideas of his resembled some she was already using herself. "It is almost uncanny how he has been seeking, in some ways, almost identical paths with many principles of dissonant counterpoint."[5]

Ruth's sensitivity to new ideas led her to think seriously of trying to experiment with some of them. She described some interesting instrumental effects she heard at a concert where Frederick Trautwein demonstrated his electrophonic instrument, the Trautonium (invented in 1930), one of several experiments which appeared after the Russian scientist, Theremin, introduced the first such instrument in the twenties. "The Trautonium produces notes from the air according to the chromatic scale by means of a special device."[6]

> Imagine a kind of glissando starting from the low beat tones keeping the same speed of beats per second but rising in pitch to a high xylophone through the entire huge range; or else, starting again with the percussion effect rising and modulating in a wide sweep into the cantabile of a cello, or on one tone modulating through an infinite variety of tone qualities. I'm wondering if this modulation from the percussion to the cello, and myriad other effects can be notated and played. I feel tempted to attempt a composition for it.[7]

Ruth frequently mentioned Wladimir Vogel, a Russian musician and a student of Busoni, who was in Berlin during her stay there. His compositions reportedly show the influence of both Scriabin and Schoenberg.[8] Ruth probably heard his cantata, <u>Wagadu</u>, when it was performed in Munich on May 19:

> Vogel, whose Toccata you heard, asked me to a little musical evening last week, requesting that I play. Luckily, I had been practising somewhat this month. Unluckily, Stuckenschmidt, the critic, arrived after I played (perhaps luckily). Hans Gutman of the cold Egyptian face was there; Nicolai Lopatnikof, whom I am to visit tomorrow night, Wiener, an important man in radio and a number of others of varying interest and importance.[9]

Why Ruth did not make meaningful contacts with either Hindemith or Schoenberg during these months needs to be addressed, however briefly. She did arrange to have one short meeting with Hindemith which, however, she felt was unproductive.[10] And a projected meeting with Schoenberg did not even take place, due largely to difficulties in arranging the time for the appointment.[11] Although she understood and fully appreciated the important theoretical contributions of each of these composers, she felt no particular rapport with their approaches to composition. Under these circumstances, she apparently did not consider it vital, or perhaps, even appropriate to pursue their acquaintance further.

Ruth did, however, enjoy two visits with Josef Rufer, who had been a Schoenberg student and who was, in 1931, his assistant at the Akademie der Kunste in Berlin. He was also an important writer on the theories of Schoenberg and of composition with twelve tones, and Ruth thoroughly enjoyed hearing his discourse on these matters. She mentally compared his theoretical ideas with those of Charles Seeger and would have liked more time to discuss counterpoint with him. Her talks with Rufer made her anxious for Seeger to finish his book on dissonant counterpoint, on which she had worked with him the previous summer:

> Important. Josef Rufer has just finished his book collecting Schoenberg's ideas on counterpoint,

so I hear. And it is ready to be published. Your
book should not come out later; it must be finished
soon.[12]

Did I tell you of my second meeting with Josef
Rufer: I find him extraordinarily sympathetic. In
fact, we talked so long, agreeing and discussing and
sometimes not quite agreeing, that the time was gone
and we had only a short time for his manuscript of
the counterpoint book. He showed me a few examples
which looked like the continuant idea, but really
weren't....[13]

As her stay in the German capital drew to a close,
Ruth entertained high hopes of being able to visit Russia.
An acquaintance, a Dr. Ernst Chain,[14] tried to help her arrange such a trip at comparatively little cost; but although
she considered it seriously, she was not able to carry out her
plan.

I should like to meet Feinberg, if possible, show
some of my works to him and others. What [goes]
on in Russia always interests me more--it seems truly
like a land of the future. I may become a Communist
yet. What do you think of my plan? I am rather
thrilled over it. If through Chain and Henry I could
get in touch with a few composers and people who
interest themselves in new music it would be very
worthwhile. I should enjoy this too for a change.[15]

And so Ruth left Berlin for Paris--by way of Vienna,
Budapest, and Munich where she enjoyed many interesting,
important, and challenging musical experiences. She went to
Vienna first, where she visited the Universal Edition headquarters and was lucky enough to find the director, Emil
Hertzka, in his office. He received her kindly; however, he
did not offer any hope for publication of her music. She began to feel that if she had cultivated the acquaintance of important people or had studied with a well-known composer she
would have received some recognition for her work and would
perhaps have been successful in getting it published. But
this concept was repugnant to her, and the gradual realization of its importance to a budding composer became a strong
factor in her attitude toward striving for commercial success.[16]
Too, Ruth had seldom encountered discrimination because of

her sex, so when Hertzka intimated that this might make it hard for her to get her music published, she was understandably distressed. "What is this for reasoning? He did not see my music."[17]

Ruth's assessment of Berg's opera <u>Wozzeck</u> as probably "the most towering of a very few master works in Europe today"[18] shows clearly her great admiration for this giant of twentieth-century music. Her respect for his achievements prompted her to try to make his acquaintance and, if circumstances would permit, to show him some of her compositions. Her informal way of attempting to meet people brought only frustration at her first effort, although she was able to arrange to have a good visit with him the following week.[19] In the meantime, she managed to arrange for visits with both Egon Wellesz and Josef Hauer. Wellesz, who had been a composition student of Schoenberg, was at the time Ruth visited him, a musicology professor at the University of Vienna. Hauer, who like Schoenberg, worked with the idea of twelve-tone music, claimed priority in the development of such a system. In 1931, Hauer was working in Vienna as a conductor, teacher, and composer.

> Wellesz lives near. I have made no appointment. I like taking chances and have learned that I am most at home in the informal manner of approach. I give Foss's name of the Oxford Press which he had told me to do. Imre's and Marion Bauer's. Wellesz received me with charm and we had a delightful time. I am to call him again next Thursday. We will get together again.[20]

Later that same afternoon she enjoyed a long conversation with Josef Hauer:

> Four-thirty. Hauer talked to me almost three hours about his twelve-tone system. An intense man, who believes intensely in truth he has found for himself; who is colossally sure, who says himself that he is the only man in the musical world who can teach anyone anything about what modern music should be. He is seeking in his way what you speak so much of--more unity--something to hold the structure together--a new system to replace the old.[21]

The European Experience   81

Ruth's three-day visit to Budapest proved to be quite
successful and satisfying, as she was able to see several
composers of some importance and interest to her with whom
she wanted to exchange music and musical ideas. Her
ability to ingratiate herself with people who interested her
seems to have stood her in good stead, despite the fact that
she seldom made formal appointments to call on them. This
lack of pretense and her genuine interest in people was often
disarming to the point of being an effective approach to the
attainment of her goals.

She found a room the evening of her arrival and set
out on her adventures the following morning. She visited
with Lázló Lajtha, a Hungarian composer with strong interests
in ethnomusicology, and showed him some of her music (not
specified). That evening she visited with Antal Molnár, who
was active not only as a composer but who was also interested
in the sociological aspects of music:

> A dear and fine person he is; critic--has written
> a book on modern music, teaches harmony. He is
> very neugierig [anxious] to see "the book." Was
> too, very much interested in my music and asked me
> to leave more of it at the Academy the next day.[22]

Again, Ruth did not specify which of her scores she
showed to Molnár. The following morning she met Kadosa,
"a charming, sweet, unassuming person who plays piano
electrically."[23] Kadosa, a composition student of Kodály,
taught piano at a music school in Budapest for many years.

Ruth's efforts to meet and visit with Bartók were
realized on the second day of her stay in Budapest. He
talked to her only briefly at the Academy, but was very kind
and seemed interested. Later she met him at his home and
enjoyed a more extended visit, although she did not mention
any discussion of either his compositions or her own:

> He asked me into his work room and we spent a
> delightful while. Childlike, he showed me his Arabian
> and Hungarian flutes and other things; turned his
> back, told me not to look, and asked me to guess
> while he played a Jew's harp. From the subject of
> overtones, I excitedly branched to undertones and
> told him what I also forgot to tell you--that Imre and

I with a tuning fork on the edge of a piece of paper
got the undertones as far as the seventh. He was
surprised--said he understood they were only theoretical, etc. And I was inside tickled to be able to
tell him something. He is a dear, quiet, shy, little
person, isn't he?[24]

    The third day in Budapest, Ruth was able to call on
György Kósa, a composition student of Bartók and a piano
student of Dohnányi; also Hugo Kelen, a minor figure on the
Budapest scene in the early thirties. She was not successful,
however, in meeting Kodály who, along with Bartók, was
probably the most important of the Hungarian musicians at
the time of Ruth's visit. She was told he was out of town.
She then took the train back to Vienna where the following
day the long-awaited visit with Berg finally took place.

    Ruth's rather extended account of this meeting points
up two aspects of her personality: her efforts to overcome
her shyness around people she felt were superior to her
seemed to be bearing fruit in the ease she felt in Berg's
presence; her failure to bring with her the manuscript to
what is considered one of her most important compositions,
her String Quartet, emphasized the idea that making an impression on the "right" people and commercial success were
not uppermost in her mind. It also gives valuable insights
into Berg's specific thoughts on western and American composers of that time:

> ...At his house at ten. At first, he was more
> sympathetic than later. Very much interested--
> seemed surprised that America had that kind of a
> Richtung [direction]. With the datum of six years
> old stamped in words on my Preludes, I played two,
> just to give a historic idea of my development. His
> face was gleamingly, genuinely pleased, but after
> the choruses came a discussion, pleasant enough,
> started by my statement that Schoenberg, until Op.
> 25, pleases me more than his later work. I am
> trying to develop a polite frankness and make myself
> lose my fear of expressing an opinion.... We then
> continued work on the chorus. He made a suggestion
> which seemed very good. We worked over it quite a
> while.
>   Then he said he sees in my music still further

> proof of the difference in direction between German
> and western music, and western music comes more
> from Debussy. Too homophonic, too harmonic! I
> then showed him the suites and pointed out a few
> things. He still was not of the feeling that it was
> contrapuntal in his sense of the word. I told him
> how sorry I was to have forgotten the quartet which
> has crabs, canons, contraria, and everything German
> (I didn't say that). He still advised me to study
> German music more and to write something in a
> larger form demanding more coordination and develop-
> ment of ideas.... Though, as he said, I don't need
> to write German music just because I study it. He
> was really sympathetic, but not so much as I had
> hoped. He is more German and more of a Schoenberg
> worshipper than I would have thought--a grand,
> towering, rich personality, yet very simple.[25]

Ruth spent several days in Munich where she attended a number of concerts given during a contemporary music festival. Malipiero, prominent Italian composer, educator, and editor of the time, who prepared a collected edition of Monteverdi's works, was represented at this festival by a performance of his opera Torneo Notturno. Ruth heard this work and also met the composer and talked with him briefly. She characterized the opera as romantic, both musically and textually, and compared Malipiero's treatment of the theme with Berg's treatment of a like theme in Wozzeck.[26]

Die Mutter, a quarter-tone opera by the Moravian composer Alois Haba, was likewise performed in Munich during Ruth's stay in that city. She not only attended the performance of the opera, but also heard Haba deliver an illustrated lecture about it the night before the performance:

> You should have seen the German audience bristle
> when he said a bit hesitatingly, but with conviction,
> that the Slavic race--he is from Prague--is naturally
> more able to appreciate and understand the quarter-
> tone than the people farther west, because the Slavs
> are nearer to the east and have, in their folk songs,
> heard the smaller intervals for centuries.... The
> opera itself, the strangeness of sound, is fascinating.
> One feels, as many laymen must feel when they first
> hear dissonant twelve-tone music, one swims in a sea

of unaccustomed relations and floats about not seeing land anywhere, yet not drowning either. Hába uses many of our old chords, but one scarcely recognizes them. Asked if he observes the tonal relations when he uses them, he said emphatically that once the quarter tones are introduced there are no more the old tonal relations--new ones are created. He bristled when someone asked if his music were atonal. He said, "there is no term."[27]

Ruth's experiences in Vienna had provided one of the highlights of her year--her meeting with Alban Berg. Her great admiration for the music of Berg was reinforced by her personal encounter with him--she respected his ideas and felt that her short contact with him was profitable musically. Budapest had been a whirlwind of new faces, many of whom were friends of Imre Weisshaus. Her meeting with Bartók gave her added confidence that she need not fear personal confrontation with composers of considerable renown. Bartók, throughout practically all of his life, successfully combined his researches into the field of folk music with his art music composition--a situation with which Ruth grappled much later in her career. She gave no indication, however, that she was at that time familiar with his accomplishments in this area. Ruth's few days in Munich had afforded her more opportunities to absorb new sounds and ideas before she went on to Paris (via Venice for a short holiday), where she arrived early in June.

In Paris, Ruth found much the same situation as far as "connections" were concerned. She met some more of her old friends from America here: besides Adolph Weiss, she met Varèse and the Rudhyars, both of whom she had seen in New York the previous winter. Ruth continued with the same pattern of work and relaxation that she had followed in Germany. Interspersed with her composing--working further on the first two movements of her string quartet and on the first two of the three Sandburg songs (<u>Rat Riddles</u>, enlarged version and <u>In Tall Grass</u>)--she continued to attend concerts and to seek out important musicians with whom she visited and to whom she showed her music. She heard some American music in Paris (Cowell, Copland, Ives, Weiss) at two concerts conducted by Nicolas Slonimsky, given under the auspices of the Pan American Association of Composers. After one of the concerts, she enjoyed an exhilarating conversation with Varèse:

The European Experience 85

> Varèse pitched into you tonight--we had quite a
> discussion. Ruth didn't agree with Varèse and some-
> times said so emphatically but apparently impartially.
> You might have enjoyed my matter-of-fact, yet firm
> holding of my ground smiling into the gripping green
> eyes and telling them I didn't agree. And several
> times, enigmatically, kept silence. We got on quite
> well in spite of not agreeing ... I like him....
> Through Adolph I learn he thinks I have come to
> study with him.... Perhaps if the Guggenheim comes
> and I stay a few fall months, I shall after all do some
> work with him.[28]

In Quebec the previous August, when Ruth and Charles took leave of one another, they made plans for him to come to Paris for a visit, probably the following summer. As the time for the visit drew ever nearer, they both entertained high hopes for the work they could thus accomplish together. Ruth wanted to get a projected orchestral work well under way, and Charles expected to put the finishing touches on his book on dissonant counterpoint. Seeger, who arrived in Paris the last of June, made the following brief reference to his stay:

> We spent a marvelous summer in Paris, but I must
> get personal to this extent that one day we went
> down to the American Express to get our mail and
> there was a letter from the Guggenheim Foundation
> informing her that her fellowship would not be re-
> newed for the next year. As we walked by the wall
> of the opera the tears ran down and she said "What's
> going to happen to me?" So I put my arm around
> her and took her across the street to the Cafe de
> Paris where we had a nice little alcove in the wall and
> ordered some refreshments, and I told her what was
> going to happen to her was that we were going to get
> married and that we would have some lovely children,
> but I can imagine the passersby seeing the older
> man--I was fourteen years older than she--with a
> weeping young woman and all the thoughts they would
> have and, of course, was delighted with the picture.[29]

As for their planned projects, they simply did not get done. Ruth had applied for the Guggenheim fellowhsip for a second year--even though she did not want another year away

from Charles Seeger--with the faint hope that somehow she
could have the fellowship renewed and perhaps spend at
least part of the year in New York, since she knew that
other grantees had been given this privilege. Seeger's
comments on this matter, made at a later date, show the be-
ginnings of a shift of emphasis in things musical in both
Ruth's and his life:

> I think things worked out for the best, although
> she would have written some more compositions per-
> haps if I hadn't gone over in the summer. I think
> it was that summer that knocked her out, knocked
> me out too. It knocked us out from my making the
> examples for the book [Tradition and Experiment in
> Twentieth Century Music] and her continuing compo-
> sition of the fine art of music. But in the light of
> our later life it was just the time when it was be-
> ginning.[30]

After Seeger returned to New York Ruth settled back
into her pattern of seeing people and hearing music. The
disenchantment she had felt in Berlin with the professional
music world persisted and increased when she came to Paris.
Even so, Ruth occasionally visited with these people. At
both the Eschig and Senart publishing houses, Ruth showed
her quartet, songs and suites, hoping for some interest in
their publication. Nothing developed from these interviews,
however.[31]

One critic in Paris, Irving Schwerke, who was music
critic for the Paris edition of the Chicago Daily Tribune
from 1921 until 1934, held weekly gatherings of an informal
nature to which promising young composers were invited and
were often asked to perform their own compositions. Ruth
attended a number of these recitals and although she was
asked to play, she declined,[32] a refusal which was doubtless
prompted by her gradually changing attitude toward the accepted means of receiving publicity, her natural shyness,
and her lack of self-confidence.

Ruth enjoyed a pleasant visit with Honegger, the Swiss-
born member of the so-called French "Les Six," whose stage
work, Judith, made a strong and favorable impression on her.
She found him to be unpretentious and human. He looked at
her cello and oboe suite (one of the Diaphonic Suites) but

The European Experience   87

spent most of the time looking at Rat Riddles. "Then, after
telling me he felt it was bewusst [knowledgably written],
that one felt, as one does not feel in so much modern music,
that there was a reason for everything being there and that
I knew what I wanted." Ruth had written to Honegger prior
to her departure for Europe and had suggested, although
indefinitely, that she might study with him. Even though
that had been quite a long time ago, Ruth felt in talking
with him, that he had not forgotten her suggestion. Since
she had decided not to study with any one person, she once
again found herself in a rather uncomfortable situation.³³

Ruth became acquainted with several other leading
musicians during her stay in Paris. She visited with and
showed her music to Roussel who taught counterpoint at the
Schola Cantorum and who counted among his students the
eccentric French composer, Eric Satie, and Edgard Varèse,
her old friend. He received her kindly and showed interest
in her work. She also made brief acquaintances with Koechlin, an important and prolific writer on music as well as a
very effective teacher, and with Prunières, the eminent
French musicologist. Ruth had an appointment to see Martinot as well as one short talk with Ravel, the most important
living French composer at the time; her plans to see Milhaud
were unrealized, because of a schedule conflict.³⁴ Ruth's
contacts with Boulanger, one of the most famous private
teachers of composition in the twentieth century musical
world, were brief but reasonably productive for such a short
time. She spent only a few minutes with her during which
Boulanger talked much. At that time, Boulanger was in
Paris only one day a week--the rest of the week she spent
in the country. Boulanger was already familiar with Ruth's
Preludes, Numbers 6-9, which had been published in New
Music, and she asked Ruth to send her anything else of hers
when it was printed. Boulanger and Ruth also discussed
briefly the role of music in general education.³⁵

Seldom did Ruth ever make any show of vanity concerning her growing reputation as a composer. The following
comments are all the more delightful, made as they were as a
result of her pleasure at being recognized as such:

> Yesterday on my way home I paid a visit to the
> music library to get Edwin Evans' address if possible
> as well as to ask Miss Huchet [the librarian] casually

for Carl Ruggles' Portals, since I noticed they have
only three New Music copies ... I am taking some of
my things to her. You'll be amused at my little
vanity. After talking with Miss Huchet she said:
"Oh, are you Ruth Crawford, the composer?" Emphatically, and it wasn't through New Music because
she didn't know about it. Boulanger knew my name
at once, but through New Music. Vanity, vanity.[36]

Ruth's stay in Paris, which brought her contacts with
several important French musicians--composers, teachers, and
members of the press, gave her a fairly clear idea what life
would be like should she choose to enter the competition for
public recognition and compounded the doubts she had already
entertained concerning it during her months in Germany and
Austria. Both she and Charles Seeger were becoming more
and more conscious of their growing dislike for the business
aspects of music--Charles from years of probing into the relationships between music and society and Ruth largely from
an inborn tendency to shy away from public involvement, as
well as her distaste with the role that "pull" and publicity
played in achieving commercial success as a composer.

Throughout her stay in Europe, Ruth's love for Charles
Seeger--and his for her--had occupied her thoughts unceas-
ingly. And there were complications which had to be resolved
in that situation also. Although Seeger had been living apart
from his wife for several years, the separation had not been
made final through divorce. However, Ruth and Charles
planned to be married as soon as that action was taken. Ruth
had loved children from her very early years and hoped some-
day to have a houseful of her own. Her conflict of interests
between a career and a family, long theoretical, began to
take a more realistic turn as she pondered the future.

The advantages which Ruth had enjoyed during this
year were many: freedom from financial worry, the opportunity to hear all the important experiments and developments
in contemporary music, a chance to meet and discuss music
with most of the prominent European composers of the day
and to show them her own music; time and opportunity to
absorb new ideas, time to reflect, to mature, to gain confidence in herself, and to change her conception of the place
she wanted for herself in the musical life of her world. Although circumstances, rather than the objectives stated in her

The European Experience

Guggenheim application, often dictated her actual accomplishments during this year, and although her musical output was rather small, the work that she did accomplish was of very high quality. Some of Ruth Crawford's finest compositions were either written or completed during her year in Europe--when she was not under the direct tutelage of any one person, but was completely free to work out her own musical salvation. In retrospect, it becomes evident that she was a wise choice as recipient of the first Guggenheim Foundation fellowship granted to a woman in the field of musical composition.

Chapter Six

BACK IN NEW YORK
(1931-1935)

"And of course--my marriage ... That is more important than all these two pages put together." (Ruth Crawford, letter to Nicolas Slonimsky, New York, January 29, 1933)

Headlines give a vivid description of the conditions which faced Ruth on her return to the United States--"Juilliard Benefit for Unemployed Musicians" (January 17, 1931), "London Orchestra in Trouble" (April 2, 1932), "Metropolitan Opera Prospects Uncertain for 1932-33" (April 2, 1932), "Economy the Watchword in Vienna" (April 11, 1931), "Bush Conservatory in Bankruptcy" (August 27, 1932). In the wake of economic disaster came noticeable changes in musical activities, with headlines such as "Peoples' Chorus Concert" (February 13, 1932), "Virginia White Top Festival Draws Audience of 6,000" (September 3, 1932), "Freiheit Mandolin Orchestra," directed by Jacob Schaefer in Town Hall (April 22, 1933), "20,000 Attend Folk Gathering at White Top Mountain," (August 6, 1933). The repertoire of surviving groups reflected current emphases on American composers in headlines proclaiming "New Blood in American Music" (September 16, 1933), "American Composers Concert Given by Rochester Orchestra" (January 6, 1934), "Aaron Copland Program" (October 19, 1935). A few scattered attempts were still made to present "new music"--"Eleventh International Festival Attracts Visitors to Amsterdam" (July 8, 1933), "Pan American Association of Composers with Martha Graham and Her Group" (April 28, 1934), "New Forms of Electrical Music Heard in Brussels Concert" (March 17, 1934). Blaring head-

Back in New York

lines foreshadowed menacing events--"Political Doings in Berlin Push Music into the Background" (March 25, 1933), "Berlin Police Guard Hall for Hearing of Berg's Lulu score; First Performance Possible Only by Assent of General Goering" (December 22, 1934), "Festivals and War Clouds" (April 20, 1935).[1]

And so Ruth came back to a changed world! Gone was the brilliant musical life she had enjoyed in Berlin and Paris which had provided in some ways, the climax to her experiences of the previous year in New York when, for the first time, she could feel herself a part of the international music scene. Although the stock market crash of 1929 had badly jarred the foundations of musical activities in New York--and to a certain extent in Europe--Ruth had not personally felt its effects. She had lived in pleasant, congenial and stimulating surroundings and mingled with the great and near great in the field of modern music where her interests lay. In Europe, she had continued much the same kind of living as in New York, and although in neither New York nor Europe did she have any more than just enough money to supply her with basic needs of food, shelter, and clothing, she thrived in this kind of situation. Her personal friends saw to it that she was supplied with tickets to concerts and other cultural activities; occasionally, when her economic situation got worrisome, they would give her small sums of money, as did her brother, Carl.

Besides the new professional friends she had made in Europe, she had encountered some of her personal friends from her homeland, such as Marion Bauer with whom she had visited in Liege. Bauer, who was there for the ISCM festival, continued to be solicitous for her welfare.[2] Both Madame Herz and Ruth's cousin, Nellie Hastings, visited in Europe while Ruth was there, and both kept in touch with her. Her cousin continued to supply Ruth with a small monthly stipend, and Madame Herz conveyed to Ruth her willingness to help her try to find some piano pupils on her return to New York, which Ruth hoped would help her survive financially.[3] Also, on board ship coming home, Ruth met a young woman who was to be a good friend for many years, Margaret Valiant. Margaret, who had been studying music (opera in particular) in Europe, was returning to New York also, and she quickly learned that Ruth had been a Guggenheim fellow in composition.[4] Their mutual interest

drew them together and they enjoyed each other's company on
the crossing. When the ship docked in New York, however,
Ruth had eyes for only one person, Charles Seeger, who was
waiting at the pier. Friends, musical composition, money
problems--all faded quickly into the background as she and
Seeger were reunited after their long separation. Although
Constance still refused to consent to a divorce, Charles and
Ruth made plans to set up housekeeping together, and they
found a small apartment in Greenwich Village. Charles introduced Ruth as his wife and she, in turn, recorded in subsequent autobiographical notes that their marriage took place in
November 1931. This situation can best be explained by referring to a later statement which Ruth made in the introductory remarks to her book Animal Folk Songs for Children.
Animal stories can perhaps contain elements of untruth. Her
statement there "There is the lying which is more like a wish
to believe in something," seems to fit nicely into this catego-
ry and helps explain Ruth's actions.[5] Even though she had
willingly and happily shared with Charles Seeger the decision to live together, it cannot help having created a stress-
ful situation for Ruth given her background and upbringing.
Finally, on October 2, 1932, Seeger was granted his divorce,
and he and Ruth were married the same day.[6]

    Charles was away much of the day with his teaching,
even though the economic situation had reduced his work
load considerably (and with it his income). Ruth's plans for
teaching private piano did not materialize, and Charles's hope
that she might teach harmony at the New School for Social
Research came to naught. So the Seegers began their married life with a bleak financial outlook. Ruth had a piano at
her disposal in the apartment and also had her time free to
spend on her music. Nonetheless, she did not do extensive
creative work.[7] She was naturally preoccupied with adjusting
to her new life and love; musically she occupied herself
largely with putting on finishing touches and copying the
works she had written previously. She also wrote the third
of the Three Songs to Sandburg texts, Prayers of Steel, and
completed the optional orchestral ostinati for all three.[8] The
performance notes which Ruth appended to the score state
that "the concertanti [solo] section is complete in itself."[9]
Cowell had been planning for some time to publish these songs
in his New Music Orchestra Series and since Ruth could not
afford to hire someone to do the copying for this purpose,
she had to do it herself. They appeared as Number 5 in the
orchestra series in 1933.

Charles Seeger (New York City, 1932)

Arrangements were soon under way to record the slow movement of Ruth's String Quartet for the New Music Quarterly recordings series. This project naturally involved rehearsing with the performers and demanded time and patience as the score was far from easy, if it was to be given a sensitive, musically satisfying reading. The recording appeared in 1934--the first, and for many years, the only recording of her works available on discs.

Ruth's music continued to receive a hearing throughout these years in New York. Performances were given in New York, Philadelphia, at the Yaddo Festival (Saratoga Springs, New York), and Palo Alto, Oakland, and San Francisco, California, with mixed reviews by the critics. Also on December 9, 1931, her Diaphonic Suite No. 4 for viola and cello was played at a concert in Hamburg. The program consisted entirely of works by women composers, with Ruth and her friend and former student Vivian Fine representing the United States. On this occasion, Fine's Four Pieces for Violin and Oboe (1930) were performed, regarding which Ruth commented, "It is by far the best thing she has done. Coordinate, unified, and with very intelligent use of dissonance and much more use of consonance."[10] In 1932 Ruth's Three Songs were sung on a program given in Berlin under the auspices of the Pan American Association of Composers,[11] and again the following year to represent the United States at the ISCM festival in Amsterdam.[12]

But not all of Ruth's time was free to spend on her music. In August of 1933, Ruth and Charles's first child, Michael, was born, which happy event was to provide another and drastic change in her life. She had had no experience with babies except to admire them from a distance and none with small children other than to teach them piano. The problems involved in receiving a domestic education such as that provided by Michael's advent, soon absorbed much of Ruth's time and energy, and composition was forced into a secondary role. Ruth's former active social life--concerts and recitals, with attendant receptions, parties and such--was reduced, or at least changed in nature--not abandoned--as such friends as Vivian Fine, who moved to New York in 1931, and Djane Lavoie Herz, also in the city at that time, kept in rather close touch with her. Both Vivian and her mother visited Ruth in the hospital at the time of Michael's birth, as did her friend Margaret Valiant, who was then working as a dress designer in New York. Margaret shared her pleasure at Michael's imminent arrival by designing clothes for Ruth to wear during her pregnancy. Margaret recalled Ruth's great joy in her condition and her pride in confirming it to the world.[13]

Ruth and Charles continued to participate in the activities of avant-garde music circles as much as time and opportunity allowed, but such opportunities were rapidly decreasing. The Depression was deepening and would continue to affect the country for many years to come. One of the first areas to feel the economic pinch was that of the arts. People were jobless and hungry and music study did not assuage these needs. Nor was the market for the publication of new music in a thriving state, especially music of an experimental nature. The unrest which pervaded the country affected the Seegers, and they soon found themselves interested socially and politically, as well as economically, in the problems thus created. Both Ruth and Charles had earlier in their lives been introduced to and become interested in "the people." Ruth's friendship with Carl Sandburg and his strong influence on her has already been noted in some detail, as well as her interest in becoming acquainted with the music of Soviet Russia expressed in her hope of visiting that country while she was still in Germany.

Charles Seeger's interest in social and economic concerns dates from an even earlier period. Seeger, born in Mexico City of American parents of some affluence and educated at Harvard, accepted as his first teaching assignment, the position of Professor of Music and head of the department at the University of California at Berkeley. There, he became acquainted with people involved with socialism, both at the University and in San Francisco.[14]

When Seeger and his family left California to return to New York in 1918, he and his wife, who was a concert violinist, attempted to reach the underprivileged sector of American people by living in a trailer and giving concerts from New York to North Carolina. They were unable to make a go of this project financially, so they abandoned the idea and returned to the city. After his separation from his wife, Seeger continued to try to reconcile the art music, which he still composed and taught to select groups of individuals, with his increasingly strong conviction that music must somehow relate to the political and social situation in which he was living.[15]

Although Seeger had met Ruth via art music circles, they had each gradually become aware of the other's interest in music of the people. It is not surprising that Ruth's disillusionment with the commercial aspects of being a composer and her new role as a family person, together with Charles's questions about the place of music in society and the economic situation in which both Ruth and Charles found themselves, all helped bring about a change of emphasis in their musical thinking and activities.

It was not only the Seegers who were affected by the times; many other creative artists replaced their interest in avant-garde ideas with social and political concerns. Eric Salzman aptly characterized the times when he said that "in the 1930s ... under the influence of populist idealogies, avant-garde ideas and forms were set aside."[16]

Although economic factors exerted a strong influence, both political and social concerns commanded their share of the Seegers' attention. The social implications of the Depression were forcefully drawn to their notice many times, as they observed the pathetic conditions under which many people were forced to live--homeless, hungry, eking out an existence on the streets. Both Charles and Ruth felt constrained to make an effort to help those less fortunate than themselves and to try to discover music's place in their lives.

The conclusions reached by Seeger that music must be made to relate to people and not exist in a social vacuum, led to the abandonment of his and Ruth's long-projected book (<u>Tradition and Experiment in Twentieth Century Music</u>), still waiting for its final examples. Seeger and Ruth both realized that the book dealt with only half of its title, the part that related to experiment; the element of tradition had been left untouched.

> So more and more we were drawn in to the attempts to do something about the Depression by people like ourselves, and this suspicion of mine had been growing that music didn't exist by itself.... Musicologically I know perfectly well that music exists in the context of general social and cultural development.[17]

In line with these attempts, Charles and Ruth, at the instigation of Henry Cowell, became involved in 1931-1932 with the organization of a small group of musicians who called themselves the Composers' Collective and whose chief interest in music was tied to the political, social, and economic problems of the United States. The group was affiliated with the New York Chapter of the Pierre Degeyter Club which was, in turn, an affiliate of the Workers' Music League, a local federation of about eighteen or twenty workers' organizations in New York City.[18] This latter group, founded in 1921, provided musical association with the American Communist Party through the mid-1930s.[19]

The Collective was guided in its efforts to provide music suitable to the workers' needs by Hanns Eisler, a German composer and Schoenberg student, who had successfully written music for the labor movement and for Socialist and Communist political activities in pre-Hitler Germany. Eisler had come to the United States in 1933, where he lectured on music at the New School for Social Research in New York City. Seeger was generally sympathetic with Eisler's idea that the texts must have revolutionary overtones while the music should attempt to educate and uplift the workers' cultural taste through the use of art music sources. They and others in the group rejected the use of folk music for the Collective's purposes as being unacceptable artistically and musically. The result was that much of their music proved to be too intellectual to achieve its intended goal--their intentions and their understanding of the situation were not the same. The later appearance of Aunt Mollie Jackson, the widow of a coal miner and a militant organizer, at the Collective meetings made Seeger realize the rightness of the folksong approach. Aunt Mollie used Kentucky ballad melodies which were related to the Old English tunes, for her songs, for protest marches and for union gatherings; the Composers Collective had tried to use the music of the intellectual elite.[20]

Charles took an active part in the Collective, discussing philosophical concepts, attending meetings, helping to organize activities, writing newspaper reviews of musical events (under the pseudonym Carl Sands) and composing music for group use. He participated in the production of the Workers' Songbooks I and II, which continued the group's utilization of bourgeois music coupled with revolutionary words.[21]

Ruth's part in the Collective was a minor one. She attended a few meetings and contributed two songs with timely texts and contemporary compositional techniques (Sacco, Vanzetti, and Chinaman, Laundryman,) which were sung in 1933 at a concert called Workers' Music Olympiad, by Charles and Ruth's old friend Radiana Pazmor.[22] Perhaps the most successful musical efforts of this group were the rounds, satirical in character, written by various group members, and on the writing of which Ruth and Charles seem to have often worked together. Their catchy and humorous qualities are exemplified in the round titled, "Not If, But When," in a version by Charles, and "When, Not If," in a version by Ruth.[23]

The entire Collective gradually accepted the folk-song approach, influenced in part by the deepening Depression, which brought about an emphasis on American nationalist spirit, and an interest in the country's grassroots as of cultural importance, with its stress on folk arts and crafts. Although interest in folk music in America had been developing throughout the century, the impact of the Depression changed the character of this development, causing it to mature rapidly, so that by the 1940s, folk music was considered an important element of our cultural heritage.[24] The politically radical elements in society also finally espoused wholeheartedly the utilization of folk music for their purposes.

Charles' teaching at the New School for Social Research also helped draw the Seeger's interest away from experimental art music to that of more socially oriented musics. The New School, instituted in 1919, provided fertile ground for the germination of ideas and concepts congenial to the leftist tendencies of many American intellectuals during the twenties and thirties when communism held a strong appeal for these people. The school's devotion to innovative programs and ideas in all areas was attractive to Charles Seeger, who felt somewhat repressed by the conservative curriculum he had worked with at the Institute of Musical Art. The music program at the New School, directed from 1930 to 1936 by Henry Cowell, stressed liberal tendencies. Its roster of instructors during this time included people who were sympathetic with the aims of the Composers' Collective, and contained such names as Aaron Copland, Wallingford Riegger, and Elie Siegmeister.[25] The school's catalog for 1933-1934 showed rather strong emphasis on fine arts courses, with impressive attention to

Back in New York

contemporary music (13 courses). The generally adult student body, in which the New School was and is still basically interested, not only attended these classes but also provided the nucleus of the audience for the many concerts of contemporary music, both American and European, which the school sponsored. The New School also provided the setting for the premiere performance of Ruth's String Quartet, which was played by the New World String Quartet on November 13, 1933 in a concert of North American music of the Pan American Association of Composers.[26]

Two other events about this same time helped point the way for the Seegers' renewed interest in the music of the people:

> George Pullen Jackson's book, White Spirituals in the Southern Uplands (1933) came out and that showed us that thousands, and hundreds of thousands, even millions of Americans had been singing a kind of hymn which we didn't know existed, that is, the shape note hymn, and as we looked at those shape note hymns, especially those in three parts, we suddenly realized that there had been going on in the United States for over 130 years, a type of singing that showed some kind of an approach to the dissonant counterpoint we were most interested in. There were parallel sevenths and seconds and fifths and fourths, and there were cadences from seconds and sevenths straight into bare fifths and octaves at the ends of hymns.
> About this same time, Tom Benton, the painter, had showed me some commercial records of American folk singing (which I thought was practically moribund) and pointed out to me that it was a million-dollar industry in the United States and that there were singers all around the place who could sing, not only the old ballads, but contemporary songs of labor, protest, and all kinds of things; and especially I was struck with a record by Doc Boggs singing Pretty Polly and The Danville Girl. Ruth and I were completely flabbergasted by the situation--that here we were--people who called ourselves American composers and we didn't know anything about America or American music, so we simply decided that we would lay aside for a while our interest in dissonant coun-

terpoint and try to find out something about America.[27]

As far as can be ascertained, the Seegers were never personally acquainted with George Pullen Jackson (1874-1953), despite the strong influence his book had on them. On the other hand, the Bentons and the Seegers maintained active social contacts until the Seegers departed for Washington, D.C., and the Bentons returned to Kansas City, both in 1935.

Actually it was through the New School that Seeger's friendship and fruitful association with Benton developed. Benton, who also taught at the New School, had for some time been interested in the popular music (not just Tin Pan Alley tunes) of the day, and both played and collected it. He interested Charles in playing guitar with a group which performed at the dedication of one of his murals which decorated the walls of the New School.[28] Charles and Ruth, along with Henry Cowell and Carl Ruggles, soon became members of the "gang" that met at the Bentons' Greenwich Village apartment on Saturday nights. Benton later remarked that "Charles Seeger is now one of the first authorities on American folk song but he found his first strong interest in them at our house."[29]

It is not surprising that the Seegers and the Bentons became good friends, as they shared many similar attitudes and convictions regarding the relationship between the arts and life. Benton, like Seeger, had started out as a modernist. Both came from socially rather prominent family backgrounds and both broke out of the artistic mold in which they had been trained, to pursue aims of an entirely different nature, tending to identify themselves with the interest of "the people," each in his own way. Benton and Seeger shared an interest in the social and political overtones of the economic situation brought about by the Great Depression, and they were both involved in the efforts of the government to aid artists and writers during this difficult period.

Finally, their families were congenial and they became personal friends and enjoyed many pleasant times together talking and singing folk songs. Margaret Valiant, who was a frequent member of the group which gathered at the Bentons' place, tells an amusing story of one such gathering.

> There were a whole group of us at the Thomas
> Hart Benton apartment in Greenwich Village, a very
> small place ... there were two rooms ... and the bed
> was covered with coats. It was wintertime and here
> came Charlie and Ruth with baby Michael in arms.
> Well, there was no place to put baby Michael, so
> they emptied out a bureau drawer, and carefully
> wrapped in a blanket, we placed dear little Michael
> for his nap ... maybe that's the first time he ever
> heard folk songs.[30]

Margaret was probably Ruth's closest personal friend during the New York years, and they often visited together, presumably during the day when Charlie was working. Margaret stressed the earthy qualities--"close to the warm earth"--in Ruth and the fact that she was an instinctual person, whereas Charlie was the highly trained intellectual, though not without his earthy qualities too. "They made a person feel like a creature of Nature."[31] Margaret also became interested in the same ideas and activities which had attracted the Seeger's attention, and the three spent many a pleasant hour discussing their emerging interest in American folk music. She was to become and to remain involved in its utilization for social purposes along with the Seegers during the ensuing difficult Depression years when Americans were seeking solace in music.

Another incident relating to the Seeger's interest in folk music occurred when Macmillan asked Henry Cowell and Charles Seeger to look at a new book they were considering for publication, American Ballads and Folk Songs, by John A. and Alan Lomax. They were fascinated by the music, and Ruth soon shared in their enthusiasm. Inspired by the new insights they received from the music collected by the Lomaxes, both Charles and Ruth began to immerse themselves in their newly espoused interest, giving special attention to authentic singing styles and the many problems involved in their notation.[32] Thus the groundwork was laid for Ruth's eventual involvements in this field.

Neither Charles nor Ruth Seeger gave up interest in a more esoteric approach to music, however. Charles's involvement in the new (for America) interest in musicology, which he had begun years earlier in his classes at the University of California, Berkeley, had simmered for a number of years,

but bore fruit during this thought-provoking, if difficult and
hectic, period. During Ruth's winter at Mrs. Walton's, he
and several other interested people, including Joseph Schillinger, Joseph Yasser, and Henry Cowell, had organized the
New York Musicological Society[33] and had held meetings at
Mrs. Walton's apartment, so Ruth was familiar with their
activities.[34] Seeger had also served during the mid-thirties
as president and editor of the American Library of Musicology.[35] He was also a prime mover in the 1933 organization
of the American Society for Comparative Musicology, which
tied in nicely with the Seegers' burgeoning interest in folk
music. Together, Seeger and Henry Cowell had taught the
first course in ethnomusicology given in the United States at
the New School for Social Research in 1932.[36] It was also
during this same period that Seeger and Cowell prepared
their contributions to the 1933 edition of the Encyclopaedia
of Social Sciences.[37] Charles was thus able to organize the
activities of his life in such a way as to encompass his interest both in things sociological and musicological, and in
both their practical and intellectual aspects. And while it
is true that he had practically given up interest in his own
composition, as long as he lived, he occasionally indulged in
compositional activities.

Although Ruth's participation in Charles's widely diversified activities was restricted, she was nonetheless interested in them. She supported Charles in his work with the
Composers Collective at the same time she cherished his realization of a long-standing dream to help organize groups devoted to musicological studies. And she shared his interest
in Americana through folk music studies. She seems to have
been very happy during these challenging times. She did
not lose interest in composing--she simply did not have the
time necessary for such concentrated work. Her family responsibilities and joys were increased in the summer of 1935
with the advent of their first daughter, Peggy. She had always loved children and having Michael and Peggy, as well
as her Charlie, gave her great happiness and satisfaction,
even though times were hard. Ruth had learned early in her
life to get along with whatever was available to her, and as
long as she lived she had to do without as often as she had
to do with. As she remarked, "Our last three years had
been about as empty of dollars as they had been full of fun
and the enjoyment of life."[38] These years of her life were
very full of meaningful activities and very rich in human re-

lationships. Her own brand of head and heart meshed with that of Charles, and life was good.

The years in New York seem at first glance to have been unfruitful, but they were, in reality, a period of transition both professionally and socially. Of the "old" (Walton) New York crowd, only Henry Cowell remained and would continue to remain as a close friend and associate through the coming years. Although at the time the Seegers felt somewhat uncertain about the changing ways of their life together, in retrospect, Seeger realized that they were building a new life:

> We didn't realize until years afterward that those days when we just seemed to be wasting time we were really getting started on our second lives.[39]

Chapter Seven

LIFE AND DEATH IN WASHINGTON, D.C.
(1935-1953)

"For the ability to feel comfortable with oneself and with music, even under ordinary circumstances, is a thing we are seeking not only for our children; it is a thing many of us have spent years in seeking for ourselves." (Ruth Crawford Seeger, lecture notes, probably for a demonstration with a group of children, not long before her death)

Life was good for the Seegers, but it was also hard. It was a constant financial struggle simply to have enough for the necessities, and bills were an ever-present fact of life. Relief from daily uncertainties came with a telephone call in November 1935 offering Charles a position in Washington, D.C., where he would be responsible for organizing the music work of the Resettlement Administration. The Seegers decided to accept the offer and prepared to make the move to the nation's capital, headquarters for the federal government's efforts to provide aid and relief to millions of needy Americans. They eventually settled in the suburb of Silver Spring, Maryland, and Charles began his work in the Special Skills Division of Resettlement. The "second life" which had budded during the difficult days in New York began to unfold, and they started their "discovery" of America in earnest. They began immediately to enjoy a degree of financial stability and even some small luxuries, such as a house with sunshine and light, often missing from New York apartments. Their house also had "a comfortable deskroom [where] a composer hopes to be able to work again."[1] Ruth's hope remained just

Charles Seeger (Silver Spring, Maryland, ca. 1940)

that and gradually became less than that, as new patterns of
living emerged.

Charles Seeger's experiences with the Resettlement Administration utilized some of the experiments from the Composers Collective which, although it had been a musical failure, had at least been useful in pointing out some dos and don'ts for similar situations. In addition, the work of the Lomaxes, not only in the collection and publishing of folk songs but also in helping to build up the folk song archives in the Library of Congress, had fueled the Seegers' growing interest in folk music, and they soon found themselves exploring the rich resources contained in this collection. These things all contributed to Ruth's background for her later folk music activities;[2] they also dovetailed with Charles's new responsibilities. Ruth soon found herself working at making transcriptions and arrangements of archival materials for various folk music projects in a kind of learn-as-you-go situation; at the same time, Charles supervised various music projects ranging in geographical areas from Florida to Texas to Maryland. It was during this period that the Seegers gained firsthand knowledge of the context of the folk music they were both to be closely involved with during the following years.[3]

A glance at the kinds of activities undertaken by various segments of the New Deal shows that the artists, photographers, and writers were all attempting to portray America at the grassroots level. At least some of the music projects attempted to work in the same way by insinuating music into the daily activities of the people. In these there was no attempt to superimpose music of a European art culture onto the lives of the underprivileged; rather, the kind of music these people knew and understood was presented so that they themselves could take part in the performance of it and could associate it with their own mode of living.

Not long after Charles started working with the Resettlement program in Washington, he was able to get an appointment for Ruth's friend Margaret Valiant (who had made the trip with them when they moved to Washington) as a field representative on one of the projects. The story of one of their joint efforts (1936) will serve to illustrate the way in which Resettlement Music projects could be presented, as well as the kind of exposure to the American people which both

Ruth and Charles were experiencing. Seeger related the following story:

> She [Margaret Valiant] landed in January on a cold, drizzly night in West Florida in a group of 150 to 200 families who were living in chicken houses. On this cold, rainy night the manager of the project called the community together. They had a lot of business and at the end of it he said, "and now, folks, you know what we want from Washington. We want a couple of nurses, we want drugs, we want a specialist in some kind of fertilizer--what do they do? They send us a music teacher. Here she is." And he walked off the stage. Well, she did her best to face it out and she had a little piece of paper telling them what she was to do. She was to present herself to the people as a human being, not as a music teacher ... a human being with a lot of human beings who were in terrible trouble....[4]

Margaret, whose past experiences included designing clothes for such fashionable houses as Bergdorf-Goodman in New York City, set about organizing a fashion show among the women. During the show, each woman took a step or two onto a little platform, either singing her favorite song or while Margaret sang it. The women responded well, and the show was a success. Next, some members of the local hillbilly band came around to see Margaret, bringing their instruments with them. At first, they sang familiar songs, then Margaret gradually introduced new ones. She won them over easily, and soon they were all singing and playing together at community gatherings. Then the music teacher was asked to help with band music to be played between the rounds of a prize fight, a project designed to raise money for equipment and uniforms for the baseball team. This was duly accomplished.

After that, she was told to involve the whole community in a script to be written on the spot, which would fit their own personal situations. After about four months' work, the show was finally given. It included square dancing, clog dancing, storytelling, harmonica playing, hymn singing, and the hillbilly band.

And it all proved acceptable, because by this time

> music was beginning to perform the function that
> Mrs. Roosevelt and Rex Tugwell and the others who
> started the Resettlement wanted music to serve.
> They wanted somebody not to bring music into the
> lives of the people, but to use their own music to
> bind the conflicts and smooth over the troubles, and
> make people get along together.[5]

This kind of music making among the poorer elements of the population also fitted in with the Seegers' evolving ideas about the sociological function of music. Ruth and Charles were beginning to pull together several of the strands of music that belonged to the people. They had cut their teeth on this sort of thing in the Composers Collective and had become acquainted with religious folk music and country popular music, all of which they had discovered in New York before they moved to Washington.

When the Resettlement program was phased out in 1937, Charles moved on to the Federal Music Project of the WPA, acting as assistant director where he helped develop the folk music and recreational aspects of the program.[6] In 1941 he became Chief of the Division of Music and Visual Arts at the Pan American Union, a position he held until the year of Ruth's death (1953).[7] Here Charles worked through various channels toward the development of international music organizations. He gradually became known as a musicologist who stressed the importance of music as a worldwide and social-class-wide system of auditory communication among people. For Seeger, folk music was one of the most important aspects of the music vernacular of a people.[8] Ruth deserves to be recognized at least as a serious student and researcher in this area. The Seeger children knew their mother through her folk music and related teaching activities (their two oldest children are professional performers of folk music) rather than as a composer of "classical" music, and they are pleased when Ruth's folk music activities are correctly described as folk art. Her years of working in this area are not regarded as an unproductive time.

Although Ruth and Charles Seeger were not unaffected by the interest shown by many intellectuals in the leftist political point of view often found during this time, their best efforts were directed toward the broader concept of musicology, which included ethnomusicology, and which considers all

Life and Death in Washington

the musics of the world to be worthy of serious consideration. Essentially, Charles and Ruth spent many years of their lives trying to satisfy themselves of the relevance of all kinds of musical endeavors to all the other activities of man.

In both high school and college, Ruth had helped to support herself by teaching piano. By the early to mid-forties, she also resumed this activity in an effort to offset the burgeoning expenses of a growing family--Barbara had been born in 1937, and Penelope in 1943. Ruth brought to her piano teaching the same intensity and devotion she displayed in all the major activities of her life, and she soon developed a deep rapport with her students of all ages, but especially with young children. Further, she enjoyed teaching problem students--they were a challenge to her.

Ruth's philosophy of piano teaching, based on solid musical values, was directed toward development of the student's enjoyment of music as well as of his technical abilities. Charles Seeger has made some interesting comments on her approach to teaching piano:

> She'd play a good deal to them and put them up against unusual things in music and she'd make them sing a lot and improvise. With the two pianos, as soon as a child could do much more than just play with one finger, she'd put them at one piano, and she'd take the other piano. And she'd harmonize what they played, and that sort of thing.... With any student who could play, who had any degree of fluency on the piano [she did] a lot of improvising and we recorded it. We recorded it on tape and then played it back. And it was very interesting to listen to your own improvisation when it was played back to you. It sounded entirely different from what you thought you were playing.[9]

Ruth was also an innovative teacher. In the case of one of her students, a fourteen-year-old boy who was a talented jazz pianist, Ruth asked him to teach her how to play jazz. As the experiment progressed, she kept introducing into the jazz fabric, tunes of Bach which the boy liked and wanted to know more about. Through this means, she introduced Bach to one who might otherwise have not taken any interest in him. He became one of her prize pupils at playing classical music and still remained as good a jazz pianist as ever.[10]

One of her students recalls Ruth's approach to presenting basic harmonic relationships as being both effective and pleasurable:

> ...she taught harmonic relationships on the piano and supplemented that by using the autoharp, which operates on the principle of depressing one labelled chord-bar for a total chord, thus making it easier for beginners to grasp the chord changes by ear immediately without having to worry about finger placement on so many individual notes as on the piano--and also the autoharp added fun and variety for the student.[11]

Many of Ruth's students returned year after year, an indication that she gave them something to look forward to each lesson and to cherish for a long time to come. Another of her pupils, who studied with Ruth from 1945 (age eight/nine) until her death, recalled with great pleasure his association with her as his piano teacher. He has kept, these many years, the notebooks in which Ruth wrote his weekly lesson assignments. His personal reminiscences and his lesson plans combine to show that Ruth's approach to teaching was many-sided. His assignments stressed technique, sight-reading, rhythm problems, theory, transposition, transcription from orchestral scores, composition (e.g. the writing of canons at various intervals), and conducting.[12]

Ruth's oldest daughter, Peggy, recalls her mother's approach to the inevitable student recitals as a most pleasurable affair:

> She'd give a party once a year for any of her pupils who wanted to come and whichever students wanted to play would play.... People would bring their grannies and their husbands and their sisters and brothers and if she would have, say, twenty or twenty-five pupils, nearly a hundred people would come and they'd just mill around and talk and drink.

Peggy's comments on her mother's approach to piano teaching are also of interest:

Ruth Crawford Seeger with a group of nursery-school children enjoying folk songs (Silver Spring, Maryland, ca. 1941-42)

> She never had anything bad to say about anybody and this is a very important thing about teaching because it means that you teach the person with a sense of optimism. You teach them with a sense of compassion and with a sense of communication.[13]

Although Ruth taught both adults and children and both at home and at school, it was perhaps in the nursery school situation that she made her most unique contributions. The nursery schools were cooperative ventures organized by groups of women who were interested in providing these kinds

of educational opportunities for their children. These
schools emphasized principles of progressive education in
dealing with the young-approaches which appealed to Ruth,
such as,

> Confidence in the young child's innate interest in
> and response to music and poetry, and undoubtedly
> other arts; opportunity for adults to guide and in-
> crease the child's unique capacity to enjoy <u>and</u> to
> <u>create</u> in those fields; conviction that the adult teach-
> er should proceed by helping each child develop
> in his own way at his own rate, <u>not</u> by imposing any
> standards or patterns; determination to involve the
> parents or at least the mother of each child in the
> training pattern and process, as not only observer
> but active participant <u>with</u> the teacher.[14]

Ruth had been asked to join with such a group from
Silver Spring, Maryland, the Washington, D.C., suburb
where they lived. (She later taught at other schools in the
area, including the Foxhall Nursery School, Whitehall Country
School, and the Potomac School). In August of 1941, Ruth
made some notes which indicated she was considering seriously accepting the invitation from the Silver Spring group,
where her chief duty would be to work with the children in
their music activities. They are incomplete, but start with
the title, <u>Diary of a "Corporating" Mother</u>, with the sub-title,
"Mother has improved since she went to cooperative nursery
school."

Ruth had never particularly liked belonging to clubs
or organized groups of any kind, and she felt unsure about
getting involved with the mothers' organization, which decided
on and helped with the activities of the nursery school
children. When one of the mothers called her about a meeting
one evening, she hesitated to go--she did not like meetings,
and she did not like being away from home in the evenings
when Charles could be there, as they had so little time together during these busy years. However, she decided to
go to the meeting where policies, problems, and experimental
techniques were discussed. "Changed my mind and went after
all. I think I may like these meetings if they are like this."[15]

And four-year-old Barbara quizzed her mother almost
constantly about her chances of going to (nursery) school.

Ruth felt she was too busy to help start the school, but agreed that she would be interested if someone else would organize it:

> How can anyone with three children and no maid and a few ideas for books and compositions on the side, expect to cooperate with anything except her own intertangled can-do's and can-not-do's. On the other hand, it would help both Barbara and me (and I might be able to get back to my own music every morning at least) if Barbara could be in school.

Ruth finally decided in favor of sending Barbara to the nursery school which, of course, meant she herself would also become involved in its activities:

> I have called up the powers-that-organized and started the ball rolling for Barbara. One of the rules I cannot comply with: every mother is required to drive her "unit" to school one day a week. The second rule I can manage, and it will probably be good for me, though I'm not sure it won't bore me: I must participate at the nursery school one day a week. It is a tenet of these cooperative nursery schools that the child and the mother benefit by doing things together at school. It sounds logical, and I can improve plenty as a mother, heaven knows. But I hate to give up the time. I wanted it for my music, here at home.[16]

As it turned out, the nursery school provided Ruth with an excellent opportunity to incorporate her current preoccupation with folk music into the group's activities. Ruth's ability to control the children in the classroom, to anticipate their reactions and to suggest musical activities to respond to these has been noted by those fortunate to witness some of her classes. The cooperative apparently issued an occasional newsletter. One edition carried the following delightful story titled: <u>With a Song in Her Heart</u>:

> Ruth Seeger's love of American folk music is contagious. The few weeks she worked with our children left its happy mark. December 27, seven of the 4's ... illustrated Mrs. Seeger's theories of the preschool child and American folk music at the Shoreham

Hotel for the annual Music Teachers National Convention. Well-poised, hardly self-conscious but rather audience-conscious, the children gave their all for their school and themselves. To <u>Joyce Wore a Red Dress</u>, young Miss Carney stated, "It's not a red <u>dress</u>, it's a red <u>jumper</u>!" Mrs. Seeger sang, <u>Tie My Shoe</u> and David Kramer, foot way out, insisted, "But <u>really</u> tie <u>my</u> shoe." The only person the least bit nervous was a silver-haired gentleman in the audience who kept worrying about the dirty knees being accumulated.[17]

Sidney Cowell, who was associated with Ruth during this time through their mutual involvement with folk music, felt that Ruth had great talent for this kind of teaching:

> Not long before she died I had the pleasure of seeing a demonstration of Ruth's work with a group of children, presented I think for the MENC or some such organization. I had done a lot of similar work myself but was greatly impressed with Ruth's talent for this sort of thing: she made the session a kind of small drama, with climaxes, diminuendos and changes of pace, but always moving directly from one thing to another so that the session made a continuous flowing pattern of activity, movement or song: I had never seen anything like it nor even imagined such a thing. She led in a quiet voice, mostly from the piano, like the conductor of a small and receptive orchestra of children.[18]

Throughout the Seegers' years of residence in Washington, there runs a continuous if fine thread of Ruth's involvement with her art music. Not only did she make several written references to her hope of finding time to compose again, she often received word of performances of her compositions, e.g., a letter from Marion Bauer telling of Helen Traubel's singing two of her songs (1936),[19] letters from Radiana Pazmor about her performances of Ruth's songs (1937),[20] a letter from a flautist in Sao Paulo reporting his performance of her Diaphonic Suite No. 1 for unaccompanied flute (1942),[21] and one from Wallingford Riegger regarding the successful use of the andante movement from her string quartet as accompaniment for a dance (1945).[22] She also received various requests in connection with her music, such as permission to copy parts for any of her scores that had appeared in the New Music Edition as part of a WPA project in San Francisco (1938). From the year 1938 also comes Ruth's formal application for a job on a WPA project (June 24). It is doubtful that anything ever came of this application--perhaps it was never even submitted. The application stands alone as testimony to Ruth's willingness to help with the family finances.

On April 6, 1938, Ruth's works formed half of a program presented by the Composers' Forum-Laboratory, Fifth Series, directed by Ashley Pettis. (The second half of the program presented works by Hanns Eisler.) The Composers' Forum-Laboratory consisted of a series of concerts originating in New York City as part of the Federal Music Project of the WPA. These concerts were designed to give composers' works a public hearing and to provide a forum for subsequent discussion of them.[23] Included on the program were Ruth's String Quartet, Five Preludes, and an Etude for piano, and her Three Songs for contralto, oboe, piano, and percussion. After the concert, Ruth took part in a question-and-answer session regarding her works that had just been heard as well as her future plans. This interview is important in establishing some signposts in Ruth's musical career and musical development during her first years in Washington.[24] It shows that she was beginning to think in terms of a simpler kind of music, even though traces of her more sophisticated style of writing persist. This "simpler kind" involved not only Ruth's utilization of folk music materials in her arrangement of a number of American folk songs for piano, elementary grades (mentioned earlier) but also her composition of Rissolty, Rossolty, which drew on her folk song experiences. This composition, which utilized several American folk tunes transcribed from recordings in the Library of Congress, was commissioned by CBS and played over the "School of the Air" at that time.

She was to be allowed time for only one further essay in the art music field, the Suite for Wind Quintet, (1952), which won first place in a competition for a woodwind quintet sponsored by the District of Columbia chapter of the National Association for American Composers and Conductors and was first performed in Washington by the National Woodwind Quintet, December 2, 1952.

As if teaching both in the nursery school and privately at home, in addition to extensive research and transcription of folk materials at the Library of Congress, sitting on advisory boards, writing and preparing folk song books for publication, was not enough to allow Ruth little time for composition, she also managed to take care of the voluminous correspondence that went along with all these activities. She also continued to write to her brother, Carl, and his family and friends from earlier days.

Of particular interest is Ruth's continuing, if intermittent, correspondence with Carl Sandburg, who always had time for his old friend and unofficially adopted daughter. Letters to Sandburg in the late 1940s reveal plans for an <u>American Songbag for Children</u>. Ruth hoped to interest Sandburg in taking part in this project. Apparently it never got beyond the planning stage, as there are no extant sketches or other written notations concerning it.[25]

Ruth's long friendship with Edgard Varèse, recognized as one of the major seminal forces in twentieth-century music, was reinvigorated in the late 1940s, when Varèse advised Ruth that he had been invited to lecture on twentieth-century music at Columbia University and that he would like to include her as a representative composer. He asked her to send him information regarding her musical credo and to select a work of hers (recorded) which she considered most representative. He also asked for a score and for her own analysis of this work. In response to his request, Ruth selected her String Quartet and sent Varèse the score with the third and fourth movements "analyzed as to tone, rhythm, form, and dynamics."

In reply to Varèse's request for a credo, Ruth admitted she found this difficult to formulate because she herself was not completely sure how she would manage to dovetail her interest in folk music materials with her desire to continue her art music composition.[26]

The problems of raising a family loomed large in Ruth's activities during the years she lived in Washington, D.C. From her early resolve to have thirty-five children, to her actual bearing and rearing of four, she loved children and was able to gain their love, respect, and admiration in return. That her own children were, indeed, a big responsibility and

Life and Death in Washington

The Seeger family in Chevy Chase, Maryland (ca. 1950).
From left to right: Michael, Peggy, Ruth, Penny, Charles, and Barbara

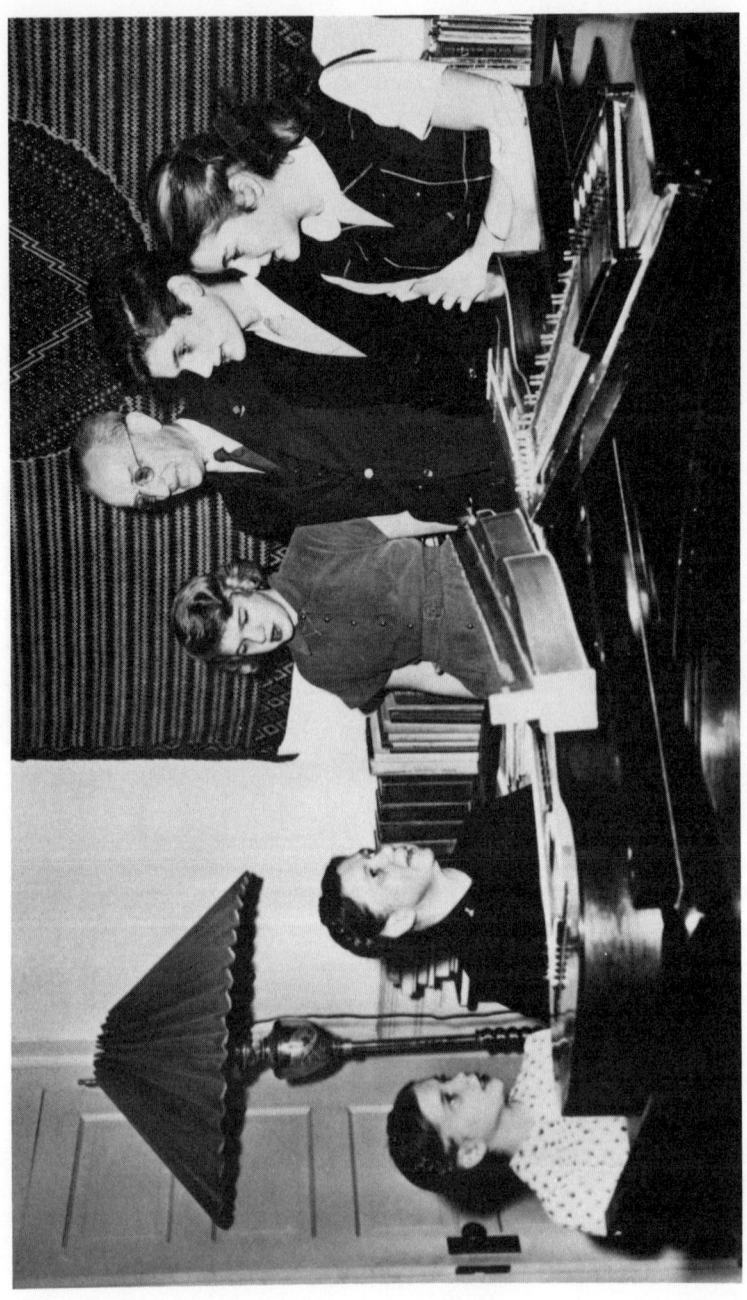

Life and Death in Washington

source of frustration is nowhere better set forth than in a long letter to Miss Prink, who was the editor with whom Ruth worked on the Lomax book <u>Our Singing Country</u>. The letter delineates in a hilarious manner, the endless minutiae involved in caring for a large house, a husband, and three children while continuing numerous activities in connection with her writing, her teaching, and her music. It is a classic of its kind and provides eloquent testimony that a woman's work is never done, if she does it conscientiously. It also shows that they were a real family, a congenial group that worked and played together.[27] There was no generation gap in the Seeger household, and everyone managed to survive the inevitable growing pains. Both parents taught by example; there were few long, serious conversations, but there were many good times together.

Ruth's children recall their mother's loving and caring relationships with them, expressed not often through words--more apparent through such activities as singing their favorite songs to them at bedtime, as an indication that they should go upstairs to bed. It is interesting to note that Ruth's own mother had provided the model for this activity when she was a child by playing the piano for her to go upstairs to bed.

Activities in the Seeger household, already enumerated in some detail, were augmented during Charles Seeger's last official position in Washington, as Chief of the Division of Music and Visual Arts at the Pan American Union. During these years, the Seeger household became a favorite gathering place for the innumerable visitors who came to Washington in connection with the cultural activities of the Pan American Union. Naturally, Ruth, as hostess, became involved in these affairs and although she thoroughly enjoyed them, they were one more drain on her already severely taxed time and energy.

What of Ruth's problems as a woman composer and her attitude toward the male-dominated society in which she lived? Many people have been intrigued with these aspects of her

---

[Opposite:] The Seeger family at home in Chevy Chase (1952). From left to right: Penny, Ruth, Barbara, Charles, Michael, and Peggy

career and have given much thought to possible explanations. Her irritation at women's lack of freedom to go where and when they chose, chronicled in her Chicago days, and her indignation with editors she met in Europe who pointed to her sex as a barrier to publication of her music, have already been mentioned. Also, comments made at the MacDowell Colony record her concern over the fate of her career should she decide in favor of marriage. Even at this early date, she was reconciled to the thought that pursuing both a career and marriage would involve compromise. "I can have a career and life too, but even though the former will be enriched by the latter, there must be sacrifice."[28] Obviously, she had cheerfully accepted and rather easily fallen into her role as a traditional housewife, even while she still entertained hopes of continuing her art music activities, which she had never consciously relinquished, but rather had, in her own mind, just postponed.

    The following comments from Ruth's own family expand her references to possible friction between the career of housewife and mother and that of a professional person. Peggy, herself a professional musician and the mother of three children, thought that the real problem is trying to be a mother and a composer. "Time just doesn't exist for doing things on your own. Being a wife is a problem only if one has an overweening husband ... but my father was never like that. He absolutely gloried in her [Ruth's] independence ... she wanted her freedom to compose but she wanted her children." Peggy also felt that in the late 1940s, Ruth's piano teaching took time away from her composing,[29] and Michael sensed that there was a definite conflict in Ruth's mind about "how to spend the limited time in one's life--difficult for a woman who could do so much."[30] Obviously, Ruth was aware of and deeply concerned with the problems she faced in her many-faceted existence. In a review of her book, American Folk Songs for Christmas, the reviewer refers to an essay by Ruth on this subject which reveals Ruth as

> ...torn between the worlds of editing, teaching, composing, and home-making. I have before me an undated letter of 1951, in which she apologized for not writing me on business: "I'm sorry. This week has been such a precious thing. I have done a rare thing: turned off the feeling of weight and conscience

Ruth Crawford Seeger's music room at 7 West Kirke Street, Chevy Chase, Maryland

about letters and deadlines, and spent two solid days, and parts of others, just writing music. I don't know whether I'm a lost soul or a found one.... I think I'll work much better for this orgy of vocal silence and pianistic noise."[31]

Ruth herself has thus acknowledged her personal dilemma in sorting out her priorities among her manifold responsibilities and sometimes conflicting desires. Folk music provided a true parallel interest to her art music for the decade of the forties and consumed much of her time; it would eventually have added an enriching dimension if she had had more years at her disposal to implement her projected return to the writing of art music. In the meantime, it supplied the family with much needed income as did her piano teaching, which Ruth sometimes felt was an imposition on her time, especially the long hours (13 hours on Saturday) that that activity required.

The Seegers' home at 7 West Kirke Street, Chevy Chase, Maryland

If she was on occasion a bit "peppy"--to which all members
of her family testify--she had reason enough to be that way.
She worked untiringly and was utterly unselfish, but she
was also human and sometimes felt she was over-extending
herself. After many years of financial struggles, the Seeger
family enjoyed a short period of comparative affluence when
they were able to afford a larger house (they moved to 7
West Kirke Street, Chevy Chase, Maryland, in 1944) and
domestic help, and to send two of the children, Michael and
Peggy, to private schools. These additional niceties were
also an additional expense, and Ruth worked very hard to
help supply the money necessary to provide them.

Ruth chronicled practically nothing regarding her personal health during these hectic years in Washington. Indeed
she had little time to consider her own needs and wants.
Except for occasional references to her desire to resume her
art music composition, she seldom spoke of herself. Her remarks to her brother and sister-in-law indicate that by 1950
things were beginning to weigh her down so that she felt she
was working less effectively:

> It's been a sort of slow, low year for me. I took
> on a few too many things to do, and instead of doing
> them faster so as to get on to the next one, my perverse self wouldn't let me think fast, and the introduction to the book which is just out, and which will
> reach you soon, took three times longer to write than
> I thought it would.[32]

It was probably late spring or early summer of 1953
that Ruth began to notice that her physical condition, generally good throughout her life, was beginning to change for
the worse. One might safely assume too, that Ruth's driving
of herself for many years had begun to lower her physical
resistance noticeably. Her condition apparently began to deteriorate seriously so that by midsummer, when she went for
medical consultation, her trouble was diagnosed as cancer, at
which time she submitted to an operation. As with her
mother, Ruth had about three months to live.

Her condition improved briefly and she attempted to resume her work, but her health then gradually worsened till
her death on November 18. Libba Cotten, well-known folk musician and their beloved and faithful companion for many years,

stayed on with the family during this difficult time when Charles was overcome with grief and utterly distraught and the children were brokenhearted and bewildered.

That this woman of tremendous drive and energy, who gave of her time and talent freely and unselfishly, should be cut down by terminal cancer at such an early age was indeed a tragedy; she had so much still to give and so much still to live for. Peggy, who was called home from college about a week and a half before Ruth died, recalled that she never complained. "She was a person who loved life and I seem to remember when I came home there was a manuscript which was floating about her sick room which was a book which she had nearly finished while she was ill; while she knew that she had absolutely no hope." Peggy further related that Ruth offered herself to an experimental clinic that was trying to cure cancer by X-ray because she felt this might be of some value to other people.[33]

Her indomitable spirit persisted to the end. The day she died she had been scheduled to appear at the Washington Post's Children's Book Fair in downtown Washington.[34] The two older children, Peggy and Michael, both of whom are now very successful professional performers of folk song, appeared in her place. (What a source of pride and comfort it would have been to Ruth to know how ably her children have perpetuated the legacy she and her husband bequeathed to all concerned with America's cultural heritage.)

One of the finest of the many tributes paid to her after her death was that written by a friend and coworker, Sidney Robertson Cowell, which appeared in the International Folk Music Journal. Mrs. Cowell wrote at some length of Ruth's work in the field of folk song, of her teaching ability, and of the extreme warmth of her family life. She concluded her remarks with a picture of Ruth in her favorite place, her home:

> The Seeger home in Washington was an unforgettable centre of warmth and hospitality to musicians, especially those working with folk music anywhere in the world. The stimulus of an evening with the Seegers has been described over and over again by foreign visitors as their most important musical experience in the United States. For all her great

creative gifts and wide musical knowledge, Mrs. Seeger was a sturdy personality of the utmost simplicity and naturalness. She had the widest possible sympathies, the quickest loyalty and kindness--a memorably rich and generous human being who was a most rewarding friend.[35]

Ruth's life was inextricably interwoven with her music, and its course can be seen as an attempt on her part "to feel comfortable with oneself and with music." She was fairly certain that her ambition was to be a pianist and composer until she went to the MacDowell Colony in the summer of 1929, en route to New York, but even here, under the influence of her first serious love affair, she felt that marriage and a composing career could be compatible; doubtless she did not correctly evaluate the factor of raising a family, which she had always wanted. The question of career versus marriage remained largely theoretical throughout the early stages of Ruth and Charles's relationship, and although he maintained that he did not want to influence the course of Ruth's career unduly, he nevertheless played a decisive role in most of her planning. He was fourteen years older than she, and from the first she had looked to him for guidance; she deferred to his judgment throughout most of their life together. When he was interested in dissonant counterpoint, Ruth made it the center of her efforts in composition; when Charles became interested in music and politics during the days of the Composers' Collective, she took part in these activities at least mentally and spiritually; as folk music gradually assumed a major role in her husband's thinking, she developed a strong interest in it.

"We are all looking and longing for understanding and love when we marry. Do more than two out of every ten thousand find it?"[36] Judging from all available testimony, Ruth and Charles were two such fortunate people; Charles Seeger himself freely admitted that he could not tear himself apart from Ruth.[37] Ruth had a deep and genuine liking for people, although she had no social aspirations as such. She had always demanded of her friends, if they were to be close friends, that she must respect and admire them intellectually as well as personally. When she began her study of composition with Charles Seeger, there was quickly established a sympathetic intellectual bond between teacher and student. The intellectual bond remained important, but Charles was destined to be more than an advisor and friend. After Ruth met Charles, she never again felt alone; she knew (as did he) that their rapport was unique and irreplaceable.

Ruth's association with Charles was an enriching experience in many ways for them both. They were both teachers and were both interested in the intellectual side of music, Charles as a musicologist and Ruth as a researcher. They were both composers: he as one whose ideas dominated his creations; she as one whose talent was perhaps more intuitive, who took ideas and developed them into vital and significant musical substance. His educational and social and professional connections had led him into a rather select circle of acquaintances which Ruth also enjoyed and which opened doors for her that were extremely valuable to her ambitions. His endless fund of ideas and his many interests made him a stimulating friend and companion whom Ruth could admire and enjoy as well as love.

In turn, Ruth brought out the best in Charles Seeger. Ruth's references to herself as a child seem a reflection of her diffidence and should not obscure the fact that in most ways she was--even from her early years--quite mature and an unusually deep and thoughtful person. Charles not only loved her intensely, he was also constantly goaded by her intellectual curiosity and her great talent to maintain a high level of accomplishment in all his endeavors. She helped him to mature in his personal relationships, not only with her but in his general outlook on the world; her strong feelings for him, which contained elements of non-possessiveness and honesty, appealed to Charles Seeger and gave him new insights into the power and meaning of love. The great difference in their ages helped them both--association with a younger woman gave Charles a new lease on life and association with an older man helped Ruth gain the self-confidence she continuously sought; his natural intellectual and philosophical bent complemented and reinforced hers.

Avant-garde composers, the world of musicology, a heightened awareness of the social and political overtones of music, and, above all, the search for tradition in American music were all explored by Ruth with Charles's help, to the enrichment of her own talents and life. Ruth's sturdy values inherited from her parents naturally underwent variations as her experiences broadened, but her sense of values

remained strong. Her strength of character was a boon to
Charles who found her support to be a stabilizing factor in
his life. Ruth's unassuming and unpretentious attitude appealed to the human side of Charles Seeger, whose natural
reserve did not make it easy for him to expose this side of
his nature. Charles and Ruth worked effectively and sensitively with each other from the time Ruth started studying
composition with him in the fall of 1929. Ruth gave constant
help, advice, and criticism throughout the time Charles spent
on his book, <u>Tradition and Experiment in 20th Century Music</u>,
and in turn, Charles encouraged Ruth in her nursery-school
activities and in the writing of her folk song books for
children. Ruth did her best to make life comfortable for
Charles, and he often helped with the care of the children
and of the house. Together they explored and became deeply
involved in the world of folk music, discussing various problems and experimenting with their solutions. They inspired
each other to do their best in all their undertakings.

One cannot help speculating on one aspect of Ruth's
musical life. If Charles had used his influence over her to
encourage Ruth to continue with her musical composition
rather than to channel her energy, time, and talent into folk
music, would she have continued with her fine art composing?
She would probably have composed more than she did, but
other factors must be considered. She would still have been
influenced by the times which did not favor avant-garde experiments; folk music was in the air and she would have been
aware of its values, though probably not in the same ways.
Also, in 1935, Washington, D.C., did not offer a composer
the stimulation and performing possibilities to be found in
New York. The musical life of our nation's capital could offer
no competition to the lures of our nation's cultural center
which she had known and enjoyed. Raising a family and
helping support them remains as probably the most obvious
and the greatest obstacle to the pursuit of a career which offered no hope of providing monetarily for the responsibilities
which Ruth had willingly assumed. True, she wanted to compose, but she also wanted children, and she never really
relinquished the hope of being able to do both.

Ruth Crawford was a determined, talented, and ambitious woman, trusting, unafraid, and filled with tremendous
energy. She achieved each goal in turn and then set her
sights a little higher. In her own quiet way--without fan-

fare--she became a successful composer, whose true stature is just becoming known. Ruth Crawford Seeger was all this and more. She became known for her authentic and artistic transcriptions of folk music and for her books of folk music for children, and in the words of her husband, "she was an inspiring teacher of children. And an unbelievably wonderful mother and wife."[38] The years since her death continue to enhance the image of Ruth Crawford Seeger as a person of integrity and quality both as a musician of lasting importance and as a great American woman.

PART II:

THE WORKS OF RUTH CRAWFORD SEEGER

Chapter Eight

ART MUSIC

"Would I think much of my own music, if someone else had written it? What would my criticisms be?" (Ruth Crawford, diary entry, November 1, 1927)

Ruth Crawford's interest in composing goes back to her high-school days, even before she studied harmony (briefly) at the School of Musical Art in Jacksonville, Florida. None of her very early compositions are extant, although some apparently had enough merit to warrant Weidig's query as to where she had received her early music training. At the American Conservatory of Music in Chicago, Ruth's interest in her harmony classes soon rivalled the piano for her time and attention. The discomfort she experienced from the tense arm muscles at the piano possibly helped turn her thoughts seriously toward composition, although this was not the decisive factor. Rather, it was Weidig's pronouncement that she had serious compositional talent which should be cultivated that gave her the confidence she needed to consider seriously a career as a professional composer.

Ruth did not study composition formally until her third year at the conservatory though both Weidig and John Palmer, her two theory teachers, introduced creative work in their classes for their beginning students. Very early Ruth evinced an interest in writing for the violin--her brother had played the violin, and Weidig, whom Ruth admired and respected, was a professional violinist, playing with the Chicago Symphony orchestra and teaching violin at the conservatory. This interest is reflected in the sizable number of her scores which use this instrument. Her friends, Alfred Frankenstein and Adolph Weiss, played clarinet and bassoon, respectively, thus giving her occasion to become familiar with these instruments. Further, her close association and friendship with Alice Burrows, a singer whom Ruth accompanied on occasion, provided opportunity for familiarity with the problems in vocal writing. Ruth's thorough training in piano and theory provided useful basic tools. Doubtless her participation in the percussion section for a part of a season in the training orchestra sponsored by the Chicago Civic Association gave her needed additional experience in the practical workings of the orchestra. These things, besides the regular conservatory curriculum and the expected contacts with all kinds of student performers, provided a background for serious creative effort. Ruth supplied the talent, and even more important, the desire, the drive, and the willingness to do the hard work necessary to achieve her goals.

During Ruth's second year at the conservatory, Weidig, the man who would be her composition teacher and guide for the next several years, published his book Harmonic Material and Its Uses (1923). This book embodied his classroom teaching and thus gives a good idea of the approach to harmony which Ruth studied. It presents a very thorough (one might say "Germanic" in its thoroughness) exposition of traditional harmony, with creative exercises for the student at every turn. It also stressed the necessity for analysis of everything, especially of original work. Weidig's assignments to find specific examples of harmonic usage in the literature itself aided students in developing a meaningful acquaintance with a wide range of musical compositions. In its exploration of the far-reaching possibilities offered by the use of altered chords, the text approaches closely the concept of atonality and allows extensive use of dissonance. Besides the usual items expected in such a text of the day, Weidig discusses creation of new scales (p. 280), undertones (p. 35), speaks much of the concept of "melodic" as opposed to "harmonic" element in chord tones, and of the feasibility of moving units of sound with the same freedom as a single tone. It is reasonable to assume that Ruth was thoroughly acquainted with the material in this book, given her studious nature, her deep interest in the subject matter, and her very evident high esteem of Weidig, whose every word she cherished.

Several of Ruth's early conservatory attempts at writing

survive in manuscript despite her avowal that she had destroyed them all. Compositions from as early as 1922 may be found in the Seeger Collection. These include Little Waltz (1922) and several other probably teaching pieces with no date, but in the same longhand writing and giving the street address, 4736 Woodlawn Avenue, Chicago. One is a study in short trills, one a study in triplets, some have fingering written in the score. Only one with the above street address is longer and more elaborate; its title page, <u>Caprice</u>, is handprinted. Perhaps it was intended for a somewhat older student. These pieces possibly date from 1922-1923, when Ruth first started her piano teaching on Chicago's south side. Two songs, <u>To One Away</u>, and <u>Return</u> are dated 1923, as are <u>Nocturne</u> for violin and piano, Theme and Variations for piano, and the first movement of a piano sonata. These are probably outgrowths of class assignments. Theme and Variations--of some interest--is imaginative, highly chromatic, with rather strong dissonances; it shows understanding of keyboard techniques and idioms. Five Canons, doubtless a class assignment, and <u>Kaleidoscopic Changes on an Original Theme, Ending with a Fugue</u> are both dated 1924. The latter was probably Ruth's first composition to receive a public hearing in Chicago, when Weidig placed it on his annual composition recital in Kimball Hall on May 31, 1924. These events were considered of some importance locally and were reviewed by the Chicago press. <u>Kaleidoscopic Changes</u> is by far the most ambitious and technically advanced of Ruth's work thus far. The romantic sounding theme exhibits typical nineteenth-century traits--extensive use of dynamics, chromaticism, pedal markings, and a sweeping, dramatic approach to the keyboard. The thirteen-page work also shows a dense fabric, with generous servings of dissonance and touches of Scriabinesque harmonies.

Ruth continued to receive Weidig's support for her efforts as she worked on her master's degree in composition (1925-1927), even though he did not necessarily share her enthusiasm for the new and the experimental, especially her strong attraction to dissonance. She seemed to be naturally drawn to unconventional sounds and through a series of new acquaintances, she soon began to try to incorporate them into her own compositions. Through her new piano teacher, Madame Djane Lavoie Herz, who was not connected with the American Conservatory, Ruth became steeped in the music of the Russian composer and mystic, Alexander Scriabin. Madame

Herz had been his student in Europe and had become attracted not only to his music, but also to his interest in theosophy and Oriental mysticism. Herz was thus able to give her students firsthand information about Scriabin personally as well as about his music. Possibly they discussed such things at Ruth's lessons and on other less formal occasions. Certainly Ruth had a good opportunity to become knowledgeable about Scriabin and immersed in his ideas. And although his strong influence later dissipated under Charles Seeger's instruction, Ruth did not forget his music. Her desire to visit Russia while she was in Europe stemmed at least partly from her hope of making the acquaintance of Samuel Feinberg, a Scriabin student, who played piano concerts which featured his master's compositions.

The hand of Scriabin lies rather heavy on the works which Ruth composed from 1924 to 1929, even while she continued her composition study with Weidig. She had become acquainted with his works early in his conservatory training, so when she was exposed to a massive dose of his music as well as his philosophical and esthetic ideas, she was conditioned to absorb them. Ruth's piano preludes and the several chamber music suites, as well as the violin and piano sonata, share Scriabin's tendencies toward panchromaticism, atonality, use of serial procedures, preference for the tritone, and wide-spaced chords or vertical structures laced rather liberally with numerous added tones to produce an almost pseudo-contrapuntal texture, in effect wiping out the distinction between the vertical and horizontal aspects of the musical fabric. Their music often sounds improvised, but close analysis reveals a high degree of organization with some constructivist tendencies (at least, in their later works). Scriabin, in his later works, and Ruth throughout practically her entire composing career, abjured the use of a key signature; both made extensive use of dissonance--Scriabin with an almost romantic touch, whereas unrelieved and sharp dissonance seemed central to Ruth's style almost from the beginning. Also, they each introduced material which reappeared in later movements of a composition, although this of course, had been used at least since Beethoven. Both used cell-like motives and melodic whipsnaps (short decorative notes preceding a strong beat); both avoided triads in favor of fourths and fifths, and favored the device of ostinato. Most of these techniques were used by the leading composers of the time, but Ruth's close association with Madame Herz and her friendship with Rudhyar impressed Scriabin's interpretation of these ideas rather forcibly on her musical consciousness. Well established, too, during these years were Ruth's use of dynamics, tempo, and ostinati as form-building devices, and her avoidance of fixed forms, of exact repetition, and of development technique.

Esthetically and philosophically Ruth was curious about Scriabin's theosophical ideas as new and different from and as a possible substitute for the religion she had experienced in her family life, and which had far-reaching effects on her spiritual outlook. She was probably aware of Scriabin's experiments with inventing a new language for his Mysterium, a never-completed work which was to be a synthesis of all the arts. The language "had Sanskritic roots, but included cries, interjections, exclamations, and the sounds of breath exhaled and inhaled."[1] Ruth later did her own experimenting with the creation of original sounds for her choral works. She also considered using the Bhagavad Gita as a programmatic basis for a composition but got no further with this idea than the use of the sacred word "om." Other than her connection of Prelude No. 9 with Lao-tzu's Tao, Ruth did not say whether she associated her sound combinations with theosophical doctrines as Scriabin often did. Despite his personal philosophical extravagances, which tended to militate against wide acceptance of his musical ideas, Scriabin has proved increasingly to have pioneered many of the avant-garde theoretical concepts of the twentieth century, all of which held a strong interest for Ruth.

Dane Rudhyar, French-American composer whom Ruth had met through Madame Herz, was also attracted to Scriabin; Ruth and Rudhyar thus shared an interest in the Russian master as well as a friendship with the Herz family. Rudhyar also had a personal influence on her. She had never taken the narrow view of any subject, so it is natural that she was drawn to his concept of the "encyclopedic" man; she responded to Rudhyar's interest in the music of long ago (pre-Palestrina) and the far away and exotic (non-European, especially Hindu, art and culture). She sensed the implications of Rudhyar's rejection, not only of neo-classicism, but the whole concept of music as expressed in the Western European harmonic system, as a narrow and confining approach to a subject allowing worldwide interpretation.

In his music, Rudhyar avoided counterpoint in favor of chords, often heavy and full, and Ruth herself later admitted she had been influenced by his style;[2] his emphasis on the moment rather than on sequential events affected Ruth's use of rhythm during these years. Rudhyar felt inhibited by the inadequacies of Western notation as inexact and incomplete, suggesting as one alternative, the use of neumes (which interestingly Ruth later considered for use in notating folk song transcriptions) or the use of electrical machines as less restricting than our present notation.[3] Along with Cowell, Varèse, and others, Rudhyar obviously grasped the possibilities which would later be developed in electronic music. It is apparent that Rudhyar made a deep and lasting impression on Ruth's artistic development, not only through his own music and his own personal charm, but also through his observations about future developments in music.

In spite of the very real influence of Scriabin, and to a lesser degree of Rudhyar, and--probably through Adolph Weiss--of Schoenberg, with whose atonal works she was familiar, Ruth's music does not sound like theirs. It is a measure of her talent and her artistic integrity that she developed very early her own individual and personal approach to the world of sound which she would continue to perfect and to intensify. More than once during her composing years she dwelt on the difficulty faced by creative artists in striving for originality; in avoiding imitation of other composers. This was an ever-present concern to her and may perhaps account for the impression occasionally received of a studied and constrained effort, of a lack of spontaneity, in some of her compositions. Significantly, to a friend Ruth once said words to this effect: "How does one ever write a work without a reminiscence of something that has been written before?"[4]

As early as 1924, Ruth began to write works she felt were worthy of public scrutiny and which embodied the new kinds of sounds which expressed her unique musical thought. The Five Preludes for Piano (1924-1925) (7:40, Ms., R) are all short and generally express very intense moods. No key signatures are used, conventional scales and triads are avoided, foot-tapping regular beats seldom appear, dynamic and tempo changes abound, as do involved rhythmic patterns. The often chromatic, searching quality in the melody is generally non-lyric in character and the whole set is shot through with mild dissonances. In addition to Scriabin-like traits, Debussy's spirit is not very far away from these preludes, felt both in the relaxed rhythm of some and the sprightly elfin charm of others. Prelude No. 2 is a cohesive and effective essay in the subtly humorous scherzo-like style for which Ruth had a natural affinity (as in No. 8 in the second set). Prelude No. 3 (Example 1), which offers a pleasing combination of late Romanticism and Impressionism, shows many traits of Ruth's style.

Ex. 1: Prelude No. 3, measure 1. Courtesy of the Estate of Ruth Crawford Seeger. Used by permission.

Gitta Gradova, outstanding young concert pianist of the time, gave the first performance of these preludes in Town Hall, New York City, on December 12, 1925, for a League of Composers concert.

Preludes 6-9, a second set of four, (1927-1928) (6:55, P, R) show many of these same traits and influences, but they tend to become more dissonant and complex rhythmically and harmonically. They show frequent use of heavy, low chordal sounds, which relate rather easily to the music of Dane Rudhyar, with whose scores Ruth had become acquainted during this time. Prelude, No. 9 (Example 2), which emphasizes such chords, also testifies to Ruth's admitted groping for new means of musical expression.

Ex. 2: Prelude No. 9, measures 4, 5, and 6. © 1941 Merion Music Inc. Used by permission of the publisher, Theodore Presser Company.

Richard Buhlig, American pianist who received his early training in Chicago and to whom the somewhat lugubrious Prelude No. 9 was dedicated (the second of only two such dedications in Ruth's works), performed these preludes at a Copland-Sessions concert in New York, May 6, 1928. Four Preludes by Ruth's Chicago friend, Adolph Weiss, appeared

Art Music 139

on the same program. In reviewing this concert, Edward Burlingame Hill wrote concerning Ruth's preludes: "Miss Crawford's preludes were surely meritorious in workmanship and style, but presented a singular union of 'influences'--a sort of esthetic mésalliance, Scriabin and Schoenberg."[5] Ruth's own comments on two of these preludes are especially interesting because programmatic ideas associated with her compositions are rarely found. In response to a friend's inquiry as to meaning in her music, she said: "Having just finished playing my wild Prelude No. 8 in primitive fifths, I answer smilingly, 'This one represents a human laugh.'"[6] Regarding Prelude No. 9 she told another friend its program was related to Lao-tzu's Tao.[7]

Ruth wrote her prize-winning composition, The Adventures of Tom Thumb (11, Ms., NR) for piano and narrator, in 1925. The author of the text is not identified; probably Ruth adapted it from the Grimm Brothers. Written in a musical idiom designed to please children, it is one of two of Ruth's mature compositions to utilize tonality. All movements are definitely tonal and use key signatures. It also contains several characteristic traits, such as the use of dissonant and conventionally forbidden intervals. Her fondness for patterns that are not quite the same on repetition is also in evidence. As in all her works that use words, she takes great care to make the accompanying music expressive of the texts. This composition also reflects a trend of the times in writing music of immediate appeal and ready accessibility. J. A. Carpenter's Adventures in a Perambulator (1915), his Krazy Kat ballet (1921), Hindemith's Let's Build a Town (1930), and Prokofieff's Peter and the Wolf (1936) are a few such titles which come quickly to mind.

Ruth's earliest orchestral work, the Suite for Small Orchestra in two movements (1926) (7:42, Ms., R), is effectively written for the modest instrumentation of flute, clarinet, bassoon, strings, and piano. It appears to be an interval study, concentrating on small skips (half and whole steps) and generally avoiding the large skips Ruth often favors. The first movement uses only a few tritones (conventionally forbidden interval which bisects the twelve-tone scale in half rather than the conventional proportion of seven to five); the second is full of it. The somber mood of the first movement, marked "slow and pensive," contrasts sharply with the second, which is almost frisky. Here, the music's easily felt beat works its way to two climaxes toward which tempo, dynamics, and texture gradually build. Both movements show the use of layered rhythmic and melodic ostinati and tone clusters, which became characteristic traits of her style. The following excerpt (Example 3) shows the beginning of the second movement; these eighth- and sixteenth-note patterns provide the basis for ostinati which appear in every measure thereafter, save the last. Note the rearranged chromatic scale pattern found in the first eight notes of the piano part, whose cell-like twisting design becomes typical of Ruth's melodies.

Ex. 3: Suite for Small Orchestra, second movement, measures 1, 2. Courtesy of the Estate of Ruth Crawford Seeger. Used by permission.

The Sonata for Violin and Piano (1925-1926) (15:28, P, R) is one of Ruth's most impressive works and without doubt the most important of her scores written in Chicago. In four movements marked 1) Agitated, vibrant and Andante lusingando, 2) Buoyant, 3) Mystic, intense, and 4) Fast, with bold energy, Ruth allows her naturally warm and frankly romantic nature to show in a brilliant technical display behind which are carefully worked out sound and effective musical ideas, couched in a highly dissonant fabric.

After a short but arresting introduction, the first movement features large non-triadic upward skips, which dominate the melodic line played by the violin and contribute to the intensity of the music. Ruth relies rather heavily on late nineteenth-century devices, using numerous changes in tempo, dynamics, expression marks, and time signatures to achieve her effects in a formal pattern approximating a classical sonatina.

In the second, scherzo-like movement, a syncopated rhythmic ostinato, again featuring wide non-triadic melodic skips, is bandied about by the piano and violin while a second melodic idea runs lightly in between and around it. These two ideas are deftly transposed and inverted in a rondo-like design. In the piano part, left hand, Ruth makes use of the whipsnap pattern often found in her writing for piano.

The brief third movement starts with a feeling of subdued intensity, using a syncopated four-note chromatic motive against which Ruth poses a counter melody in halved time values. The slow pulse and the soft dynamics gradually give way to a rather brilliant climax which leads without pause to the last movement of the sonata.

Numerous changes in time signature (thirty in forty-nine measures), tempo, and dynamics, intermingled with many expression marks and an intense driving quality, give the fourth movement a strongly romantic cast. The principal theme (there is really only one--a second idea acts more or less as a bridge) is characterized by large non-triadic skips, found in much of the sonata (the third movement only excepted) which give it a typical Ruth Crawford touch. The opening measures of the last movement (see Example 4 on page 142) contain the germinal motive on which the entire movement is based--a motive which bears an affinity to the motivic material used in the first and third movements of the sonata.

The Sonata for Violin and Piano provides a good example of Ruth's constant striving for originality and her concern to preserve her artistic integrity. It is a strong, convincing and artistically sound piece of work which effectively demonstrates her ingenious methods of construction. One cannot help but wonder why she felt constrained, by her own admis-

Ex. 4: Sonata for Violin and Piano, fourth movement, measures 1–3. © 1984 Merion Music Inc. Used by permission of the publisher, Theodore Presser Company.

Art Music 143

sion, to burn the score for what is surely one of her finest compositional efforts. To be sure, Scriabin's presence can be detected in its aesthetic qualities, but it is Ruth's own true self which speaks from these pages.

The first performances of the Sonata for Violin and Piano[8] apparently took place on a program of works written by members of Weidig's composition class in Kimball Hall on May 22, 1926, with Ruth playing the piano and Mrs. Ruth Parker Lilien the violin. The sonata was also played in New York in 1927, and in Chicago in 1928. Following the New York performance by Josef Stopak and Irene Jacobi at a League of Composers concert, the Musical Courier reported:

> The most ambitious work on the program, Miss Crawford's Sonata for Violin and Piano, is boldly energetic and virile, with a bittersweet harmonic flavor. The composer writes with palpable sincerity and poetic intent.[9]

After the Chicago performance of the sonata at the Cliff Dwellers Club, February 18, 1928 (Amy Neill, violinist, and Lee Pattison, pianist), under the auspices of the International Society for Contemporary Music, the Chicago Journal commented, "The young Chicago girl's violin sonata easily deserved its place in its famous company."[10] Its "famous company" included Milhaud's Sixth String Quartet, Louis Gruenberg's Four Indiscretions, Stravinsky's Serenade in A, and Castelnuovo-Tedesco's Alt Wien.

Of even greater interest than the newspaper reviews are Ruth's own comments:

> Last night I longed to write, but was too weary. My violin sonata was played by Amy Neill and Lee Pattison at the first concert of the International Society for Contemporary Music, Chicago chapter. What I wanted to set down for memory's sake were two occurrences. One, when Stock, after the performance, came to my seat, led me to the front, gripped my hand several times, saying "very beautiful." The other occurrence has gripped me all day and brought me several times to the verge of tears.... Stella Roberts, at the end of the evening ... told me how much she had been moved by the sonata.... Later, in the

dressing room she said, with a terrible seriousness, "Ruth you must not let anything interrupt you; you must go on and on; there are things which can stop you; you must not let them...."[11]

Ruth herself made one further reference to this sonata in a biographical resume. Commenting on the over two hundred poems she had written by the time she was sixteen, she stated: "Fifteen years later I burned most of them, together with a violin sonata which had been played in New York at a League of Composers concert and in Chicago at the Cliff Dwellers, with Frederick Stock present."[12] Luckily for us, Ruth had given a copy of the score to her pupil and friend, Vivian Fine. Ms. Fine, who had attended the performance of the sonata at the Cliff Dwellers, cherished and preserved her copy of the work through the years. When the opportunity presented itself, she planned and successfully carried out her project to perform this sonata. With Ida Kafavian as violinist, she gave a definitive performance of the work at the Coolidge Auditorium in the Library of Congress (November 12, 1982) and then donated the manuscript to the Music Division of the Library of Congress.[13] This work, so recently restored to us, can only add stature to Ruth's already solid reputation as an important American composer.

The manuscript of the Suite for Five Wind Instruments and Piano bears the notation, "composed in 1927, revised in 1929" (12, Ms., NR). It can be assumed with some degree of safety, that the revised version of this suite was made after Ruth left Chicago for New York in the fall of 1929. One of a series of letters to Alice from New York City mentioned that Ruth's suite for winds and piano was to be played by the Pan American in the near future. Ruth commented: "After giving them the parts, I decide it is time for me to make some drastic changes and insert a few climaxes here and there." The work was then performed by the Pan American Ensemble at a musical soiree of Ruth's works given at Blanche Walton's home during the concert season, 1929-1930, probably January.[14]

Ruth made several remarks which indicated that she was having trouble with the composition of her Suite for Five Wind Instruments and Piano. Not only was her attention to detail limiting her conception of large sections,[15] but she also felt herself handicapped in writing extended works.

Work on my piece for wood winds and piano with
little gusto and no inspiration.... Almost everything
I write lacks skillful development; it is more a repetition in different voices of the same theme, unchanged
except for pitch.[16]

The suite, which consists of an introduction and three
movements, calls for flute, oboe, clarinet, bassoon, horn, and
piano. Thematic material from the Introduction is used in the
first movement, from the Introduction and first movement in
the second, and from the Introduction, first, and second
movements in the third. This material appears in various
guises, with changes in rhythm, tempo, pitch levels, dynamics, tone color and mood. The almost unrelieved dissonance
of the supporting lines is softened by the catchy and involved
rhythms which permeate much of the suite. The score shows
extensive use of tone clusters, the tritone, novel scale patterns, and traces of polytonality, all infused with the concept
of panchromaticism. The work lacks cohesion--perhaps a result of revision under different influences and conditions.
Possibly Charles Seeger was thinking of this score when he
said her works from Chicago were diffuse.[17] Speaking of
Ruth's Chicago compositions, Seeger said: "I looked everything she had over ... and I gave her detailed criticisms."
Seeger stated that he criticized very severely the Suite for
Five Wind Instruments and Piano and that her 1929 revision
incorporated some of his suggestions.[18]

Also from the year 1929 comes the Suite No. 2 for
Strings and Piano (9:45, Ms., R). Although no exact date
is given for the writing of this work, it was probably completed while Ruth was still in Chicago (possibly until around
the last of June).[19] The work is more highly organized than
the Suite for Five Wind Instruments and Piano, although
both utilize the thematic materials presented at the beginning
of the first movement throughout the entire composition.
Close study of the score shows extensive manipulation of a
narrow range, highly chromatic motive of three to four to
five notes. Subtleties and permutations abound, but the
suite is compounded of many facets of the germinal motive
used with considerable ingenuity and sophistication. Ruth's
affinity for rhythmic variety is likewise apparent in this work.

If the influence of Schoenberg can be detected in Ruth's
compositions of this period, it is not hard to read into her

Ex. 5: Suite No. 2 for Four Strings and Piano, first movement, measures 1-2. Courtesy of the Estate of Ruth Crawford Seeger. Used by permission.

Ex. 5 (continued): First movement, measures 3-4.

Suite No. 2 for Four Strings and Piano, as it shares Schoenberg's preoccupation in his early scores (the ones with which Ruth would probably be familiar at this time) with manipulation of a germ motive. She also shared his avoidance of mere repetition to lengthen a composition and of octave doublings, his use of sharply dissonant intervals--often widely spaced--and his blurring of the distinction between melody and harmony. A certain self-consciousness pervades both this suite and the Suite for Five Wind Instruments and Piano; she was admittedly struggling to find a new compositional approach and she felt unsure how to solve some of her problems, especially those related to the handling of form, texture, and dissonance. The opening measures of the first movement of the Suite No. 2 for Four Strings and Piano (see Example 5 on pages 146-147) show her emerging athematic and atonal tendencies.

Chicago had been good to Ruth Crawford. It had given her time and opportunity to mull over and absorb what she heard and read and learned and experienced and to develop herself musically. In the summer of 1929, Ruth left the midwest metropolis to seek her fortunes in other, perhaps more renowned, musical centers. New York was to add dimensions of importance to her musical career, as was Europe, and in its own way, our nation's capital. But Chicago had not only introduced Ruth to most of the major composers and the major concepts that would shape twentieth-century American music, it had also seen the appearance of the basic components of her musical style.

On leaving Chicago, Ruth spent the summer at the MacDowell Colony, during which time she wrote several songs to poems of Carl Sandburg. Although her diary makes specific mention of only three of these songs (<u>Joy</u>, <u>Sunsets</u>, and <u>Loam</u>), two others (<u>White Moon</u> and <u>Home Thoughts</u>) were probably written either before she left Chicago or while she was still at the Colony, but almost certainly prior to her study in New York. Ruth's manuscript containing all five of these songs as a set shows the same handwriting and bears the title, Five Songs (9, Ms., NR). Further, she makes no mention of these in any place other than the diary notes she made at Peterboro. The songs are set for a voice of moderate to moderately low range and are appropriate for performance by either a man or a woman. Musically, late nineteenth-century styles here blend with emerging twentieth-century

Art Music

techniques, such as extensive use of the tritone. They are all declamatory in style and show Ruth's constant concern to make her musical settings emphasize the meaning of the text. The song Loam (Example 6) illustrates these points.

Ex. 6: Loam, measures 5, 6, 7, and 8. Courtesy of the Estate of Ruth Crawford Seeger. Used by permission.

After a summer of working without guidance, Ruth was reinvigorated on her arrival in New York in the fall when she began her study of composition with Charles Seeger, friend and former teacher of Henry Cowell, and at that time teaching at the Institute of Musical Art. Seeger's concepts, especially his approach to dissonant counterpoint, which he had been formulating and teaching for a number of years, fitted in almost perfectly with Ruth's strong liking for dissonance. As he explained his concept of dissonant counterpoint:

> It reversed the traditional approach of Fux in that it had prepared consonance and then resolved dissonance. The first species was entirely in dissonance, that is, major and minor 2nds, 7ths, and 9ths, and tritones. Octaves were forbidden; and unisons, in the first species, as of course, were 5ths, 3rds, and 6ths, that is harmonically. Melodic-wise, any interval was alright provided it was not followed by a second interval which would make a consonance. That is, you could skip from--except octaves, which you could never skip--you could skip a 5th, for instance, if,

afterwards, you would either reverse that fifth to a tritone or to a major or minor 9th, a major or minor 7th. The plan was to produce dissonant combinations, both harmonically and melodically. The object was to purify the style--get the sentimentality out of it--get away from consonance.[20]

Since Ruth's Chicago compositions were full of just such dissonant intervals, their use proved no problem to her. Seeger helped her to control more tightly her use of dissonant intervals and to become conscious of the place and importance of every note she used, in an effort to avoid diffuseness. Melodically, he helped her to vitalize the concept of the lean line, and he worked with her to learn control of a single melody and then of its combination with other melodies. She quickly learned Seeger's idea that pitch repetition is permitted only after approximately eight different pitches have been heard. He taught her that to keep the melodic line from coming to a cadence or close, required purifying the line of unwanted, undesirable consonances.

Seeger's ideas regarding rhythm used similar concepts. Dissonant rhythm required that one rhythmic design not be allowed to persist lest it become a pattern, and a feeling of accent become established. A design such as an eighth, two sixteenths must be followed by another such as eighth-note triplets or a quarter note, or any of a number of other possibilities. By varying the number of beats in a measure, the feeling of meter can also be quickly destroyed, so they systematically pursued this idea. Ruth's Chicago compositions had featured complex, often non-pulsatile rhythms contrasted with rhythmic ostinati, which she used as a form-building device. In New York, she learned to incorporate Seeger's concept of dissonant rhythm into her scores which helped to organize these traits more tightly.

Seeger also worked with Ruth on the problem of form, a major concern of all composers who substituted a new approach for the conventional harmonic one with its form-building characteristics--how to achieve unity and coherence in a large design. To help her overcome her former sometimes hazy concept of the phrase, they worked from the smallest unit, the motive, to the molding of the entire line. Seeger was endeavoring to get back to the balanced phrase, rather than just allowing the music to flow in an undifferentiated stream, as he felt had often occurred in the recent past. He felt that a network of overlapping rows had a tendency to obscure the phrase. Seeger stressed not only the structure but the function of the phrase in the overall pattern of the composition. He worked to get away from the all-pervasive four-measure phrase found in much nineteenth-century music, so they experimented with the use of asymmetrical patterns.

Seeger was obviously trying to do in his own way what many other composers were attempting, i.e., to abandon the way the elements of music had been used in the common practice period and to experiment with various other possible ways to organize sound. And although Ruth had, as we have seen, been previously exposed to similar ideas, she responded to his personal presentation of them. He was a composer of some merit who was well equipped to understand the new approaches to all parameters of music, and thus he quickly sensed what it was that Ruth was interested in and what her possibilities were. Especially was Seeger able to direct Ruth's strong experimental tendencies into productive channels. He had been an experimenter himself during his active years as a composer. He liked to reminisce about the two pageants which he wrote during his Berkeley days, one of which (The Queen's Masque, 1915) featured the performance of four separate pieces of music simultaneously, an early example of the use of layers of sound,[21] a concept which Ruth incorporated into a number of her later works.

Ruth soon felt a strong hand guiding her, helping her organize her work and giving her a sense of direction which she felt had been lacking heretofore. Her initial indignation at Seeger's distrust of women's compositional talent ("I'll show that cocky man, Seeger")[22] soon gave way to a feeling of complete confidence. He called her compositional ideas a discipline, a term which appealed to Ruth; she had tried to discipline herself from a very early age and thus responded easily to this approach. She quickly recognized and respected his acute musical intelligence. He soon had an avid student on his hands, who not only grasped his ideas with alacrity, but who began to utilize them in compositions of real merit. It appears that Seeger taught Ruth to use, in a highly organized manner, what she had already used instinctively and not necessarily efficiently, but often effectively.

Since his Berkeley days, Seeger had been formulating his ideas of dissonant counterpoint, and his year of working with Ruth gave him the impetus to put this material into a more or less definite shape. At the end of Ruth's year of study with him, he dictated to her a book containing the gist of his ideas on the subject. Titled <u>Tradition and Experiment in 20th Century Music</u>, the book set down most of the concepts he had taught Ruth the previous winter. He dedicated the book to her--she had helped him by her constant suggestions and even more by her encouragement of his efforts to finish and publish it. Actually the work was never completed to the point where the needed examples were inserted into the text, nor polished to the point where Seeger felt he was ready for it to be published. He apparently felt that Ruth's part in the book was vital enough that she should be acknowledged, perhaps as coauthor. Wisely, she declined this honor--[23] she knew that it was his book, in the same way that her compositions were her own, despite the fact that he often made suggestions regarding them which she utilized in their working out. Their ability to complement each other musically (and otherwise) was almost uncanny and emphasized the major talents and strengths they each possessed. The dedication reads: "To Ruth Crawford, of whose studies these pages are a record and without whose collaboration and inspiration they would not have been written." Seeger referred to the second part of the book as founded upon the principles of dissonance. He called this approach a "frank stylization of technique [which] is not recommended as an ideal or even as an inevitability, but rather as one possible discipline in a field where discipline of every kind has broken down."[24]

Weidig had apparently given his composition students a fairly free rein to do as they wished and then offered his suggestions. This is in sharp contrast to the approach Seeger took with Ruth Crawford. He disciplined her talents and helped her develop them. She already had good musical ideas; Seeger offered concrete suggestions for their realization, which she was free to accept or reject. In retrospect, Seeger stated that if he did affect Ruth's compositional life, "it was in persuading her she was a good craftsman, and matured enough to strike out on her own without all this wondering whether she was as good as someone else, and substituting the bad habit of waiting for inspiration to a daily writing of notes regardless of how one felt about the prospect as one tried to write them."[25]

Art Music

In addition to the aforementioned revision of her Suite for Five Wind Instruments and Piano, Ruth completed several other compositions during this winter of preoccupation with new compositional techniques: three of the four Diaphonic Suites for small chamber music combinations (No. 4 was completed in Berlin, December 1930), the Piano Study in Mixed Accents--all studies in dissonant counterpoint or a single melodic line--and the first of the Three Songs to poems of Carl Sandburg, Rat Riddles. Further reference to Rat Riddles will be made in connection with the other two songs in the set, the last of which was completed in New York in 1932.

The word "diaphony" has two generally accepted musical meanings: 1) in Greek theory, it means dissonance in contrast to "symphonia," which means consonance; 2) the term was used by medieval theorists to mean two-part polyphony. Both meanings of the term can be applied to the Diaphonic Suites, which are studies in two-part polyphony as well as studies in dissonance, except the suite for unaccompanied flute (No. 1), which embodies the Greek meaning only (5, P, NR). The second suite features bassoon and cello (or two celli) (3:57, P, R), and the third, two B-flat clarinets (3:20, P, NR). No. 4 is set for oboe (or viola) and cello (8, P, NR).[26]

The four suites share many qualities. In them, Ruth apparently cut her teeth on Seeger's discipline of writing dissonant counterpoint and dissonant rhythm. Almost without exception, they place little emphasis on dynamics and tempo changes, all are infused with a basic three-note motive (cell or twist); and most of them contain movements which are through-composed. Experiments in asymmetrical phrases appear in all four suites; the second, third, and fourth contain a variety of approaches to two-part texture, while Diaphonic Suite No. 1 reveals considerable skill and imagination in the manipulation of a single line. The third movement of this suite is built on an eight-measure seven-note pitch pattern, which is then transposed, presented in retrograde, in inversion, and in retrograde inversion. Example 7 (page 154), which gives the opening measures of this movement, shows the pitch set and also illustrates Ruth's practice of deliberately omitting or altering one note in the sets she used. This was apparently done to indicate lack of perfection in human beings--only the Supreme Being is perfect!

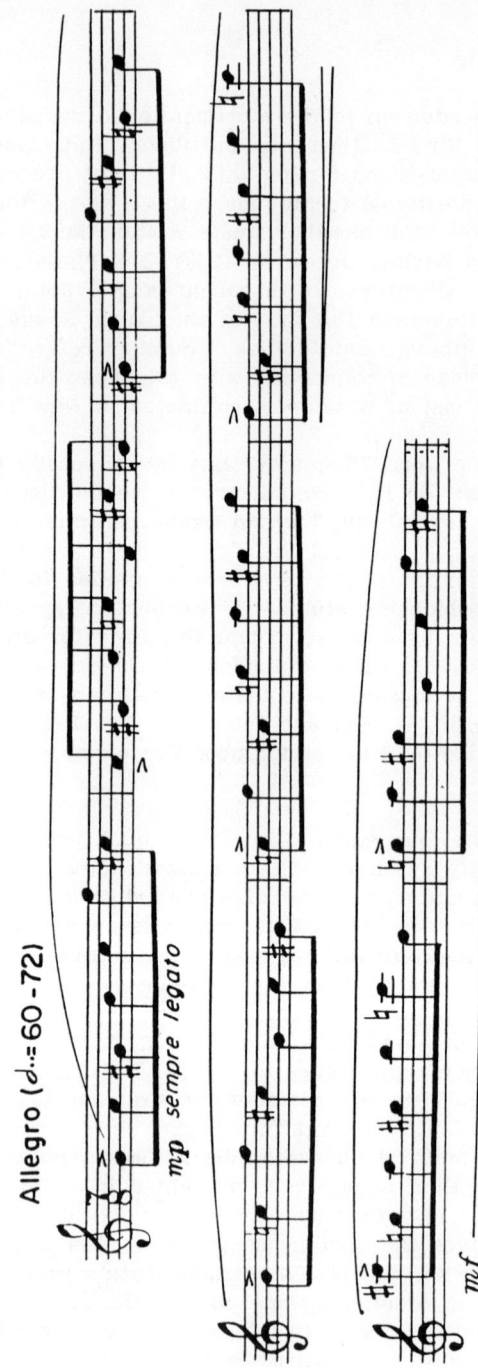

Ex. 7: Diaphonic Suite No. 1, third movement, measures 1-8. Copyright © 1972 Continuo Music Press, Inc. Used by permission.

Frances Blaisdell gave what was probably the premier performance of Diaphonic Suite No. 1 for a League of Composers' concert on March 1, 1931, with Charles Seeger present. To Ruth, who was at that time in Europe, he wrote the following comments: "I was impressed with the excellence of the conception, the cleanness and the leanness of it, its nice balance and unbalance, but also with the difficulty of writing it so that the virtues might be apparent enough to the performer for him to do a good job."[27]

Shortly thereafter Ruth wrote to Seeger from Berlin concerning the progress of Suite No. 4 which was written there and which was scheduled for a performance by the Novembergruppe in that city:

> But the suite for viola and cello is going exceedingly well. The two players are willing and work hard. We had a probe [rehearsal] a few days ago in which we worked over an hour without stopping and I, among other things, was delighted with myself for actually, first of all, knowing a raft of things I wanted and secondly, being able to tell the players about it. We got on well.... The first piece is entirely rewritten, only the first nine notes remaining, though it still is in the form of a much-disguised canon. It is much better now. The second movement is frightfully romantic and I revel in it. I like the numerous sixths and thirds spread throughout, do you? The third I haven't heard yet.[28]

In an article devoted largely to Ruth's music, a Berlin correspondent of The Daily News offered sympathetic but discerning comment on the actual performance of this work by the Novembergruppe. He wrote, in part:

> Miss Crawford allows a viola and a cello to talk simultaneously, with the effect of hearing two telephone voices at once. At the end of the second movement the two speakers begin to coalesce. Her aim, so she stated, was to achieve new effects in atonal music and her success was apparent. Perhaps it is necessary for her to plunge ever more deeply into "visible music"--meant rather to be read than heard--before again realizing that the ultimate criterion must be the ear.[29]

The critic of the Morgen Post was not so kind. He dismissed the work with one sentence: "The work of a lady, 'Diaphonic Suite' for viola and cello, by Ruth Crawford, had such an anemic effect because completely inconsequential material was being performed."[30]

The Piano Study in Mixed Accents (1:05, P. R), which requires considerable keyboard agility and control for its effective performance, provides another striking example of the almost continuously dissonated melodic line (Seeger's term for a non-triadic melody). Further, the melody which starts from the lowest pitches on the keyboard and works gradually to the very highest, reverses its direction at midpoint and, in retrograde, returns to its beginning point. This etude, written in octaves throughout, also shows Ruth's increasing interest in rhythmic and dynamic organization which becomes more and more prominent in later works. The perpetual, unmetered sixteenth notes are barred together in groups ranging from two to eight, with an accent on the first note of each group. The score also suggests three possible dynamic patterns. The first five groups (Example 8) show most of its features.

Ex. 8: Piano Study in Mixed Accents, first five groups of sixteenths. © 1932 New Music Edition. Used by permission of the publisher, Theodore Presser Company.

Before Ruth left for Europe, Seeger helped her lay out plans for several compositions and to set up a tentative course of action. Rat Riddles, the first of the Three Songs (Sandburg), had already been written; the second, In Tall Grass, she wrote in Europe; the third, Prayers of Steel, was finished back in New York in the autumn of 1932. The first

Art Music

three of the four Diaphonic Suites were completed before she went abroad; the fourth she completed in Berlin (see p. 153 for further comments on these). One of the three chants for women's chorus was partially finished before she left; she wrote the second and third in Berlin. The third and fourth movements of the string quartet were started before her departure; the first and second were completed in Berlin and Paris.[31]

The Three Songs (9:20, P, R), set to poems of Carl Sandburg, are Ruth's finest vocal works. She wrote them for contralto, oboe, percussion and piano, labelled <u>concertante</u> in the score, and optional ostinati--for strings and for winds. These strong, if whimsical poems receive here extremely effective settings and are her most imaginative works. They enhance the poems in startlingly innovative ways, notably the use of layers of sound and her treatment of the voice in a speech-song, near-<u>Sprechstimme</u> manner. There are elaborate pitch patterns, often serialized and full of strongly dissonant intervals. Her treatment of the instruments, particularly the strings, is unusual. The string ostinato parts use many glissandi, which are frequently marked <u>alto possible</u> and tend to run off the high end of the fingerboard. <u>In Tall Grass</u> also provides a rare instance of the patterned use of vibrato. In all three songs, the instrumental parts are highly organized; the vocal lines, which are quite demanding from the standpoint of pitch discrimination and intonation as well as of their extensive range, are free and highly declamatory. Example 9 gives a brief excerpt from the string ostinato parts of <u>In Tall Grass</u>.

The Three Songs received their first performance as a group when they were sung in Amsterdam at the ISCM Festival, June 15, 1933. Frederick Jacobi, who conducted the performance, wrote Ruth the next day:

> Your songs went simply excellently last night and were one of the only things which seemed to interest and amuse an otherwise apathetic public at an otherwise pretty lousy concert! The first song evoked a most spontaneous applause (conspicuously lacking at this festival) and at the end there were again signs that your work had made its impression. I am so sorry you were not here; it would have given you happiness, I am sure, and I really doubt whether

Ex. 9: In Tall Grass, string ostinato, measures 70-73.
From: Three Songs, © 1933 New Music Edition. Used by permission of the publisher, Theodore Presser Company.

> you will hear your work more carefully and skilfully given.[32]

Nicolas Slonimsky had, the previous year, conducted a performance of Rat Riddles in Berlin, after which he reported to Ruth:

> Your delicious Ratriddles had such a success that we had to repeat them--sneezing and all. The Kammersängerin Frau Ottilie Metzger-Latterman sang them very well, in English....
> You know, of course, that our first concert was a very turbulent affair--the extra concert on the door keys lasted for about five minutes, and Imre

Weisshaus nearly killed some hissing Americans in the hall. I am still receiving various clippings from all over Germany encouragingly entitled: Skandal in Beethovensaal, Krach in Berlin, u.s.w. Frau Schmolke has sent out all criticisms without sparing anybody's feelings.[33]

Some reviews were not so warm in their praise of these songs, however, nor so perceptive regarding their fine, if intricate, workmanship and high artistic qualities. An unnamed reviewer for Musical America offered the following bit of biting criticism:

One of the most far fetched compositions which has ever been placed on our reviewing desk is Ruth Crawford's Three Songs (San Francisco: New Music Edition) consisting of settings of Carl Sandburg's Rat Riddles, Prayers of Steel and In Tall Grass....
Cast in the extreme Left idiom, this work is but another manifestation of the paucity of creative urge possessed by so many of our younger composers. Miss Crawford is probably sincere in her desire to add to the literature of modern music works which shall be as far as possible from well trodden paths. It is as fascinating to note the meticulous care with which she scores her music, leaving nothing to the imagination in the way of minutest detail in the matter of expression marks, etc., as it is deplorable to observe the blind alley in which she is working. There is no future for this kind of music. There is hardly a present.[34]

Ruth had already become acquainted with choral music which experimented with unconventional texts, and she was fascinated by the possibilities, so she decided to try her hand using such materials. She wrote for Gerald Reynolds, conductor of the Women's University Glee Club in New York, the three chants--both texts and music--which constitute her sole contribution to choral literature.

The first chorus (2:40, Ms., NR), originally called To an Unkind God, is scored for three parts, a cappella, labeled one, two, and three. The text consists solely of meaningless phonemes--all intervals are used both vertically and horizontally, and the resulting melodic lines exemplify the concept of dissonant counterpoint as well as the idea of a constantly dissonated melody.

To the second chant (2:30, P, NR), later published as Chant, 1930, Ruth first gave the title, To an Angel. Besides changing the title, she also changed the original setting for women's chorus to a four-part mixed chorus, a cappella, with soprano solo. It shares with the first chant the same type of text, as well as its essential nature as a study in intervals of all sizes and kinds, and its use of dissonated melodic lines. Chant, 1930 differs from To an Unkind God in that only the soprano solo sings syllables--all the other parts hum throughout. After its performance in 1931 by the Women's University Glee Club in Town Hall, a reviewer for the New York City Post commented: "There were also first performances of ... Ruth Crawford's wordless and vaguely alluring "To an Angel."[35] Reporting on the same concert, the Brooklyn Daily Eagle critic less kindly opined the chant was "a singularly sterile, meaningless bit of harmonic improvisation as stupid as it was brief."[36] Ruth's comments on this chorus are of some interest:

> The Reynolds chants have lost their titles and I think it's much better. It occurred to me the other day that I ought to write an extra chant to some special god to help the singers to sing them. Regarding the second chant, I vary between an objective viewing of it as bad, impressionistic, and worthless and a secret liking for its simplicity and slightly fascinated interest in the fact that the second part wanders about naively in its own tonality while, which was not planned, the effect is dissonant vertically. When these are done, I want to write a couple more short songs to accompany the "Rat Riddles."[37]

The third chant (3:25, NP, NR), which never had a title, is the longest and most complex of the set. Its twelve independent parts include a soprano solo and a contralto solo which combine at the climactic mid-point in the chorus. Texture provides probably the strongest formal element; the number of parts employed at any one time ranges from seven at the beginning, middle, and end, to twelve in the intervening periods. The dynamic pattern, also of interest, provides a good example of Ruth's fondness for the structuring of this element.

Art Music   161

To the same kind of meaningless phonemes found in the other two chants, Ruth has added the Hindu sacred word "om," which is repeated throughout, appearing in different voices at different times, while various other voices intone the syllables which Ruth made up for use in this composition. All this is made more intricate by the fact that voices seven through twelve sing an ostinato tone cluster on A, B-flat, C, D-flat, D, and E-flat, changing not quite halfway through to another tone cluster a whole step higher, and then back to the original pitch in the closing section. When Ruth sent the score for the third chant to Gerald Reynolds from Berlin, she accompanied it with a letter of explanation and suggestions for its performance, and also sent him helpful diagrams (see below and page 163). She told Reynolds that since the

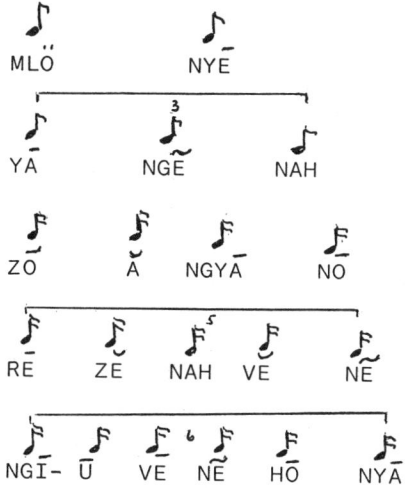

Rhythmic patterns for text syllables in Ruth Crawford's Chant Number 3

syllables which she concocted had no meaning, they would not need to be printed in the program.[38] Excerpts from

Ruth's letter to Gerald Reynolds from Berlin, November 10, 1930, follow:

1. The idea back of it is that of chanting done in far-eastern monasteries. I understand the Pranavi Or. . U. . M (the prolonged OM), "is pronounced by each voice chanting at the pitch most suited to that individual voice regardless of any harmonic relation to the pitches of other voices sounding at the same time." The effect I wish from these voices is that of a "complex veil of sound," half-intangible, out of which the chanting voice rises. I use the half steps to effect a kind of new composite mass-pitch.

2. The seemingly complex counter-rhythms have I think been made almost simple by the fact that each group of two eighths is always accompanied by the same "word," each group of three 8ths by the same word, and the groups of 4, 5, and 6 accordingly. Thus, the unit of beat being felt, the singer simply fits that word into it, the effect desired being that of a group of people chanting quite independently to a central idea or emotion.

If the finding of the pitches is too difficult (especially on page 24, where all rise) I suggest as an effect from the beginning, six violins entering a beat before on the six tones on which the piece begins, pp throughout, sustaining throughout; and, a beat before each new voice entry, the entry of that same tone on the violin (12 violins altogether) the tone being always quite cold and aloof. I believe this need not sound like a help--that it can be an interesting effect. Perhaps even the violins might be situated each one near or within the group of singers who pronounce its particular tone!

The breathing I have arranged purposely so that each voice breathes as independently of the other as possible, giving thus a continuous uninterrupted flow of resonance. There would be possible many small dynamic nuances, especially when the voices leave the long Or. . U. . M and wander into groups of 3, 4, 5, etc.

The enclosed diagram [see page 163] is an attempt to place the singers of adjacent half-steps as far from each other as possible.[39]

Art Music

	XII	VII	X	III	
<u>A</u>	IX	IV	II	V	
	XI	VIII	VI	I	

Better	XII	IV	X	II	
<u>B</u>	IX	V	VIII	I	
	XI	VI	III	VII	

Seating Chart for the Twelve Voices of Ruth Crawford's Chant No. 3

Ex. 10: Chant No. 3, measure 44. Courtesy of the Estate of Ruth Crawford Seeger. Used by permission.

Art Music   165

Measure 44 from Chant No. 3 (see Example 10 on page 164) illustrates Ruth's "new composite mass-pitch" which she used to give the effect of a "complex veil of sound," mentioned in her letter of explanation to Reynolds.

The musical and textual treatment in all three chants is experimental and advanced for the year 1930. Both Milhaud (Les Choephores, 1959) and Vaughan Williams (Flos Campi, 1923) provide earlier examples of unconventional choral techniques; however, since 1930 such treatment has become common in the works of many composers (Dallipiccola, Nono, and Penderecki, to name a few).

Ruth sent Charles Seeger the scores for two of the chants, both of which pleased him highly. He told her: "It looks as if you had found yourself. There is a consistency, I mean a coherence in both these pieces (as in Rat Riddles) that spells maturity. There are good plans in both of them and no aimless wandering."[40]

Ruth's best known and probably most important composition, String Quartet (9:47, P, R), has now become a classic in string quartet literature. Composed in 1931, it has enjoyed many live and several recorded performances since its first performance in 1933, sponsored by the Pan American Association at the New School for Social Research. These have allowed its unique qualities to become widely known. When New Music Quarterly Recordings recorded the Andante movement in 1934, H.K. (Harrison Kerr) wrote a sympathetic, if brief, review which appeared in Trend. He said: "The Crawford piece is to me the outstanding example of her creative work to date--as far, of course, as I am acquainted with her music. It is an homogeneous, expressive movement written with seeming fluency and with deep emotion."[41] Members of the Juilliard Student Club heard the recording soon thereafter where the music aroused various reactions, ranging from its being sentimental to mechanistic. In his report of the club meeting, George Grossman quoted Ruth as saying she was attempting "to develop the use of dynamics to the nth degree, to make music without the 'old-fashioned' aids of harmony, melody, and rhythm."[42]

Henry Cowell's New Music continued its interest in the quartet by singling it out for publication in the January 1941 issue, thus allowing for even wider acquaintance with this important work. Virgil Thomson, whose assessment of contemporary music was as astute as Cowell's, wrote the following after the New Music Quartet's performance of the <u>Andante</u>, March 6, 1949:

> A slow movement from a quartet by Ruth Crawford, composed in 1934 [<u>sic</u>] was striking for intensity and elevation. Consisting entirely of long notes closely juxtaposed in slowly changing chords of high dissonance content, the piece seemed scarcely to move at all. And yet it was to this listener and I am sure, many others thoroughly absorbing. It is in every way a distinguished, a noble piece of work. It is also a daring one and completely successful.[43]

The four movements of the work reveal varying stages of organization, from the seemingly random to the obviously almost rigid. The rhapsodic first movement shows a number of tempo and meter changes, extensive chromaticism and dissonance, irregular rhythmic groupings and syncopation. The almost constant use of large skips provides aural unity.

A strong rhythmic drive dominates the second movement in which the various instruments imitate each other with great verve and rush relentlessly to an abrupt end. Ruth's great admiration for Bartok can be detected in her use of rather acid dissonances and her contrapuntal style.

Almost from the beginning, the third movement has aroused considerable interest and comment largely because each of the four parts has its own elaborate and constantly changing pattern of dynamics. Charles Seeger has called this movement a study in "dynamic counterpoint."[44] Pitch is also treated in an unusual manner; all parts change pitch slowly and in a generally stepwise pattern. The quality of pitch movement might be described as the gradual shifting of blocks of sound. A note in the score states that the Andante can be performed separately by string orchestra which includes double bass. Measures 13-17 from this movement (Example 11) illustrate the "dynamic counterpoint" and the treatment of pitch.

The last movement provides a striking example of total organization of the musical materials. Pitch, rests, rhythm, dynamics, tempo, instrumentation, texture, and form are all

Art Music 167

Ex. 11: String Quartet, Third movement, measures 13-17.
© 1941 Merion Music Inc. Used by permission of the publisher, Theodore Presser Company.

worked out according to a prescribed design, and, as in the 1930 Piano Study in Mixed Accents, the second half of the movement is a retrograde version of the first.

The String Quartet has justifiably been accorded an important place in contemporary string chamber music literature not only because of its technical innovations, but also because of its intense emotional qualities.

The work Ruth did in Europe was in many ways a continuation of that of the previous winter, although her year there provided her with time to put her work with Seeger to actual writing test without his direct supervision and to compose at her leisure. It also gave her the opportunity to discover new ideas through her contacts with many of the outstanding composers of the day. She was already pretty well aware of what was being written in Europe and the whys and wherefores of the theories behind these works. Actual hearing of much new music filled her consciousness with new sounds and new effects, which doubtless helped enrich her tonal resources. Very little specifically European influence can be noted, however, in the works she completed in Berlin and Paris, and what there is, she had, for the most part, absorbed before she went abroad.

Ruth's return to New York, November 1931, was filled

with momentous happenings which allowed her little time for
composition. And too, she had to spend many weary hours
copying the scores she had finished in Europe while adjusting
to her new life situation in New York. She also wrote the
third of the Three Songs, Prayers of Steel.

After her marriage to Charles Seeger, October 3, 1932,
she composed two songs titled Sacco, Vanzetti (4:30, P, NR)
and Chinaman, Laundryman (3, P, NR) to poems by the
Chinese poet H. T. Tsiang. These songs reflect the Seegers'
involvement in the Composers' Collective, with its Leftist
orientation, and Ruth's real concern for social justice, re-
kindled by the memory of the famous trial (1921) of the two
unfortunate Italian workers. The Society for Contemporary
Music in Philadelphia scheduled their performance on March
27, 1933, which provoked generally unfavorable reactions in
the press. The Philadelphia Ledger commented typically:
"The two songs were fearful and wonderful creations unless
you are so constituted that for a thing to be 'different' is to
excuse all else."[45]

Although Sacco, Vanzetti and Chinaman, Laundryman
were written shortly after the completion of the Three Songs,
they are worlds apart aesthetically and artistically. In contrast to the poetic whimsicality of the Three Songs, these
two carry a definite social message. They represent the work
of Ruth Crawford Seeger at its most sophisticated, if also its
most self-conscious, level. The accompaniment for Sacco,
Vanzetti, with its clanging, dissonant chords, is highly, almost rigidly, patterned, whereas the voice part is characterized by endlessly changing rhythms and patterns. The song
contains interesting examples of indefinite pitches--the composer uses arrows only to indicate the highness or lowness of
the desired sound. Even though it is constructed with remarkable ingenuity, Sacco, Vanzetti fails to impress the
imagination and stir the emotions as much as Chinaman, Laundryman, although it is a powerful, intense song. Both songs
use the same general vocal range and compositional techniques
and the same highly patterned piano accompaniment and free
vocal line; however, Chinaman, Laundryman seems more successful musically. The piano simulates the tinkling sound often associated with Oriental music as well as its ambiguous
tonal and rhythmic qualities. Also, the ear accepts Chinaman,
Laundryman more quickly, perhaps because the dissonances
occur contrapuntally, rather than harmonically as they do in

Art Music

Ex. 12: Chinaman, Laundryman, measures 4-7. © 1973 Merion Music Inc. Used by permission of the publisher, Theodore Presser Company.

Sacco, Vanzetti. The declamatory vocal line with its indefinite pitches, as well as the exotic touches in the piano accompaniment, can be seen in measures 4-7 from Chinaman, Laundryman, (Example 12).

After writing these two songs, Ruth entered into a long period in her life filled with activities which made musical composition difficult--the birthing and raising of Michael, Peggy, and Barbara, and later, Penelope. Also, with the move to Washington, D.C., in 1935, where Charles Seeger worked in various government-sponsored music programs, Ruth's musical interests became diffused as she and Charles began in earnest to find out something about America and American music. Diffused, but not radically changed! Although she was to spend the next several years of her life concentrating on the use of folk materials, she kept her in-

terest in composing art music and planned to continue it when
time and circumstances permitted.

In the late thirties and early forties, Ruth began to experiment with the combining of her two interests, art music and folk music, an approach popular at the time with many American composers. These efforts will be discussed in the consideration of Ruth's folk music activities. Throughout the late thirties and early forties, she also continued to speak of her hopes and plans to return to what she called "my own music." In the late forties, she became almost totally involved with the production of her children's books of folk songs. Even then, however, in a letter to Varèse in May 1948, she explicitly stated her musical goals "when I write more music." These included melodic clarity, rhythmic independence, experiments with ways to fuse the use of dissonance with organic unity and, very interestingly, a feeling of tonal and rhythmic center. In 1948 she reaffirmed her desire to combine folk music elements, which by then had become an important part of her musical thinking, with her art music. At that time, she made certain statements which, in retrospect, would seem to indicate that perhaps her years of abstinence from art music composition served, among other things, as a period of ingestion of various ideas and approaches to her personal solution for the use of folk materials in any future art music compositions.[46]

Tragically, circumstances allowed Ruth time enough for only one more essay into the art music field. In 1952, the year before her death, she completed the composition of the Suite for Wind Quintet (11, P, R) in which she, however, abjured the use of folk materials and returned to her earlier more abstract, linear, dissonant style of the thirties. The suite also shows a definite effort to incorporate her 1948 goals into this score. Many favorite techniques of long standing are found--use of dissonant intervals, and ostinati (both of which, incidentally, are present in her folk song settings), interval inversion and alternation between a high degree of organization and a rather rhapsodic presentation.

In the first movement, rhythmic complexities are combined with an unusual approach to tone-color, and texture. Touches of the early Scriabin influence are found in the second movement, while the cool, brittle quality of the third suggests neoclassical chamber music. Both the first and third movements contain a strong feeling for tonality by assertion. In Example 13, note the subtle relationship between the pitches in the bassoon ostinato and those used in the flute and oboe.

Ex. 13: Suite for Wind Quintet, first movement, measures 10-12. © 1969 Continuo Music, Inc. Used by permission of the publisher, Alexander Broude, Inc.

The compositions of Ruth Crawford Seeger help to illuminate the musical thought of her lifetime in the United States. She not only knew and understood the past and the present, but she also anticipated the future as far as musical innovations and developments were concerned. The new held a natural attraction for her. Thus, the experimental atmosphere of the time inspired her to make an intensive and extensive acquaintance with what would make tomorrow tick. Some of her techniques, unusual for their time, have now many years later, become commonplace, such as serialization of all parameters of music and unconventional use of glissandi, both vocal and instrumental. She shared in the vanguard investigation of chord clusters, the systematic use of dissonance, the expressive use of silence, motivic and intervallic rather than thematic manipulation, variation of the serial principle, use of monophonic lines, juxtaposition of layers of sound, and unconventional treatment of the voice.

She did not attempt large-scale vocal and instrumental works--she wisely confined herself to resources over which she felt she had mastery. She had a distinctive chamber music style--that was her strength and she realized it. She avoided slavish following of the models provided by leading composers of the twentieth century. She was well acquainted with them all, but chose to work on paths she set for herself. She was a good composer and a highly original one--one who possessed and developed a very great talent, perhaps a touch of genius.

Chapter Nine

FOLK MUSIC ACTIVITIES

..."you asked for a kind of 'credo.' I found
that a little hard, for I am still not sure whether
the road I have been following the last dozen
years is a main road or a detour. I have begun
to feel, the past year or two, that it is the
latter--a detour, but a very important one to me,
during which I have descended from the stratosphere onto a solid well-travelled highway, folded
my wings and breathed good friendly dust as I
travelled along in and out of the thousands of
fine traditional folk-tunes which I have been
hearing and singing and transcribing from field-
recordings, for books and for pleasure." (Ruth
Crawford Seeger, letter to Edgard Varèse, May
29, 1948)

Ruth Crawford's involvement in folk music goes back almost as far as her serious interest in becoming a professional musician. When in the mid-twenties in Chicago and through the intermediary of Alfred Frankenstein, Carl Sandburg asked Ruth to prepare accompaniments for several songs which were to be included in his forthcoming publication of The American Songbag, a collection of folk songs, he was literally starting her off on a by-path which would one day become a main thoroughfare for her musical activities. At that time, her acquaintance with folk music was practically nil. (She had played the guitar in high school--she might have sung some folk songs then.) Sandburg, a writer, poet, and amateur musician, whose chief interest was in American culture, had for a number of years toured the country, giving lectures during which he gave poetry readings and sang folk songs. When his publishers requested that piano accompaniments be added to his songs, Sandburg asked a group of composers to supply these. He explained his procedure as follows:

> In the arranging of a song I would usually sing it for the composer--and bring out my notebook sketch, a rough affair rapidly penciled.... The composer and I usually collaborated on the main design or outline of the harmonization or accompaniment. From then on, the work was entirely that of the composer, except in a number of instances when I suggested a different mood, atmosphere or rhythm to meet the requirements of the song as I customarily heard it.[1]

It is evident from this explanation that the composers had to rely on their previous musical training and their own judgment as to the appropriateness of the accompaniments they provided. During Ruth's years of close friendship with the Sandburgs, roughly the second half of the twenties, when she was the children's piano teacher and a frequent guest in the Sandburg home, she often enjoyed hearing Sandburg sing folk songs and probably on occasion, she joined in their singing. Certainly she became deeply imbued with the spirit of folk song and soon came to have a real empathy with this kind of music and the world it represented. She set only four of the songs in the collection: Those Gambler's Blues, Lonesome Road, There Was an Old Soldier, and Ten Thousand Miles Away from Home. The romantic touches apparent in the full texture and the rich harmonies of her arrangements reflect her approach to folk song at that time. These traits are easily seen in Example 1, which gives the first six measures of Ten Thousand Miles Away from Home (0:30, P, NR).

Further acquaintance with the folk music world did not come Ruth's way until several years later when she and Charles Seeger, whom she married in the fall of 1932, became involved in the activities of the Composers Collective. Seeger, who initially felt that folk music was not suited to the purposes of the Collective, eventually became convinced of its rightness. During their years of working with this group, Ruth and Charles had also come in contact with other sources of folk music which doubtless helped influence their change in attitude. Tom Benton, American painter and folk-

Folk Music Activities

Ex. 1: Ten Thousand Miles Away from Home, measure 1-6, from The American Songbag by Carl Sandburg, copyright 1927 by Harcourt Brace Jovanovich, Inc., renewed 1955 by Carl Sandburg. Reprinted by permission of the publisher.

song fancier, who taught at the New School for Social Research during Seeger's years there, and George Pullen Jackson, folk music researcher, whose White Spirituals in the Southern Uplands they became acquainted with soon after its publication in 1933, were both highly influential in this regard. Acquaintance with John and Alan Lomaxes' book, American Ballads and Folk Songs, just prior to its publication in 1934, provided the starting point for a further and vital association which was to develop in the coming years.

With the removal of the family to Washington, D.C., in

late 1935, Ruth's serious personal involvement with the world of folk music began. As soon as they were settled, the Seegers availed themselves of the opportunity to become personally acquainted with the Lomaxes, then resident in that city. This acquaintance soon turned into a long and fruitful friendship as they continued their relationship through involvement with folk music. Seeger remarked that "the Lomax books just gave us a completely new idea of the art of music."[2] Years earlier, the Lomaxes, well-known and highly respected collectors of American folk music, had started their collections. They had traveled tens of thousands of miles to investigate the many authentic voices of the people's song which they then recorded on location. They also made extensive and invaluable contributions (over 3,000 disc recordings) to what is considered today one of the finest collections of folk music in the world, currently designated as the Archive of Folk Culture in the Library of Congress, Washington, D.C. At the time the Seegers made their acquaintance, John Lomax served as honorary curator of the Archive of American Folk Song (its title at that time) while Alan was assistant in charge of the archives.

The Lomaxes shared with Ruth and Charles the extensive and varied experiences they had gained from their numerous folk music collecting trips throughout the United States and thus added another dimension to the Seegers' continuing education in Americana. The Seegers were fascinated by the Lomax saga and quickly turned their musical talents and their acute intelligence to an intensive study of folk music styles. Ruth had a natural affinity for this kind of music; further, she possessed the necessary patience to work painstakingly at the tedious job of transcribing songs from the field recordings which the Lomaxes had deposited in the Folk Song Archive in the Library of Congress. Ruth's musical activities throughout much of the remainder of her short life were influenced by the interest in and enthusiasm for American folk song which she shared with the Lomaxes.

Ruth soon began making transcriptions and arrangements of folk songs from field recordings she found in the archives. One of her first projects using folk materials, 19 American Folk Tunes (1936-1938) (9:40, NP, NR) arranged for piano, elementary grades, combined her newfound interest with her life-long activity of teaching piano.[3] They are short, simple settings bearing such titles as The

Folk Music Activities

Gray Goose, The Boll Weevil, Sweet Betsy from Pike, and Cindy. These arrangements aimed to acquaint piano students with the folk music of their own country in a contemporary idiom whose bareness of style related both to "modern" music and to authentic folk music. Words to the songs are included, to be used at the teacher's discretion.[4] Ruth's setting of Cindy (Example 2) (0:45, NP, NR) is typical of these arrangements.

Ex. 2: Cindy, measures 1-4, from Nineteen American Folk Tunes. Copyright © 1985 Continuo Music Press, Inc. Used by permission.

In 1937 the Lomaxes asked Seeger if he would make the transcriptions for another collection of folk songs which they were preparing. These songs, chosen largely from the archives in the Library of Congress, were published in 1941 under the title, Our Singing Country. He replied that he was too busy; that Ruth could do a beautiful job and probably a better one than he could, so she was asked to take and she accepted this responsibility.[5] As Ruth worked with the Lomaxes on her transcriptions, they spent many days, even weeks, together talking out the problems--sometimes agreeing, sometimes disagreeing--that arose as the folk song experts and the musician worked together to provide the most authoritative, yet practical, transcriptions of each song selected for inclusion in the book. Their collaboration, which proved to be most felicitous and productive, was later described by Alan Lomax:

> It was a wonderful experience to work with her because she was tireless, she was a--she had a wonderful ear and she cared very, very, very much.

> And of course was, you know, the nicest woman that could possibly be imagined. You couldn't help loving her. She was like my older sister, or like my aunt, or like my, you know, my best friend, those years, and it was <u>Folk Song USA</u>, I mean, <u>Our Singing Country</u> that we worked on so long and hard together that was a testament about how good it can get if it's a folk song book.[6]

That John Lomax also greatly appreciated the meticulous care that Ruth took to make her transcriptions of their field recordings as authentic as possible is evident from his statement:

> ... Mrs. Seeger in some instances played a record hundreds of times in an effort to attain perfection in her translation of the tune.[7]

The years that had elapsed between the work Ruth did for Sandburg's <u>The American Songbag</u> and her reintroduction to folk music had seen major changes in the approach to its study. Interest and research in this field had enjoyed a great resurgence and flowering, with new emphasis on the importance of authentic performance styles as well as on the older historical-comparative approach. Improved techniques of recording in the field provided a new sound ideal for folk music scholars to try to transfer, as faithfully as they could, from the recording to the printed page. Both Ruth and Charles listened to the recordings and discussed the problems involved in using conventional notation which proved not to be well suited for use with folk music.

The transcriptions which Ruth made for <u>Our Singing Country</u> and subsequent publications embodied a great deal of study and research. As Charles Seeger explained it, the more a person tried "to make a notation be like the actual singing style the more impossible it becomes to read." This is so because it becomes necessary to have extra signs, extra little notes, and here and there frequent meter changes, so that it often takes a good bit of fluency to be able to read the notation.[8] Rather than utilize such an elaborate and possibly confusing notation, Ruth stated that she wished "to include as many characteristics of singing-style as is possible, yet to keep most of the notation simple enough to be sight-read by the average amateur."[9]

As she set out to accomplish these aims, she soon realized that, as a professional musician unfamiliar with the folk idiom, she needed not only to understand the context in which this music developed and its place in the lives of the people who sang it, but also to develop a transcription technique which would enable her to transfer the performance style heard on the recordings to the printed page as faithfully as possible. Details of this technique are set forth in the music preface she prepared for the Lomax book. In her usual thorough-going manner, she studied each detail exhaustively and eventually came up with a sixty-page treatise which proved to be far too long to be feasible or practical for its intended use. This long essay, never published, together with the published version, whittled down to seven and a half pages, as well as her introductory remarks contained in her further such writings, set forth the guidelines she used in arriving at her transcriptions.

As Ruth listened to these recordings she found that most characteristic was the use of the natural, untrained singing voice which came to have for her its own kind of beauty. Generally speaking, one mood prevailed throughout a song, sustained through the use of one dynamic level and one tempo; crescendo and diminuendo, accelerando and ritardando were seldom used; the music was not dramatic and did not build to a climax--it just stopped. She found that prolongation and contraction of a measure, of a tone, or of a rest, caused by intake of breath and/or changes in the number of text syllables in different stanzas brought about a kind of rubato effect. Non-tempered intonation of pitches and the blurring of the distinction between major and minor in the intonation of intervals were typically heard in the performances, as were sliding tones. Harmonically, Ruth encountered the use of bare fourths and fifths, even in parallel motion, and the frequent substitution of chord successions for chord progressions. Obviously, this oral tradition embodied many elements congenial to her musical tastes.

How best to transfer to the printed page the actual sounds heard became a major problem for the transcriber. In trying to overcome the limitations imposed by conventional nineteenth-century western notation, Ruth used several devices she and others had employed in their contemporary art music scores to indicate such things as sliding tones and indefinite pitches. Her ingenious stretching of the usual signs helped her indicate unconventional duration of tones and rests rather adequately. Free use of changing time signatures--or their omission altogether--proved useful in notating the rather frequent metrical irregularities. Majority usage, or the tune-pattern used for most of the stanzas of a song, provided the criterion Ruth followed in notating a melody where successive stanzas of a song were rendered in variant ways.[10]

Ruth's transcriptions for <u>Our Singing Country</u> embody her stated aims--practicality for general usage and preservation of authentic folk flavor and performance style. Although they must suffice, the few remarks that follow can give only a faint idea of the extent and variety of musical treasures which this collection holds. <u>The Coal Miner's Child</u> shows Ruth's modification of fermata signs to help portray its somewhat rambling nature as well as her notation of the rhythmic freedom and the sliding tones often found in these songs. Although most of the tunes are uncomplicated, there are occasional examples of quite elaborate and rhythmically involved melodies, such as <u>Pauline</u>. Ruth's transcription also notates the rhythmic sound of the convict's axe.[11]

By October 1938, Ruth was apparently working on a quartet, as she wrote to Charles Seeger, who was in Jackson, Mississippi, at the time:

> Yet the quartet is progressing. That is some consolation. Whether it is "good" or not I am getting some practice.... I find it very difficult to combine my two desires: to make use of the old technique but to make use also of folk material. Just introducing dissonance into the actual folk material seems superficial. Using it as it is is out of the question. (Why not just play a record?) If you were here, I could show you what I have done. You'd be sure to give me good ideas. I am thinking over your suggestion for two slow and two fast movements. The one I am working on most now is a fast fiddle tune one combined with dissonant runs. I chose "The Flop-eared Mule" feeling that its eighth note problems would less interfere with the runs which are built according to my old ostinato favorite, with a cumulative rhythmic hitch.[12]

Folk Music Activities

Since there is no trace of a score for a second quartet, it might not be too hazardous to suggest that the projected quartet was finally metamorphosed in 1939 or 1940 into a work for small orchestra, and that that work was <u>Rissolty, Rissolty</u>[13] (3:45, Ms., NR). This one-movement work also apparently represents the culmination of Ruth's hopes of many years to write another work for orchestra. She first mentioned that intent when applying for a Guggenheim Foundation fellowship, and she expected to write the work the year she spent in Europe. She made several more references to her hopes to compose such a work, but other plans and responsibilities had intervened to prevent her from carrying out the project until she received a commission from CBS for an orchestral work. During the years 1939-41, CBS conducted its School of the Air which sponsored coast-to-coast radio broadcasts for school children with emphasis on American folk music. Each of these broadcasts, which were conducted by Alan Lomax, featured an American folk song on which an American composer had been commissioned to write a symphonic composition. Ruth was among those commissioned and the resulting work, <u>Rissolty, Rossolty</u>, was played by the Columbia Symphony Orchestra on one of the School of the Air programs,[14] probably in January 1941. The work utilizes three American folk tunes transcribed from recordings in the Library of Congress. Charles Seeger has supplied the following information concerning the origins of these materials:

> <u>Rissolty, Rossolty</u> is the name of a courting song in which the boy makes fun of the girl; <u>Phoebe</u> is an old English teasing song in which the wife outdoes the husband, and the <u>Last of Callahan</u> is the English ballad of the fiddler about to be hung who is asked as he stands on the gallows whether he has a last wish.[15]

The score calls for flute, oboe, two B-flat clarinets, bassoon, two horns in F, trumpet, trombone, tympani, and a full complement of strings. The use of key signatures, missing from most of her work, comes as no surprise, given the fact that the musical materials are folk songs. Ruth's treatment of these folk songs shows incorporation of several typical folk-like touches--the ongoing pulse and pace of the music, the avoidance of ritardandos and other marks of expression (except for discreet dynamic markings), and its feeling of continuing on indefinitely with avoidance of tonal

Ex. 3: Rissolty, Rossolty, measures 156-158. Courtesy of the Estate of Ruth Crawford Seeger. Used by permission.

Folk Music Activities

finality at the end of the composition where the piece breaks off in mid-air soon after its return to the opening strain. Broken chord figures, used throughout, suggest affinity with guitars and banjos, commonly used as accompaniments for folk singing. The simplicity of the harmonizations and the straightforward statement of the musical materials are also in keeping with the style and spirit of folk song.

In <u>Rissolty, Rossolty</u> Ruth built an orchestral work of considerable ingenuity and of a somewhat complicated texture that is hidden, however, beneath an immediate charm and appeal. Example 3 (see page 182), found in measures 156-158, shows the simple harmonic fabric and the strong pulse as the horns and bassoons play one version of <u>Rissolty, Rossolty</u> while the trumpets play a second version of the same song.

As a result of their parents' involvement with traditional music, the Seeger children grew up living with it; it held an important place in many of their daily activities--it was part of their life and they developed a genuine love for it, as well as an invaluable instinctual feeling for its authentic performance. Encouraged by the children's natural attraction for this music and daughter Barbara's lively interest in attending nursery school, Ruth began in 1941 to gain practical classroom experience in using the folk music repertoire she was accumulating, as she worked with the music program in several nursery schools in the Washington, D.C., area. These materials also provided the basis for the books of folk songs for children which she compiled and edited during the next several years: <u>American Folk Songs for Children</u> (1948), <u>Animal Folk Songs for Children</u> (1950), and <u>American Folk Songs for Christmas</u> (1953)--all of which were enthusiastically reviewed by the press. They quickly won the spontaneous approval of educators and parents throughout the country for the freshness and appropriateness of their materials and the scholarly, but engaging manner in which the author presented them, as well as for the valuable introductory chapters in each book.

In the acknowledgments accompanying the first of these three books, Ruth described the genesis of the ideas for such a collection, tracing her interest in folk music from the days of her friendship with the Sandburg family in Chicago in the twenties through her experiences at the Silver Spring Cooperative Nursery School, where the book began to grow. The book also contains a preliminary chapter which explains in considerable detail the musical and educational and social concepts which guided its making. These few pages do much to describe the kind of musical involvements Ruth and her entire family were engaged in during the last ten years of her life. Appropriately, Carl Sandburg supplied a few words of commendation which appear in the initial pages of the book.

The introduction to the second book, Animal Folk Songs for Children, shows Ruth's writing style at its best with succinct, but colorful descriptions of the way these folk songs were gathered and selected and with helpful suggestions as to the most authentic performance practices. The introduction to Christmas Folk Songs for Children gives an account of the traditions associated with the singing of each of the songs presented. It is of some interest to note the name of Djane Lavoie Herz on the list prepared by Ruth to receive a complementary copy of this book. She had obviously maintained some kind of contact with her former teacher and idol.

These three delightful books for children combine Ruth's accumulated knowledge of folk song styles with understanding of their educational and cultural values and her skill in addressing the needs and desires of small children. Her setting of John Henry from American Folk Songs for Children, (Example 4) effectively incorporates the steady ring of the hammer in the open fourths and fifths of the left hand and the catchy rhythms of the tune in a manner well suited for amateur performers. Further, it is musically satisfying, stylistically acceptable, and wedded to a vocal line easily sung by children.

Several further ventures into the field of children's folk songs should be mentioned. Ruth provided the transcriptions for Folklore Infantil de Santo Domingo, edited by Edna Garrido de Boggs, published in the Ediciones Cultura Hispanica, Madrid, 1955. At the time of her death, she had also collected and partially assembled several small books of songs, including the titles, Everybody Has a Song, and Mary Wore Her Red Dress. One such small book, Let's Build a Railroad, was published in 1954, the year after her death.

In 1947 when the Lomaxes published their collection of 111 best-loved American Ballads, Folk Song U.S.A., both Ruth and Charles made the musical arrangements. In the musical foreword to this volume, the Seegers, who were in

Folk Music Activities

Ex. 4: John Henry, from American Folk Songs for Children, by Ruth Crawford Seeger, measures 1-5. Courtesy of the Estate of Ruth Crawford Seeger. Used by permission. Text copyright 1948 by Ruth Crawford Seeger. Reprinted by permission of Doubleday & Co., Inc.

general agreement on the basic concepts of folk song transcription and arranging, set those down succinctly and clearly. They discussed such things as the distinction between arrangements and accompaniments, unaccompanied versus accompanied singing, use of various instruments, alternate ways of performance, the need for harmonic simplicity, problems in using the same tune for all verses of the text, problems of "irregular" rhythms and non-tempered pitches, and the cautious use of phrasing, tempo, and dynamics.[16]

 Ruth's setting of Go Down, Moses embodies the kind of model accompaniment which she (and Charles) provided for these songs.[17] There are no unnecessary frills, and it is easy for amateurs to play. At the same time, there is also a good deal of artistry involved in its setting. Its simplicity, leanness of texture, economy of means, and the amazing pedal point on D--easily linked with Ruth's long-standing affinity for the device of ostinato--are all quite effective and show her work in this field at its best. These traits are also apparent in the art compositions that she wrote after her studies with Seeger, which stressed the lean line and economic use of musical materials.

Ruth was also involved in many other projects working with folk music materials, some of which never reached completion, such as the one started back in the late thirties when she and Charles "made up a book dummy which would have combined Farm Security Administration photos with traditional folk songs with the title, We Come by It Natural."[18] Ruth also acted as consultant on American folk music for several publishing houses and government agencies during the early forties. In the late forties and early fifties, Ruth (and Charles) worked with Duncan Emrich, then head of the folk song division of the Library of Congress, in the preparation of a book, 1001 Folk Songs (never completed).[19] There remain thirteen volumes of work notebooks in manuscript in the Seeger Collection (Music Division, Library of Congress). She also planned and chose music for a series of radio broadcasts, Music in American Life, sponsored by the State Department.[20] The forties also saw Ruth's music transcriptions for George Korson's Coal Dust on the Fiddle (1943) and his Anthology of Pennsylvania Folklore (1948-1949). She also acted as music consultant for Ben A. Botkin's Treasury of Western Folklore (1951), which contains her last published transcriptions. Botkin, who was active in the field of folklore for many years, probably became acquainted with the Seeger family during the early forties when he was involved in various folklore projects at the Library of Congress.

Ruth's transcriptions for this book reflect her many years of experience in working with folk materials with their relaxed tone, their simplicity, their emphasis on essentials, all done with naturalness and grace. Her transcription of Shenandoah (Example 5) mirrors the beauty of this old favorite, with its rhythmic and melodic finesse.

Why did Ruth become so deeply involved in folk music to the almost virtual exclusion of her art music composition? Why did it hold such a strong attraction for her? She (and Charles) were soon aware of and delighted with the similarities they found between art and folk music which, at first glance, seem so disparate. They both became professionally involved in working with socially oriented and socially useful music when they moved to Washington, D.C. And although economic factors were at least partially responsible for their initial involvement, musical values sustained Ruth's interest in this vital, straightforward art of the people. Too,

Folk Music Activities

Ex. 5: <u>Shenandoah</u>, from <u>Treasury of Western Folklore</u>, by Ben A. Botkin. Reprinted from <u>A Treasury of Western Folklore</u> by Ben A. Botkin, copyright © 1975 by B. A. Botkin. Used by permission of Bonanza Books, distributed by Crown Publishers, Inc.

it provided a strong link between her and her growing family, who were literally raised on this kind of music.

Ruth was comfortable with the simplicity and lack of formality of the folk idiom. Her natural love for melody, so strongly expressed through her work with folk music, does not show through in her art music where most of her melodic lines can best be described as non-lyric and sometimes manipulated to fit in with the concepts she pursued in writing dissonant counterpoint. Folk music released Ruth from the need she felt to write dissonance for its own sake and made legitimate her indulgence in a more tuneful and consonant approach to melody. Here, too, she could use melody without having to invent it herself. The simplicity of the style tested her ability to be creative in new ways and provided her with a new challenge. In this connection Peggy's comments are of interest:

> I think that like any creative person in the arts, she had two sides; she had one which was the more emotional side and one in which she just liked to sit

down and use her brain. And I think the folk song was the more emotive side although I'm not saying she didn't use her brain when she made those extraordinary accompaniments; of course she did.[21]

Ruth Crawford Seeger was one of a handful of people who were influential in establishing the notation of folk music on a sound basis with her stylistically authentic and artistic transcriptions and arrangements. The list of her accomplishments in this field indicates her wide acceptance by her confreres. Her time-consuming involvements with folk materials continue to draw the plaudits and elicit the thanks of the innumerable people who have profited from them as emphatically as her extraordinary accomplishments in art music continue to draw praise from the critics and enrich the repertoire of twentieth-century American music.

Chapter Ten

SELECTED WRITINGS

"And then too, after I have written more music, perhaps in a month or two from now, I shall retire into a tonal void and persist stubbornly in my feeling that I have something to say in words that would sell." (Ruth Crawford, letter to Charles Seeger, Berlin, November 12, 1930)

Ruth Crawford's ambition to become a writer preceded her aspirations in the field of music and although she is known as a composer of considerable merit and a folk music scholar of importance, she was also a writer of some skill. Changes in her personality, her values, her attitudes correspond to changes in the way she handled words--from the sensitive young girl with strong romantic inclinations and a love for flowery, involuted sentences to the mature woman who had learned economy and directness of expression.

Ruth's diaries, letters, articles, poems, and stories, interviews and lectures (preserved in printed form), written from her young girlhood throughout her life, have been, for the most part, collected and deposited in the Music Division of the Library of Congress (Wc) in the Seeger Collection. Quotations from these materials have been used extensively throughout the book. In general, quotations which appear in the previous chapters of the text do not appear in this chapter; however, exception has been made in the case of one patently important document, the Letter to Edgard Varèse, where it was felt that inclusion of the complete text would be of interest and importance for the reader. All selections reprinted in this chapter are found in the Seeger

Collection except for the Letter to Henry Allen Moe, which is from the Guggenheim Foundation.

Ruth's writings reflect her personal and family concerns as well as her musical and professional interests. They show, likewise, her vivid imagination, her subtle sense of humor, and her poetic concepts. It is particularly refreshing to read Ruth's personal reactions to many events which later came to assume importance in a wider musical sphere. The following brief commentary aims to present an ongoing record of her writing activities. Titles selected for inclusion in this chapter are underlined in the ensuing remarks.

Diaries and poems comprise the bulk of Ruth's writings through high school and until she left Florida for Chicago in the fall of 1921. Although portions of diaries from as early as age thirteen are extant, her high-school diary, kept from July 3, 1917 (her birthday) through March 4, 1918, contains the most extensive entries. It provides a good picture of Ruth's daily activities in addition to its journal-like entries, often with philosophical overtones. Several entries also dwell on self-analyses of her perceived faults and weaknesses. Many of Ruth's poems appeared in The Oracle (Duvall High School, Jacksonville, Florida) on which she worked throughout her four years of high school. "A Love Lyric" offers a charming example of her poetry.

Ruth's most important writings during her Chicago years (1921-1929) are contained in her letters to her mother (fall 1921 to fall 1923, when Mrs. Crawford joined her daughter in the midwest metropolis) and the diaries she kept from 1927 until July 1929, when she left for New York via the MacDowell Colony. During these years, the writing of poetry and short stories continued to provide outlets for further creative literary interests. Her poem "Creator," not without merit, is included here.

Ruth continued to confide her inmost thoughts as well as to record many of her daily activities in her diary when she went to Peterboro, New Hampshire, as a scholarship recipient at the MacDowell Colony. Her account of her life there is interspersed with a record of the deep depression she sometimes experienced as she faced the uncertainties of her life. Diary entries ruminate on her first serious love affair, her decision nonetheless to pursue her career in New

York in the fall, and the beginning of her long friendship with Marion Bauer.

Once Ruth was settled in Mrs. Walton's apartment in New York in the fall of 1929, she began to spill out her enthusiasm for the good new life she enjoyed in letters to her old friend, Alice, who still lived in Chicago. These letters to Alice contain an intimate account of a young woman's first impressions of musical life in New York City. They reveal Ruth's uncanny ability to give a detailed (and fascinating) account of her rich experiences during the year she spent as a guest of Blanche Walton, as well as to narrate entertaining anecdotes. No less revealing and captivating are Ruth's diary-like New York Jottings, recorded during the winter and spring months of that year. Her observations on the musical scene and her impressions of the people she met show her awareness and her sensitivity to her surroundings.[1]

Personal letters to Charles Seeger and a few business letters make up the large part of Ruth Crawford's writing activities during her year in Europe (1930-1931). Much information about her compositional efforts, her attempts to meet important composers and publishers, and the European musical avant-garde is interspersed in her letters to Charles Seeger with her lifelong habit of analyzing her strengths and weaknesses, both personal and musical. The Letter to Henry Allen Moe is in the nature of a progress report to the Guggenheim Foundation which provided the scholarship which supported her year of study abroad.

After Ruth's return to New York in the late fall of 1931 and her subsequent marriage to Charles Seeger, there was little occasion for her to put her thoughts to paper. However, one letter to her old friend, Nicolas Slonimsky, contains much valuable biographical information. Slonimsky, well-known Russian-American musicologist and lexicographer, and a long-time advocate of modern music, had conducted a performance of Ruth's music in Berlin in 1932.

With the Seegers' move to Washington, D.C., in 1935, Ruth's time and energy were consumed by a growing family and absorption in the world of folk music. Nonetheless, she often took occasion to express herself in words.

Interviews and lectures prove to be important sources of information regarding Ruth's thoughts on her varied interests and careers. The question-and-answer period following a performance of Ruth's compositions for the Composers' Forum-Laboratory in New York City in 1938 contains valuable statements by Ruth concerning her views on her own art music. Ruth still wrote an occasional story; sometimes these literary efforts took the form of feature articles. Ruth was never a militant feminist--she liked men and responded to them. However, she occasionally felt resentment at men's imposition of their standards of behavior on the women of the world. This attitude finds delightful expression in her short piece, "Why Don't They Eat Cake?" Ruth's last known diary was kept during the summer of 1941, in which she recorded her plans to take part in a cooperative nursery school project. During the decade of the forties, Ruth's most extensive literary efforts (and some of her best) were expended on the rather elaborate introductory materials she wrote for the various books of folk music which she compiled or for which she acted as music editor. A detailed listing of these materials is found in the Catalog of Works, p. 361.

Sandwiched in between her varied folk music activities and her heavy teaching schedule, Ruth also found time to carry on not only an extensive, largely professionally-related correspondence but also to write occasional highly humorous letters, such as the long Letter to Miss Prink, her editor for the Lomaxes' Our Singing Country. The letter provides intimate glimpses into the endless day-to-day house, home, and child-related chores which make up the life of a housewife, as well as the happy, if often hectic, activities enjoyed by the Seeger family. As is true of others of Ruth's letters, this one is really a literary piece, not meant to be and probably never mailed, to the addressee.

The Letter to John Becker, American composer of avant-garde persuasion, is of interest for recording the favorable reactions of musicologists to American folk music. Becker and the Seegers shared a common interest in Henry Cowell's New Music magazine as well as an involvement in government-sponsored music programs. The Letter to Edgard Varèse, a long-time friend, contains probably her most important statement regarding her ambivalence toward her two worlds of music, as well as a good résumé of her folk music activities. Ruth's continuing loyalty and gratitude to Carl

Sandburg are expressed in her note of thanks to him for his brief, but insightful inscription for her first book, American Folk Songs for Children.

Ruth left the typescript for a demonstration-lecture she presented, presumably for a group of music educators in Washington, D.C., shortly before death. The paper bears no indication of either place or date. Titled Pre-School Children and American Folk Songs, it gives a lively picture of Ruth's use of folk music with children and sums up her ideas on the educational and cultural values of this music, presented in a real-life learning situation.

Throughout her life, Ruth's creative spirit manifested itself through her written use of words as well as through her utilization of the language of music. Her ability and willingness to express herself artistically and intelligently in both fields, make it possible to trace, in some detail, the development of this woman of many talents.

* * *

A LOVE LYRIC

Thy sparkling eyes are like the stars
    In the night;
Resplendent is thy ebon hair,
    Glossy bright;
Thy countenance is sweet to see,
    Trustful, shy;
Thy every movement graceful, free:
    I love thee--
Thou are so winning,
    My sweetheart,
        My pretty--
            Kitty!

                  --R.P.C., December 1917,
                  Oracle

* * *

CREATOR

You are the lover of the creations of God,
    The buds and green things;
You will water them and love them into growing ...

    But I,
I shall myself be a god,
I shall create trees of sound and color
Whose branches reach up
    In masses of power...
Out of the great love of my heart shall be born
Flowers for others to caress
And warm into greater beauty
    Than perhaps I dreamt of...

    For you are the sun,
But I am the creator of suns.

                           --1925, Chicago

* * *

NEW YORK JOTTINGS--1930
(Excerpts)

February 14

After the Pro Arte rehearsal for the International a number of us are invited with them to the Lafayette Hotel as guests of Alma Wertheim. Hilarity and fun. The Pro Artes are real people, vigorous, wholesome, jolly, alert, interested. The cellist I enjoy very much.

February 17

The last rehearsal this morning of the International Society for Contemporary Music. At the Turnverein. Yesterday Ives, Wagenaar, Rudhyar and Riegger. The latter for ten strings, interesting experiment in sonority for high instruments.... Wagenaar is frank and boisterous, reminding one a little of the Holst humor. Middle movement French impressionism, Boulanger sighing thro the stringed sweetness. Wagenaar himself is a nice open likeable person. Strange that his mouth and that of Carl Buchman's, his pupil, are uncannily alike.... Ives is possibly much greater than I realize. But the middle movement, sounding like a band concert and a prayer meeting hymn-fest, prejudices me violently. Jeanne de Mare puckers her mouth at me, and I grin back disgustedly.

This morning, Rudhyar again, in a larger hall. I like the work. One feels tremendous sincerity. Also Scriabin, but the work is ten years old. I should like to hear it done with full orchestra, for many parts this morning were missing. Also this morning, Whithorne Saturday Child, Josten Jungle, Weiss' American Life.

I observe Smallens' conducting and realize the composer should simplify meter as much as possible. Salzedo suggests 7-8 should be written three-four and a half. My experience in conducting Henry corroborates this.

Also this morning I find interesting faces among the Russians. The violinist who looks like an old aristocrat. His bearing is dignified, autocratic, cultured.... The double bass player is the beggar for Picasso's famous bony pair. From the crown of his head to his chin, a right angle, via the forehead; via the neck a very long side of a triangle.... The little violist has all the tragedies of a race furrowed in heavy downcast wrinkles. Utter gloom, a low forehead and a great nose.... The shortest man in the orchestra plays the double bass, and stands next our tall thin gaunt Picasso beggar.... The clarinetist is dapper and four feet five, wears a Carl Ruggles blue suit, has blue eyes and a grin which is a cross between cherubic and idiotic. He is Alice in Wonderland's cheshire cat. He doesn't know it. He thinks he is New York's beau brummel.... Smallens has been troubling me. Because he looks like someone, and I can't tell who. (Alexander Smallens, assistant to Stokowsky). Gruenberg calls him Alix. He looks pure Italian. And is Russian Jew. Not tall, very dark, a black moustache, and a habit of walking head down with eyes piercing straight ahead. You can appear more stern and important if you have contrary motion between the down-tilt of your head and the up-grade of your eyes. Or you can look like a small boy post-mischievous.

Now I know who Smallens looks like. Charlie Chaplin

in make-up. Even to the loose-jointed jerky walk. Smallens could throw sparks of anger if he wants. I shall wait till I know him better before I tell him he looks like Charlie Chaplin....

Yesterday afternoon, to the Stratford House for a talk with Mrs. MacDowell. She is well and cheerful, and we talk an hour. She sweetly and impersonally tries to keep her young modernists from becoming irrationally radical ... quotes a composer who prefaced a statement with, "of course I know Beethoven and I aren't great composers." Also remembers how MacDowell wired Carreño to take that damn piece off her program. She suggests June and July for me at the colony, then an entire rest from music, and possibly September at the colony again. Lovely of her to suggest three months. Also she asks if I would again like a fellowship. My enthusiastic reply ends with the laughing statement that I don't even know how I'll get up to the colony, and that a fellowship will be the most gratefully acceptable thing in the world. To this she surprised me by saying she will be on the look-out for motorists who could transport me there!

I am Marion's child. Gnome, gypsy, monkey, she calls me. I am not young enough to be her child, in years, and yet--I am. But strange ... I wonder if she knows that often I feel very much as tho she were my child, and feel that I really am the older one?

February 22

The musicologists meet. It is decided that I may sit in the next room and hear Yasser about his new supra scale. Then when I come out for this purpose, I find someone has closed the doors. Blanche is irate, so am I. Men are selfish, says Blanche. You just have to accept the fact. Perhaps, I wonder, their selfishness is one reason why they accomplish more than women. Blanche is unhappy about it. They should have remembered you, she says. Charlie should have remembered you. They are selfish. They think only of themselves. I walk past the closed door to my room, and when I pass I turn my head toward the closed door and quietly but forcibly say, "Damn you," then go on in my room and read Yasser's article. Later, my chair close to the door, I hear some of the discussion. And afterward when every one has gone, I tell Charlie and Henry what I said to them thro the closed door....

February 22 [cont.]

Blanche calls Charlie a tragic figure. She tells me sadly that she has come to believe him to be the most utterly hopelessly selfish man she has ever met. Her sister-in-law is very selfish. But she knows it. She is selfish on purpose. Consciously. Whereas Charlie is so immersed in selfishness, that he is not conscious of it. To cover his extreme self-consciousness as a boy, his hyper-sensitiveness, his intense emotional nature, he built a wall of ice, of stone, to save himself. He was once so self-conscious that entering a streetcar was agony. There I can sympathize with him. I have been there too. Charlie deliberately killed in himself the milk of human kindness. According to Blanche. To save himself from suffering.

There are intense beauties in Charlie. There are exquisite finenesses of feeling. Can you feel that you are fond of him, Ruth? Yes, I can, Blanche.

Anyone who can be as excited as Charlie was last week over--a counterpoint lesson. Anyone who can be so emotionally upset that he can't eat and his hands are trembling and his whole evening is a flare of sparks--all because of a so-called abstract thing as a bit of new music ... they call him cold?

Is one of my worst faults avoiding large issues for small? Do I not get lost in detail?

February 27

We have a party for Henry on February 8. He talks on Russia. Mostly jokes. Adolf Weiss and his quiet German frau sit on the couch all evening. They both look tired. Radiana is radiant. She takes me aside and her news is more joyous than the bulging roses on her flowered dress. Engagements are falling into her lap abundant. Charlie is not circulating tonight with sandwiches and punch--his usual antidote for boredom at a reception. Tonight he has a better antidote. He and Yasser are off on musicology. His eyes are bright. Later he talks to Copland. Copland is elusive. But I happen in on a conversation between Henry, Copland and Achron. On Strawinsky. Copland upholds <u>Oedipus Rex</u> against Henry and Achron. As a result of the conversation, I am deluging my soul with all the Strawinsky I can get from the library. Because I realize I am swallowing opinions second hand. Berating neo-classicism when I know few examples of it. Strawinsky's Sonata, 1924, gives a sad example. Tho there are parts which I like. This gives me the impression which many amateurs express when they characterize modern music as music with wrong notes. Here Strawinsky has achieved a combination of Bach and Chopin, with each hand full of mistakes. It seems needlessly ugly.

<u>May 3</u>

Fear, I fear. I am afraid to tell others often my opinion. Not because I am afraid of hurting <u>them</u>, but because I am afraid of hurting their opinion of me. I am afraid to hold an opinion opposite to that of someone I respect. I am afraid, afraid. And always it comes back to self-centeredness. Fear always does?

I make a vow. I make a vow that I will not talk of myself for a week. Could I keep a vow not to say "I" or "me?" Shall I try?

* * *

LETTER TO HENRY ALLEN MOE

> Dresdner Bank
> Berlin W. 56
> Germany
> January 22, 1931

Henry Allen Moe
John Simon Guggenheim Memorial Foundation
551 Fifth Avenue
New York

Dear Mr. Moe:

As you see from the heading, I am still in Berlin, and

since writing to you last Fall have worked very hard, becoming quite a hermit. I am learning also how to make my previous German marks stretch far, and yet to live healthily--and am now getting ready for my third move to a still more reasonable room. It is surprising to find that, in spite of the general opinion that living in Berlin is high, one can have all one needs for comparatively little, if one looks long enough for it.

In September I attended the International Festival of Contemporary Music at Liege, which was in most ways disappointing and had mainly the negative value of indicating trends not sympathetic to me. Of far greater interest and help have been the concerts in Berlin, performances of works recently written or of works which have not yet been given in America, through the hearing of which I can experience personally trends of which I have previously only read or heard.

The first six weeks after my arrival in Berlin (the last of September) were occupied with the composing of choruses which Gerald Reynolds, director of the Women's University Glee Club of New York, had asked me to write, and which he needed at once for rehearsal. Then followed the finishing of a suite for two celli begun in New York, a piano study, and the writing of yet another suite as a further preliminary contrapuntal exercise for the orchestral work of which I spoke to you last Spring. Early in December a demand from the New Music Society of San Francisco made necessary a large amount of copying of parts and the composing of a new movement for contralto, piano, oboe, and percussion, which was finished and sent the last of December. The first weeks in January I took a pause from composing and began to make use of letters of introduction to various musicians and composers here, which I had not done before because I was so engrossed in composition. Now at last I begin work on the sketches for large orchestra--I have become more and more eager to get to them. At last I feel somewhat acclimated (I knew practically no German when I came). I feel I am just getting into my stride, and can begin to accomplish as I have never accomplished before. It is true that in Europe one can work! I think true particularly of Berlin. I have never worked so steadily nor accomplished relatively so much as I have these last months.

Yet I am seeing more and more, how little time a year contains, and how things which I had felt could be accomplished by this time are now only just launched. The orchestral work on which I am now beginning work will, I find, require a broad stretch of time for completion, and aside from that I have several ideas for a large work for mixed chorus which I am eager to carry out. Besides a string quartet and numerous small contrapuntal suites. You do know, I am sure, what a renewal of my fellowship would mean toward the fulfilling of these plans. Especially in a new country, surrounded by new customs and a new language, a first year seems like a beginning, a preparation, no matter how hard one works or how much one seems to accomplish. I have never, since I began to compose, had such a year as this for quiet undisturbed writing and study. And when I get back to America, I shall have to break ground in New York as a teacher and spend most of my time and energy again in money-earning, since I have no income whatsoever. These months of freedom from such necessity have been of immeasurable value, and an extension of my time here would have value not only in itself, but also because it would clinch and fulfill that which has been accomplished during the first year's work.

When I first came to Berlin, I decided to spend most of my time in composing rather than in making "connections," and have until two weeks ago kept myself purposely out of touch with musicians both here and in America, since there were certain ideas which I felt it necessary to work out at once with as little disturbance as possible. Therefore, at present I have very little to report definitely regarding performances of my work. The Novembergruppe of Berlin is interested in collaborating with the Pan American Society of Composers in a concert of American music, with one of my works on the program. Also there is a possibility that the Internationale Gesellschaft für Neue Musik will perform one of my compositions. In New York, Gerald Reynolds will perform the three choruses, (written in Berlin) on his Spring concert; their performance by him at the New School for Social Research has also been spoken of, though I have not heard definitely. Oscar Ziegler played a piano prelude at the New School on January 6. The League of Composers (New York) is considering one of my suites for a Sunday afternoon concert at the Art Center. I have not yet heard from Dr. Howard Hanson of the Eastman School; he is looking over some of my manuscript. In San Francisco the Suite for oboe, contralto, piano and percussion (the second movement was written in Berlin) will be performed by the New Music Society. Henry Cowell will write to you stating in which issue of New Music Magazine one of my suites will be printed. And Charles Louis Seeger will send you a few words about the book (Treatise on Modern Composition and Manual of Dissonant Counterpoint) with the writing of which I helped him during June, July, and part of August.

This letter to you has been delayed because I had hoped to hear more definite information about certain of the above possibilities before writing you this mid-year "report" about myself and my work. If there are any questions you would like answered further, or if you would like to look over manuscripts of work I have written here, please let me know.

I believe my choice of Berlin rather than Paris has proven for me best, though I scarcely have full right to say that until I am acquainted with Paris. But the longer I stay here, the more I find to admire in the spirit which I see in other arts as well as in music--notably photography and architecture. I feel the deepest gratitude, not only for the freedom for work which the fellowship has given me, but also for the privilege of experiencing closer contact with this culture which is not satisfied with its traditions but is eager always to add a new word or more to them.

With best wishes to you--and hoping you will let me call on you some summer at your farm near Patterson--

      Yours cordially,
      [signed] Ruth Crawford

* * *

COMPOSERS' FORUM-LABORATORY

Wednesday evening, April 6th, 1938, at 8:45

QUESTIONS FOR RUTH CRAWFORD

Question 1:   In composing the music on this program, were you primarily interested in <u>form</u> or <u>content</u>?

Answer: With the exception of the one piano prelude, the music on this program was written during a period when I was more concerned with form than with content. I was trying through form, rhythm, dynamics, to work out disciplines which would expand musical technique and give it wider horizons.

Question 2: When did you compose the music on this program?

Answer: The String Quartet was written in 1931; the piano prelude in 1926; the piano etude in 1931; the songs in 1931 and '32.

Question 3: Is your music exceptionally difficult?

Answer: Of course most composers think their music is difficult, but it is very generally conceded that mine is exceptionally so. The string quartet should have months of rehearsal, due especially to its rhythmical and dynamic difficulties. Of course, music which is thought horizontally is usually more difficult than that which is thought vertically.

Question 4: Are not the first and last songs by Miss Essig rich musical jokes? Are they intended to be?

Answer: It is very hard to draw a line between humor and seriousness in music.

Question 5: What poets wrote the words of your songs?

Answer: Carl Sandburg.

Question 6: Don't you think your percussion is unsympathetic to the voice?

Answer: With adequate rehearsal it is not.

Question 7: Have you written any music recently? The orchestral arrangement with voice was extremely imaginative and provocative. I think also that all your music is very finished.

Answer:	I have been composing babies the past five years. I wrote a couple of dozen piano pieces last fall, and expect to be able this next year to carry out some larger plans.
Question 8:	Precisely <u>what</u> did you have in mind in that last selection? (with voice)
Answer:	Doesn't need to be answered.
Question 9:	Did you write your Sonata in strict Sonata form? Your piano pieces have all similar harmony and treatment.
Answer:	There is no sonata on the program. None of my works performed tonight were written in sonata form. Most of them, however, are tightly organized, and a distinct form-plan has been carried out.
Question 10:	Do you really believe that your music is the future music of America? If so, then I pray for its deliverance.
Answer:	No, I do not. I believe, for one thing, that the music of the future will have more content than this music has. But I do believe that this sort of work has very great value. New techniques must be worked out, experimented with, for a long time before the balance can be reached out of which what can be called a true American music can arise.
Question 11:	Please inform one bewildered auditor the intent and purpose of your writing. Why is it so difficult to grasp at a first hearing?
Answer:	I think I have answered this already to some extent, but I can sum it up here. First, with all respect to the performers, who have done excellent jobs for the rehearsal time they were given on these works, you have not heard my music tonight. It requires a very great deal more rehearsal. Second, even listeners with wide knowledge and experience will tell you

they must hear a new work many times before "grasping" it.

Question 12: How is it possible to perform the slow movement of the String Quartet when there is no pulse?

Answer: The slow movement of the string quartet is done best when it is conducted. But, with sufficient amount of rehearsal, it can be done without. This movement is built on a counterpoint of dynamics. The crescendi and diminuendi should be exactly timed, and no instrument should reach the high or low point at the same time as any other. As for melodic line--as in the second movement, it travels from instrument to instrument; there is only one line.

Question 13: Can you explain something of your use of dissonant counterpoint on which your Quartet is obviously based? Should not the slow movement of the Quartet have gone much faster? As I remember hearing it before, the dynamic range moved faster. Also, the last movement should have been faster. The whole is a fascinating study in dynamics.

Answer: That would take too long. Yes, the movement should go at least a third faster. The melodic line is lost when played so slowly. The last movement should also have gone at least a third faster.

Question 14: How long did it take you to write the Quartet?

Answer: Several months, off and on. I wrote one of the movements in a week.

Question 15: What were the texts of the Songs? It would have been more helpful to have known the names of the songs and to have been permitted to follow the words.

Answer: It would take too long to repeat the texts. The

	names of the songs are 1. Rat Riddles, 2. Prayers of Steel, and 3. In High Grass.
Question 16:	I heard some hisses in the audience. Please, please, explain the purpose and the content of your music so they won't hiss any more.
Answer:	I think I have said enough about this already.
Question 17:	Did you try hard to be original? Did you succeed?
Answer:	Doesn't need answering.
Question 18:	Did it pour forth or was it constructed?
Answer:	All composers would, I believe, agree that the making of music combines both expression and construction. Any student of music who has looked into the works of any of our great composers will find an astonishing amount of thoughtful bricklaying and intellectual effort.
Question 19:	Won't you please write some music that a greater number of people can listen to: this seems like music for the very few.
Answer:	I will. I have become convinced during the past two years that my next music will be simpler to play and to understand. But at the same time we should not forget that it is also important to write music for the few. I regret that the direction indicated in the works performed tonight cannot be followed out more completely.

* * *

WHY DON'T THEY EAT CAKE?

"With liberty and justice for all" ... is it any wonder revolutions are in the air? Justice! What can there be left but a soap box, a delegation to the president's wife, or finally, if nothing else avail, a nationwide strike? Women of America--women of the world--arise! Unite! Claim your birthright!

Has it ever occurred to you with what blatant indifference your keenest interests are ignored? Colleges for women where they may play around with anything from calculus to cabbage soup--yes, your men have at last grudgingly built these for you (they had to--you made them). They even allow you to putter about in politics if you acquire a manly gait and seem to show an intellect almost as good, though of course not quite, as the average male. They give you card-indexes for toys, typewriters, even factories and strikes and airplanes now and then. In fact, they have dealt out to you (or made you think so) most of the contents of their much boasted and zealously guarded bag of tricks.

But not all. That most sacred, that most precious, that inalienably rightful possession of every male--they guard it with an iron grip. For female amusement--a female's college. For female education--a female's burlesque? God and the devil forbid! Let her come to a male's burlesque if she must--that is her right to make a nuisance of herself. But when she begins to ask what-the-hell good she can get out of that, and starts in campaigning for--well, just watch the male foot go down hard, hear the old-husbands-tale pop up again out of the dust, and if you haven't sneezed too vigorously, hear an outraged male rage. The purity of woman--but that is just a smoke-screen. Man trails his already wilting dignity along the desecrated boards (no, we thought they were sacred?) of a burlesque stage? Man an Exhibit A for the education (nay, defilement) of woman? Man a beckoner--woman a pursuer? A packed female audience all gathered together just for the purpose of ... O no, O Communism, O Fascism, O Dadaism, Buchmanism, anything but this.

Poor dear men! Women have stripped you of so much of your gold-braided power--you are so much less gods than you used to be (though none the less loved). Mere men now, with the clouds of grandiloquent mystery slinking inevitably away. One can't forbear a tear of sympathy--this, your last sanctum sanctorum....

I tell you, I am serious. This indispensable institution has been too long withheld from us. It can be withheld no longer; the need is too great. I ask that a campaign be launched; if necessary, a lobby in congress must be maintained. And a donor, or donors, must be found who will finance the launching of such an institution, in which there will be allowed not so much as one female leg on the stage, nor one male voice in the management. The donor can rest assured that her money will be returned to her by the car load; as for her name, it will be lisped by little girl babies while spooning in their oatmeal.

Just this last word to our frightened men. We won't love you less. We may even love you more.

> Ruth Porter[2]
> 2441 "P" Street NW
> Washington, D.C.

* * *

LETTER TO JOHN BECKER

9609 Fairway Avenue   Silver Spring, Maryland
September 22
1939

Dear John Becker:

Thank you so much for your heartening letter. I am so glad you are enthusiastic about the string quartet, and appreciate your writing to the others about it. I can't tell you how glad I would be if it were published, and hope everybody will agree on it.

My latest musical job has been a fascinating one--that of music editor for the forthcoming-at-MacMillan's book of John and Alan Lomax, "Singing Country." It is a successor to the "American Ballads and Folksongs" of some years ago, which you may know, and contains about three hundred folk songs which they personally have collected, most of them on discs with their machine in the field, in the country or small town or prison camp. I have transcribed all of them and there are some beauties.

We just came back from the Musicological Congress (International) in New York, which was quite a success from several standpoints. It was gratifying to note that, even tho they were conspicuous by their absence from the technical-historical meetings, quite a few of the composers turned out with high enthusiasm for the day's orgy in American folk music. The excitement with which some of them greet this music is in itself exciting to us, since we have been going through the experience ourselves since coming to Washington. We had been here only a couple of months when Charlie began to get his fingers on the pulse of some of this very live-and-kicking music of "unmusical" America.

Charlie is writing you a separate letter. Meanwhile, again thank you for writing us, and our heartiest good wishes to you.

Cordially
[signed] Ruth Crawford Seeger

* * *

LETTER TO MISS PRINK
(excerpts)

September 30, 1940

Dear Miss Prink:

Whenever you feel inclined to meditate on the book as a three-ring circus try the following as antidote.

Take charge of the Seeger family during such a week as that of September 21-28. Give Peggy (age 6) a few scattered sneezes and sniffles on the day when all are planning a roof picnic with an old friend atop 2400 16th Street. Decide she has hay fever, and go. Bring her home sneezing oftener.

Next day apply a cough and a bad chest and keep her in bed. It is a hot day. You must decide whether to keep her too hot (with window closed) or too breezy (with window open). Keep her well covered. But do not cover her too heavily. Above all, keep the other children out of her room. For the sake of two members of the family it is important that the germ stay with Peggy. One of these is Barbara (age 3); whooping cough last year left her susceptible. Barbara is not convinced of the urgency of this. She would like to comfort Peggy. You will, of course, keep the housework running along cheerfully, as usual.

Next day give Barbara, also Michael (age 7), slight traces of sniffle--sufficient to advise keeping each in bed in his own room, since either may or may not have the germ. This will, of course, mean giving each child his meals in his own room. You will not mind this: you have been advised to take more frequent walks. (I will explain to you in another letter just how to get your husband's breakfast (7:15), keep Barbara (upstairs) in bed, prepare the three breakfast trays (on the stove, the table, the chair), count the laundry (your husband must leave it on his way downtown), keep your coffee hot after it has been poured (you like it very hot), and remain cheerful. As you pass the desk with Peggy's tray bound for Peggy's room downstairs, you will undoubtedly think of the songs "Married Man" and "Trouble, Trouble." As you pass the desk with Barbara's tray bound for Barbara's room upstairs, and with Michael's tray for Michael's room upstairs, you will undoubtedly again think of "Married Man," and "Trouble, Trouble." You will, however, maintain a policy of strict neutrality toward the desk.

By lunchtime you should have freed all rooms of dust, and aired them. This means extracting each child during such operation. It means also contracting the cold yourself, since you are allergic to dust. You will, of course, make sure, before extracting the child, that the room to which he will be temporarily transferred is free from draught: doctors dub the summer cold especially dangerous because of perspiration and draught. And the children are perspiring, the day hot, the wind lively. You will not worry about this. You will be cheerful. You will take as a motto the discharging of all details with the patience you expend on a page of manuscript. You will likewise accept all interruptions to the discharging of these details with the same patience. This may be difficult at times, as for instance, when a fire siren (vocal) rises to emergency pitch from Peggy's room and you rush downstairs to be shown a 16th-inch spider in the far corner of her ceiling. You will do well at such a time to delay action on the spider, and on Peggy, until you have recalled (a) all the occasions on which Peggy has called you Little Honey Dio,[3] and (b) all the occasions on which your husband has killed spiders for you.

... All this time, remember your editor in New York, Miss Prink. Also the songs you promised to send her "in a day or two." Also remember the footnotes, which have received considerable change due to the last few weeks' work on the manuscript. Dread her reaction to this. Therefore, decide to postpone sending them a day or two more. Also, remember there are a few more all night sessions due on the Appendix. Remember further that the Appendix is materially longer than Miss Prink anticipates. Try to decide how, without seeming vain, you can indicate to her that, this Appendix being unique as a musical treatment of American folk music, it must go through uncut. Also, recall that you do not wish to release it until you have gone over it with your husband. This will remind you that he is in the midst of writing several papers for various meetings of various societies, plus music editing a book himself, all aside from his full time duties in town. Ponder this dilemma while hanging out the 42 socks and the 21 shorts and delicacies; also while squeezing the oranges for orange juice, admiring Peggy's mass production of pictures on your favorite onion-skin paper (due for carbon copies of the Appendix), giving Barbara (upstairs) more blocks, and suggesting to Michael (upstairs) that he cover his bed with only a portion of his toys.

You must remember, through the day, that the children are really angelic. Do not forget to be grateful for this undeniable fact. They are not whining, not crying. Peggy sticks to her bed, uses her dimples often. Michael says "I'll be glad to" when asked to put his toys away. Barbara calls you "Nice Dio." When, therefore, you find Peggy writing on the wall-paper, Michael making a large hole in his beaver-board wall, or Barbara eating her crayons, do not fail to remember this. It is, of course, hard to remain cheerful when you have begun to feel the cold creeping on you, and your head begins to ache, and you cannot read because your eyes are dizzy.

... Be lazy today; you are miserable. Forget your decision born of indecision. Forget that Peggy may get too hot, remember you did your best in warning Michael not to eat too much cake. Lie back on the couch in the cool thirty-foot living room, leave the breakfast and lunch dishes like a bad housekeeper, look up at the dust on the beams overhead and allow yourself luxury. Relax, try to read the paper without remembering the letters you owe, or the string quartet whose performance waits only an hour's correction and wrapping paper, or the plans afoot when the tentacles of this (oct)opus shall be released. Feel restless about all these, while you relax. Also about the footnotes and the Appendix. Remember the phonograph, and the songs due Miss Prink, and that you are very tired. Tell yourself that the amount of work yet to be done on this book is actually very little; that you have become ingrown and are letting details grow to mountains. Fret that this is partly due to unavoidable lack of continuity these last few months, since you cannot sit up every night in the week and all day too. This will remind you that if you rest now you might be able to work tonight. So hurry up--hurry up--shut your eyes and rest. Michael is at a party and Barbara in the sun. Ten minutes later, when you find that Barbara has filled the toilet with small and large stones, be thankful she did not flush them down. Remember she is a <u>herz kind</u>, has long yellow hair like corn silk and large blue eyes like corn flowers. Above all, listen to the curves in her voice as she tells you she is sorry. Then take the stones out of the toilet.

... Do not rebel at this point. The smell of the oil heating on the stove may bring pungent memories of your own childhood and the firm palm of your mother's hand (you will recall her patience) and a great black wood stove in place of this thing of beauty which you polish with pleasure. And, as you rub the oil into Barbara's chest while her eyes and voice reproach you for she has outlying spots of heat rash, you will remember wistfully that this operation last year and the year before that, was accompanied by the singing of newly transcribed songs, on their way into the Lomax book. You wonder if you will do that again when the last sheet of the Appendix is irrevocably out of your grip and you feel like singing again.

In this way your thoughts return to Miss Prink. You remember also that Michael calls you "Mrs. Coffeedrinker, because she drinks too much coffee." Will your pre-cold schedule of three cups at 11:00 PM revive you for an all-night session tonight? You cover Barbara's chest with flannel, give her one more hug and kiss by proxy, and take the oil to the kitchen. You had forgotten: the supper dishes are still to be washed.

... Now the next day you must finally go down town for a check-up on your ears.... Before leaving the fresh suburban country air with your husband at 7:45 in the morning, be sure to make detailed decisions as to what each child may be allowed to do during the day. Relay these to Mamie; likewise to each child.... You will, of course, wave goodbyes to the heads at the windows as you drive down the street. Your husband will be winking the rear red lights also, and waving his hand as he turns the corner. He will not forget any of these details. They combine to form another ritual. As you pass the milk truck at the next corner you will remember that, if there were no cotton in your ears, you would hear lusty goodbyes at the distance of at least two blocks. Therefore, the throats cannot be too badly affected.

You will, on the way to town, reflect on perfectionism, whether in treatment of colds or of books.

And that will bring you back again to Miss Prink. Having, on account of your husband's extra early summer office hour, arrived far too soon to see the doctor, you will then--with songs, footnotes and Appendix twelve safe miles away--write Miss Prink seven foolish pages in their stead.

* * *

LETTER TO EDGARD VARESE

May 22, 1948
7 West Kirke Street
Chevy Chase 15
Maryland

Dear Edgar [sic] Varèse:

Your first letter saying you wanted to include me in your course at Columbia was dated January 8. I ought to wait ten more days to make it exactly five months. I hope my lateness has not inconvenienced you too greatly. It seems that everything has combined to make this spring full. Teaching at two schools, plus a full private-teaching schedule (including an 8 till 6 Saturday), plus work on a book which is coming out this fall, plus proof on the Lomax book which came out this spring, plus four healthy children-and-a-house, have combined to emphasize my natural indolence as to letter-writing.

One reason I have been late in answering is, that you

asked for a kind of "credo." I found that a little hard, for I am still not sure whether the road I have been following the last dozen years is a main road or a detour. I have begun to feel, the past year or two, that it is the latter-a detour, but a very important one to me, during which I have descended from stratosphere onto a solid well-travelled highway, folded my wings and breathed good friendly dust as I travelled along in and out of the thousands of fine traditional folktunes which I have been hearing and singing and transcribing from field-recordings, for books and for pleasure. Until a year or so ago I had felt so at home among this (to me) new found music that I thought maybe this was what I wanted most. I listened to nothing else, and felt somewhat like a ghost when my compositions were spoken of. I answered no letters pertaining to them; requests for scores or biographical data were stuck in drawers. There were, of course, occasional periods during which I returned to composition, as, for instance, when CBS wanted works for orchestra utilising folk material for performance on the SCHOOL OF THE AIR. Charlie and I were among those commissioned, and his JOHN HARDY and my RISSOLTY ROSSOLTY were performed there in 1941. But for years the only instrument in the house was a guitar, a mountain dulcimer, and a special slow-speed phonograph for transcription of folk recordings.

Whether I ever unfold the wings and make a start toward the stratosphere again, and how much of the dust of the road will still cling to me, is an interesting question, at least to me. If I do, I will probably pull the road up with me.

As for a "credo" typifying my music of the type of STRING QUARTET 1931, and THREE SONGS FOR CONTRALTO AND ORCHESTRA which ISCM chose for Amsterdam festival back in 1933, I could mention a few points about which I felt strongly. And I still feel strongly about them. I believe when I write more music these elements will be there, or at least striven for:

>Clarity of melodic line
>Avoidance of rhythmic stickiness
>Rhythmic independence between parts
>Feeling of tonal and rhythmic center
>Experiment with various means of obtaining at the same time organic unity and various sorts of dissonance.

As to the works which I consider most representative, I am inclined to choose the STRING QUARTET 1931. It is the slow movement of this quartet which was recorded on NEW MUSIC RECORDINGS, a copy of which Mrs. Varèse says you have. I am sending the score of this quartet, with 3rd and 4th movements analysed as to tone, rhythm, form and dynamics. I would like to mention that the recording was made at rather short notice, and that therefore the counterpoint of crescendos, mentioned in the analysis, is not well heard on the recording.

A few of the things Charlie and I have been doing since 1933 may be of interest as a back-drop. We have four children, said by our friends to have both charm and good looks, born in 1933, 35, 37 and 44. Michael, Peggy, Barbara and Penelope. When Barbara went to co-operative nursery school in 1941 I went with her, and a book, AMERICAN FOLK SONGS FOR CHILDREN grew out of the experience (to come out this fall, Doubleday). Previous to this I worked as music editor on the Lomax OUR SINGING COUNTRY, which involved transcription into music notation of several hundred traditional songs, and the listening to many hundred more in process of choosing these for publication. In connection with this I worked on a 60-page treatise on the music of these songs, never quite finished nor published. This work really grew out of Charlie's activities as technical advisor in the SPECIAL SKILLS DIVISION of Resettlement Administration, and our close acquaintance with the music we heard everywhere during our travels among and to and from the Resettlement colonies.

We have acted as consultants for several publishing houses, in American folk music for children. I also planned and chose the music for the State Department for a series of radio broadcasts, MUSIC IN AMERICAN LIFE. Last summer Charlie and I, with Dr. Emrich of the Archive of American Folklore, Library of Congress, completed a book of 900 American traditional songs, to be published by Dial Press; half of these we transcribed from field recordings. And this spring another Lomax book, FOLKSONG:USA, was published by Duell Sloan Pearce, with 111 accompaniments by us.

Charlie joins me in warm good wishes from us both. Perhaps next time I come to New York I can know far enough in advance to be less spontaneous in getting in touch with you.

   Cordially,
   Ruth Crawford Seeger

* * *

LETTER TO CARL SANDBURG

November 20, 1948

Dear Carl Sandburg:

  I wanted to write you a note to go along inside the book. But Doubleday said you can't include a note with a book, so I said I would write it separate. Of course I didn't.

  There wasn't much of anything specific I had in mind to say. If letters could only be warmed up to feel to the touch--or made of velvet, or linen, or glass, or cloth-of-cactus, to suit.

  I know you do know already how your words give me very special pleasure every time I open this first book of my own, and how right it seems, from the standpoint of my own path since 1927, for it to be you who says God-bless-you.

  I hope you may sometime have spare moments to look over the introductory chapters. Whatever of "educational patter" is there was pulled, not from books or intellectual chatter, but from the mixture of children, songs and myself. It wouldn't be surprising if here and there some small elements of poetry got mixed up with what I have to say. Certainly I often felt that those three ingredients, mixed together, met to make something like a poem.

  Love to the family. Tell Margaret I haven't forgotten Schubert. It's just that I can't seem to wrap a package and mail it.

  [signed] Ruth Seeger

* * *

PRE-SCHOOL CHILDREN AND AMERICAN FOLK SONGS

In a few minutes a dozen four-year-olds will be with us. I am not at all sure what we will be doing. There has been no rehearsing in any distant sense of the word.

It is a question, of course, whether children of this age should be brought before a large group of people, under conditions which might be termed artificial. There is the question whether those elements which should be uppermost in the bringing of music and children together, can be retained with so many strange faces looking on.

If these children had been subjected in advance to any performance attitudes or disciplines, if they had been drilled or "taught," I would be the first to say certainly No, let's forego whatever value might come to us from having them here.

But what I hope to do this morning is to achieve with the help of the music and the children a complete forgetting on their part of the fact that there is anyone here but themselves and me. I believe we will make that happen (and I beg you to help by refraining from audible appreciation, either through laughter or clapping). What we will do this morning will be what we would do any morning if we were at school.

At school we are too busy with ourselves and the music--with fitting the songs to our thoughts or actions, and fitting our thoughts or actions to the songs--to think much about anyone watching us. At school we are never sure what will be happening next. No two mornings are ever the same. There is a skeleton plan, of course. Thought is given to balance between active and quiet music, to consistency from day to day, to awareness of weather and the seasons in choice of songs (though if <u>Jingle Bells</u> is wanted in June, let's sing it). But plans are really points of departure, to be returned to when needed but often to be stretched and occasionally to be entirely ignored. If David comes up today with a new idea, we may follow David. If Peter starts kicking his feet up and down in the middle of <u>Hush Little Baby</u>, we may even leave the quiet song half finished and let the music pick up the insistent rhythm of Peter's feet. Whether we decide to take such detours depends on a number of things. Does this child need for his own good to be acknowledged as someone who can contribute? Or is he just expressing a little more vociferously, a group need for action rather than for sustained singing (and how is a teacher to be sure, always, that it is she who is right?) Or is he perhaps on the edge of becoming a disruptive influence? (And what gives a teacher greater satisfaction than to catch such a moment and help the child and the group to make constructive use of it?)

What we are doing, then, teacher and children, is making something together, fresh each day--a sort of composition. And in any process of composition, large or small, some days are more productive than others. There are valleys and there are high places. The high places are rich with giving and taking between group and teacher. And with giving and taking, the valleys can sometimes reach to high places which are especially satisfying because they promised so little. Certainly if the teacher's first aims are a keen awareness of each child's smallest actions or words or thoughts, and a readiness to follow as well as to lead, there will be a spirit of freshness within the teacher as well as the children, a sense of exploring, of trying something a little new or doing something a little differently. To a tentative basic plan will have been added a vital element: spontaneity.

And if on a platform in conditions unnatural to small children, these qualities can be preserved, surely there must be either in this music or in certain attitudes toward its use, elements which prove themselves to be good for both children and teacher. For the ability to feel comfortable with oneself and with music, even under ordinary circumstances, is a thing we are seeking not only for our children: it is a thing many of us have spent years in seeking for ourselves.

It is my feeling that both these premises are valid. The music itself is American folk music. And this music possesses qualities which invite spontaneity, improvisation, natural participation both in singing and in action. The music itself, therefore--and this means not only the notes and the time values but ways traditional singers and players have of singing and using their music--holds within itself implications as to attitudes toward its use.

Now here come the children. . . . . .

> (A music period with the children follows. Among
> the songs used are Mary Wore Her Red Dress,
> Jim Along Josie, Old Joe Clarke, Hush Little Baby,
> There Was A Man and He Was Mad, Goodbye Old
> Paint. The children leave).

Before the children came we were speaking of qualities in American folk music and folk performance which are especially good for children--and for the teacher of children. It was through daily using of this music with children[--] and through years of listening to field recordings of it as sung by traditional singers in mountain homes, along roadsides, in fields, churches, towns--that these qualities suggested themselves to me, slowly, one by one. Several of them have been illustrated during the past half hour with the children.

The traditional (folk) singer keeps his song going without interruption of the pulse at stanza ends (though measure lengths may occasionally be irregular). Neither the rhythm nor the mood of the song are broken into by artificial pauses, breaks, ritards, or "expression." This is straightforward music.

Though his tempo is fairly fast, the traditional singer is seldom in a hurry. If he likes a song he will want to sing it over many times. If it has only one stanza, he is likely to sing that stanza over and over without stopping. The children this morning wanted to go on turning around, wanted Old Joe Clarke again and again. So we kept it going. At one school a group of four-year-olds kept this up during an entire music period.

Most American traditional music is sung or played with strong rhythmic vitality. Much of it has been used for dancing, for game playing, for work. Children do not need to be urged to let their bodies find ways of moving to music like Jim Along Josie or All Around the Kitchen or Old Joe Clarke.

The traditional singer has not been "taught" this music. He has learned these songs through hearing them. It is my feeling that with small children there should be little or no urging to sing. Mothers of children who sing little or none at school tell me of vigorous and spontaneous singing at home. At school Margie just sat on a stool or stood listening in a corner (and occasionally criticising) during the three weeks I sang with her group. At the end of the three weeks her mother told me: "We never talk at our house any more. We just sing. Margie won't put on her shoes or button her coat unless we sing about it."

For the teacher there are a number of comforting qualities about this music. It has been thoroughly tested by time and by use--often over generations, and among many people in many places. The teacher can be assured that it is of good quality, yet it [is] also for the most part simple and friendly to learn. She can also be assured that it requires from her no apology for quality of singing voice, that it is accustomed to being sung in a natural way by untrained voices, and is most at home with not too beautiful or polished a tone quality. To the traditional singer it is the song itself which is of value, not the quality of the singer's voice.

Perhaps most important of all, for both children and teacher, is the ease with which these songs can come close to and become part of a child's everyday living. They invite improvisation. To one song new words can be improvised ad lib, and a short song can grow to a very long song. The teacher can, then, know well (i.e., without having to turn the pages of a book) fewer songs--and with fewer songs can fill far greater needs. And the children will be learning tunes as the traditional singer has learned them, naturally, by hearing them and using them, over and over. For this music has grown through being used and being needed, in work, in courting, in religion, in play. It has learned to adapt itself to ever changing environments. It carries, as a result, invaluable comment on the history and customs of the people who have used it. It is a living entity. It is a thing unfinished, not crystallised; a thing to which a child no matter how small or a teacher no matter how hesitant may dare to add some part of himself, thus gaining in even a small way the sort of confidence which can come with making something of one's own. The value he gains for himself in confidence may be out of proportion to the value of his contribution to the song (and the teacher should be sure that the pleasure of adding new words to old songs does not crowd out the older traditional words, which possess values the newer words cannot supplant). But belief in our own worthiness and ability to make our own music is a thing to be nurtured, a thing too often lost early in education. Too early and too frequently music is brought to our attention as something for us to learn. It was made, we are told, by remarkable people like Beethoven and Mozart and Haydn, who when they were young were remarkable children. We are, we feel, not remarkable people. So we say, "I can't" to the making of our own music, and can sense ourselves growing smaller as we say it.

Perhaps feeling comfortable enough and free enough with a song to add their own words to it can be for many children a first step toward feeling free enough with music itself to make their own music. And the "I can" which attends the making of one's own music can be a value as important as food or drink.

PART III:

END PAPERS

CHAPTER NOTES

INTRODUCTION

1. Eric Salzman, "The Tradition of the New in American Music," Current Musicology 7 (1968), pp. 10-11.

CHAPTER ONE--Background, Early Life, and Training

1. Carl Crawford, Ruth Crawford's brother, has supplied much information concerning the Graves and Crawford families. These materials are found in the Seeger Collection, housed in the Music Division, Library of Congress, hereinafter referred to as SC.
2. Ruth Crawford, autobiographical data, n.d. SC
3. Carl Crawford, taped interview with the author, Laguna Hills, California, March 18, 1968.
4. Ruth Crawford, autobiographical data, n.d. SC
5. Ibid.
6. Ruth Crawford, diary entry, August 21, 1917. SC
7. Ibid., diary entry, August 31, 1917.
8. Ibid., September 23, 1917.
9. Ibid., October 1, 1917.
10. The Oracle, Duvall High School, Jacksonville, Florida, 1918, p. 14. SC
11. Ruth Crawford, letter to Nicolas Slonimsky, January 29, 1933. SC
12. Musical Leader, Vol. 41 (January-June 1921), p. 323.
13. Ruth Crawford, diary entry, October 11, 1917. SC Autobiographical data states that Ruth was also in charge of music at a settlement kindergarten in Jacksonville in 1918. SC
14. Ruth Crawford, diary entry, October 16, 1917. SC
15. Ibid., diary entry, dated only Monday, probably November 11, 1917.
16. Carl Crawford, letter to the author, October 7, 1971.
17. Ruth Crawford, diary entry, July 3, 1917. SC
18. Carl Crawford, letter to the author, October 7, 1971.
19. Ruth Crawford, autobiographical data, n.d. SC

20. Ruth Crawford, letter to Charles Seeger, undated, probably mid-September 1931. These materials are in the possession of the Seeger family, hereinafter referred to as the Seeger Family Collection (SFC).

CHAPTER TWO--The Chicago Years, 1921-1924

1. Cecil Smith, <u>The World of Music</u>. Westport, Conn.: Greenwood Press, 1973, pp. 152-53.
2. Rossetter G. Cole, "Adolf Weidig," <u>Dictionary of American Biography</u>, ed. Dumas Malone, X, 1936, p. 606.
3. Ruth Crawford, letter to her mother, October 16, 1921. SC
4. Ibid., November 20, 1921.
5. Ibid.
6. Ibid., October 23, 1921.
7. Ibid., November 1, 1921.
8. Ibid., March 12, 1922.
9. Ibid., November 1, 1921.
10. Ibid., November 6, 1921.
11. Carl Crawford, letter to Ruth Crawford, October 1, 1921. SC
12. Ruth Crawford, letter to her mother, November 6, 1921. SC
13. Ibid., December 4, 1921.
14. Ibid.
15. Ibid., February 2, 1922.
16. Ibid., May 19, 1922.
17. Ibid., February 22, 1922.
18. Carl Crawford, letter to the author, October 7, 1971.
19. Ruth Crawford, letter to her mother, March 14, 1922. SC
20. Ibid., June 14, 1922.
21. Ibid.
22. Ibid., May 12, 1922.
23. Ruth Crawford, letter to Carl Crawford, October 7, 1922. SC
24. Ruth Crawford, letter to her mother, October 18, 1922. SC
25. Ibid., November 18, 1922.
26. Ibid., November 22, 1922.
27. Ibid.
28. Ibid., January 3, 1923.
29. Ibid., January 20, 1923.
30. Mrs. Clark Crawford, letter to Ruth Crawford, March 18, 1923. SC
31. Ruth Crawford, letter to her mother, March 23, 1923. SC
32. Ibid., April 25, 1923.
33. Mrs. Clark Crawford, letter to Carl Crawford, November 1, 1923. SC
34. Ruth Crawford Seeger, letter to Nicolas Slonimsky, January 29, 1933. SC The <u>Chicago Sunday Tribune</u> (September 11, 1921) stated that the Chicago Civic Music Association organized the Civic Orchestra of Chicago under Stock and DeLamarter to help teach young artists how to play together. This is probably the orchestra with which Ruth was involved.

35. Mrs. Clark Crawford, letter to Carl Crawford, June 18, 1924. SC

CHAPTER THREE--The Chicago Years, 1924-1929

1. The Musical Courier (June 30, 1927), p. 32, and Ruth Crawford, autobiographical notes, n.d. SC
2. Martha Beck Carragan, letter to the author, September 5, 1983.
3. Stella Roberts, letter to the author, January 8, 1972.
4. Ruth Crawford, letter to Nicolas Slonimsky, January 29, 1933. SC
5. The Musical Leader Vol. 46 (July-December 1923), p. 562.
6. Musical America (January 10, 1925), p. 23.
7. The Musical Leader, Vol. 46, p. 562.
8. Ibid.
9. The Musical Leader (March 6, 1924), p. 233; The Musical Leader (May 3, 1928), p. 23.
10. Alfred Frankenstein, taped interview, San Francisco, California, March 1968.
11. The Musical Courier (October 30, 1924), p. 23. Gradova concertized under the Arthur Judson management with Siegfried Herz as her personal representative. On occasion she included some of Ruth's preludes on her recitals.
12. Albert Hirsh, letter to the author, September 6, 1983. Hirsh was a student of Madame Herz both in Chicago and New York.
13. Vivian Fine, taped telephone interview, June 11, 1983. Fine became a piano student of Herz in Chicago at age twelve.
14. Ruth Crawford, letter to Nicolas Slonimsky, January 29, 1933. SC
15. Ruth Crawford, diary entry, September 28, 1927. SC
16. Ibid., entry dated only Wednesday, probably November 1927.
17. Albert Hirsh, letter to the author, September 6, 1983.
18. Ruth Crawford, diary entry dated only Wednesday, probably November 1927. SC
19. Ibid., August 14, 1928.
20. Dane Rudhyar, taped recollections prepared for the author, San Marcos, California, January 23, 1975.
21. Ruth Crawford, diary entry, October 26, 1927. SC
22. Ibid., November 11, 1928.
23. Ibid.
24. Dane Rudhyar, taped recollections, January 23, 1975.
25. Henry Cowell, New Musical Resources. New York: A. A. Knopf, Inc., 1930.
26. Alfred Frankenstein, letter to Ruth Crawford, n.d. and incomplete. Identified by Frankenstein.
27. Alfred Frankenstein, taped interview, March 1968.
28. Ruth Crawford, letter to Carl Sandburg, April 1, 1946. SC
29. Ruth Crawford, diary entry, December 15, 1927. SC
30. Herbert Mitgang, ed., The Letters of Carl Sandburg. New

York: Harcourt, Brace and World, Inc., 1968. Letter to Thomas L. Stokes, December 26, 1949.
31. Ruth Crawford, diary entry, December 11, 1927. SC
32. Carl Sandburg, letter to the Guggenheim Foundation, December 5, 1929. SC
33. Charles Seeger, taped interview, March 18, 1968.
34. Ruth Crawford, diary entry dated only Saturday, probably September 5, 1927. SC
35. Ibid., September 5, 1927.
36. Ibid., entry dated only Sunday, probably September 25, 1927.
37. Ibid., November 8, 1928.
38. Ibid., August 30, 1927.
39. Ruth Crawford, diary entries, October 23, 1927; Friday 1 a.m. (1927); February 24, 1928. SC
40. Ms. Fine, who later studied composition with Roger Sessions, today enjoys a well-established reputation as an American composer of merit.
41. Vivian Fine, taped telephone interview, June 11, 1983.
42. The Musical Courier (June 1, 1929), p. 20.
43. Ruth Crawford, diary entry, October 28, 1927. SC
44. Ibid., dated only Monday, probably November 4, 1927. A telegram from Ruth Crawford to Alice Burrows, 411 Fullerton Street, Apt. 1007, Chicago, dated November 1, 1930, from Berlin, would seem to identify the Alice of this and many later references. SC
45. Ruth Crawford, diary entry, October 29, 1928 (SC), and letter from Martha Beck Carragan to the author, September 5, 1983.
46. Carl Crawford, taped interview, Laguna Hills, California, March 18, 1968.
47. Ruth Crawford, diary entry, August 14, 1928. SC
48. The Musical Courier (January 5, 1928), p. 44; (February 16, 1928), p. 40.
49. Musical America (February 12, 1927), p. 27.
50. Richard Buhlig (1900-1952) was a Chicago-born concert pianist and teacher whom Ruth met probably through Madame Herz and Henry Cowell. He performed some of Ruth's piano preludes on several occasions. One of these, Prelude No. 9, was dedicated to Buhlig, the second of only two such dedications.
51. The Musical Courier (October 21, 1926), p. 21. Listed as judges for this event were William Arms Fisher, Mary Turner Salter, Gertrude Ross, and Harriet Ware.
52. Peggy Seeger, taped recollections prepared for the author, Paris, April 1976.
53. Ruth Crawford, diary entry, September 26, 1927. SC
54. Ibid., entry dated only Wednesday, probably November 2, 1927.
55. Ibid., entry dated only Friday, probably August 26, 1927.
56. Ibid., September 25, 1927.
57. Ibid., December 9, 1928.
58. Ruth Crawford, autobiographical data, n.d. SC
59. Sidney Robertson Cowell, letter to the author, January 1, 1975,

and Ruth Crawford, autobiographical data, n.d. SC
60. Ruth Crawford, letter to her mother, November 20, 1921 (SC), and Aurelia Parmenter, letter to the author, February 20, 1972.

CHAPTER FOUR--MacDowell Colony and New York

1. Ruth Crawford, diary entries, July 13 through July 31, 1929. SC
2. Ruth Crawford, diary entry, from a letter to Alice, July 13, 1929. Ruth occasionally included copies of her letters in her diary entries. SC
3. Ruth Crawford, diary entry, August 5, 1929. SC
4. Ibid., July 23, 1929.
5. Ibid., August 16, 1929.
6. Marion Bauer, Twentieth Century Music. New York: G. P. Putnam's Sons, 1933, p. 287.
7. Ruth Crawford, diary entry, August 5, 1929. SC
8. Alfred Frankenstein, taped interview, San Francisco, California, March 1968.
9. "Blanche Walton Dies at 91," The New York Times (July 18, 1963), p. 27, column 5.
10. It may profitably be recalled here that Charles Seeger was one of Cowell's first teachers.
11. Charles Seeger, taped recollections, London, July, 1967.
12. Ruth Crawford, letter to Nicolas Slonimsky, January 29, 1933. SC
13. Charles Seeger, taped interview, March, 1968.
14. See Chapter Eight for a discussion of Seeger's theories of dissonant counterpoint and dissonated melody.
15. Ruth Crawford, letter to Alice, January 20, 1930. SC
16. Ibid., October 17, 1929.
17. Ibid., October 23, 1929.
18. Ibid. Ara refers to Ugo Ara, one-time violist with the Flonzaley String Quartet.
19. Ruth Crawford, diary jottings, February 14, 1930. SC
20. Ibid., February 17, 1930. The work was probably Riegger's Study in Sonority, for 10 violins or multiples of 10 (1927).
21. Ibid., February 27, 1930.
22. Charles Seeger, taped recollections, London, July 1967. This book remains in manuscript.
23. Peter Seeger, taped telephone interview, Beacon, New York, October 2, 1980.
24. Charles Seeger, taped recollections, July 1967.

CHAPTER FIVE--The European Experience

1. Ruth Crawford, diary jottings, August 29, 1930. SC
Ruth does not identify the songs she mentioned. By this

time, she had completed a set of five songs (1929) and had written Rat Riddles, the first of a set of three songs (1930-1932).
2. Ruth Crawford, letter to Charles Seeger, September 8, 1930. SFC
3. Ruth Crawford, letter to Gerald Reynolds, October 11, 1930. New York Public Library.
4. Program, Novembergruppe, April 8, 1931. SC
5. Ruth Crawford, letter to Charles Seeger, n.d., probably November 1930. SFC
6. Groves Dictionary of Music and Musicians, fifth edition, Volume VIII, s.v. "Trautonium."
7. Ruth Crawford, letter to Charles Seeger, n.d., probably November 1930. SFC
8. Baker's Biographical Dictionary. fifth edition, s.v. "Vogel. Wladimir."
9. Ruth Crawford, letter to Charles Seeger, March 17, 1931. SFC
10. Ibid., April 13, 1931.
11. Ibid.
12. Ibid., January 29, 1931.
13. Ibid., April 20, 1931.
14. Ibid., no date, probably July 23, 1931.
15. Ibid., March 1, 1931, and Baker's Biographical Dictionary, fifth edition, s.v. "Feinberg, Samuel."
16. Ruth Crawford, letter to Charles Seeger, May 6, 1931. SFC
17. Ibid.
18. Ruth Crawford, letter to Nicolas Slonimsky, January 29, 1933. SC
19. Ruth Crawford, letter to Charles Seeger, May 8, 1931. SFC
20. Ibid.
21. Ibid.
22. Ibid., May 14, 1931.
23. Ibid.
24. Ibid.
25. Ibid. Seeger himself had earlier encouraged Ruth to try her hand at writing in larger forms.
26. Ruth Crawford, letter to Charles Seeger, May 29, 1931. SFC
27. Ibid.
28. Ibid., June 7, 1931.
29. Charles Seeger, taped recollections, London, July 28, 1967.
30. Charles Seeger, taped interview, Bridgewater, Connecticut, October 8, 1974.
31. Ruth Crawford, letter to Charles Seeger, n.d., probably July 24, 1931. SFC
32. Ibid., October 7, 1931.
33. Ibid., June 12, 1931, and October 18, 1931.
34. Ibid., October 22, 1931.
35. Ibid., October 7, 1931.
36. Ibid., October 23, 1931.

Chapter Notes 229

CHAPTER SIX--Back in New York

1. These headlines appeared in The Musical Courier.
2. Ruth Crawford, letter to Charles Seeger, February 14, 1931. SFC
3. Ibid., October 15, 1931, and October 2, 1931.
4. Margaret Valiant, taped interview, Memphis, Tennessee, May 29, 1980.
5. Field notes: In May 1978 at his home in Bridgewater, Connecticut, Charles Seeger told his daughter Penelope Cohen and the author that after his death he wanted the date and circumstances of his marriage to Ruth known. Ruth Crawford Seeger, Animal Folk Songs for Children. New York: Doubleday, 1950, p. 9.
6. Message from Grace W. Bell, Humboldt County Clerk, Winnemucca, Nevada, 89445, March 12, 1979, to the author.
7. Charles Seeger, letter to Ruth Crawford, April 7, 1931. SFC; Charles Seeger, taped interview, Bridgewater, Connecticut, October 8, 1974.
8. Ruth Crawford, letter to Nicolas Slonimsky, January 29, 1933. SC
9. Ruth Crawford, Three Songs, New Music Edition. San Francisco, 1933. See pp. 157-159 for a discussion of these songs.
10. Ruth Crawford, letter to Charles Seeger, April 20, 1931. SFC
11. Nicolas Slonimsky, letter to Ruth Crawford, March 16, 1932. SC
12. Nicolas Slonimsky, Music Since 1900, fourth edition. New York: Charles Scribner's Sons, 1971, p. 570.
13. Margaret Valiant, taped interview, May 29, 1980.
14. Peter Seeger, taped telephone interview, October 2, 1980.
15. Charles Seeger, taped recollections, Bridgewater, Connecticut, April 22, 1977.
16. Eric Salzman, Twentieth-Century Music: An Introduction, second edition. Englewood Cliffs, N.J.: Prentice-Hall, Inc., 1974, p. 135.
17. Charles Seeger, taped interview, Bridgewater, Connecticut, October 7, 1974.
18. Charles Seeger, "On Proletarian Music," in Modern Music, March/April 1934, p. 121-127; and Baker's Biographical Dictionary of Musicians, fifth edition, s.v. "Degeyter, Pierre."
19. Barbara Zuck, A History of Musical Americanism. Ann Arbor, Mich.: UMI Research Press, 1980, p. 113.
20. Charles Seeger, taped recollections, July 28, 1967.
21. David King Dunaway, "Unsung Songs of Protest: The Composers Collective of New York," New York Folklore Quarterly (January 19, 1979), p. 9.
22. Ruth Crawford, autobiographical information, n.d. Lists of performances. SC
23. Charles Seeger, letter to the author, March 13, 1974. A ver-

sion by Charles appears in David King Dunaway, "Charles Seeger and Carl Sands: The Composer's Collective Years," Ethnomusicology (May 1980), p. 166; a version by Ruth may be found in the Seeger Collection.
24. Charles Seeger, taped interview, Santa Monica, California, March 20, 1968.
25. Zuck, A History of Musical Americanism, p. 112.
26. Howard Cushman, "A Woman Composer Considers 'Mode[rn Music],'" unidentified newspaper, Monday, November 13, 1933.
27. Charles Seeger, taped recollections, London, July 28, 1967.
28. Charles Seeger, taped recollections, Bridgewater, Connecticut, April 22, 1977.
29. Liner notes, Saturday Night at the Benton's, Decca Album A-311, p. 4.
30. Margaret Valiant, taped interview, May 29, 1980.
31. Ibid.
32. Charles Seeger, taped interview, October 7, 1974.
33. Ann M. Pescatello, "Charles (Louis) Seeger," in The New Grove Dictionary of Music and Musicians. London: Macmillan Publishers Limited, 1980, vol. 17, p. 101.
34. Ruth Crawford, diary jottings, February 22, 1930. SC
35. Charles Seeger, autobiographical data, 1962. SC
36. The New Grove, vol. 17, p. 101.
37. Encyclopaedia of Social Sciences, editor-in-chief, Edwin R. A. Seligman. New York: Macmillan, 1933, vol. 11, p. 143ff. The associate editor of this work was Alvin Johnson, then director of the New School for Social Research, New York City.
38. Ruth Crawford Seeger, letter to Dr. McCandlish, January 2 (probably 1936). SC
39. Charles Seeger, taped interview, Bridgewater, Connecticut, October 8, 1974.

CHAPTER SEVEN--Life and Death in Washington, D.C.

1. Ruth Crawford Seeger, letter to Dr. McCandlish, January 2, probably 1936. SC
2. Chapter Nine is devoted to a discussion of Ruth Crawford Seeger's folk music activities.
3. Charles Seeger, taped interview, Bridgewater, Connecticut, October 7, 1974.
4. Ibid.
5. Ibid.
6. Cornelius B. Canon, "The Federal Music Project of the Works Progress Administration: Music in a Democracy." Ph.D. dissertation, University of Minnesota, 1963, p. 250.
7. Baker's Biographical Dictionary of Musicians, fifth edition, p. 1490, s.v. "Seeger, Charles."
8. Charles Seeger, interview, Bridgewater, Connecticut, May 21, 1978.

Chapter Notes

9. Charles Seeger, taped interview, Bridgewater, Connecticut, October 8, 1974.
10. Peggy Seeger, taped recollections, Kent, England, April, 1976.
11. Kathy Shimberg, letters to the author, December 8, 1983, and January 1, 1986.
12. Charles Miller, taped interview, Washington, D.C., January 5, 1980.
13. Peggy Seeger, taped recollections, April, 1976.
14. Harriet L. Tynes, a sister of Margaret Fairley, in a letter to Charles Miller, January 10, 1980. Margaret Fairley was a close associate of Ruth during the nursery school years and a good friend for many years after.
15. Ruth Crawford Seeger, Diary of a "Corporating" Mother, August 29, 1941. SC
16. Ibid., August 20 and August 25, 1941.
17. Silver Spring Nursery School Newsletter, December 1950-February 1951, mimeographed sheet. SC
18. Sidney Robertson Cowell, letter to the author, January 1, 1975.
19. Marion Bauer, letter to Ruth Crawford Seeger, March 2, 1936. SC
20. Radiana Pazmor, letter to Ruth Crawford Seeger, February 22, 1937. SC
21. H. J. Koellreutter, letter to Ruth Crawford Seeger, September 4, 1942. SC
22. Wallingford Riegger, letter to Ruth Crawford Seeger, June 23, 1945. SC
23. Barbara Zuck, A History of Musical Americanism, p. 168.
24. The complete text of this interview is found in Chapter Ten, pp. 201-205.
25. Ruth Crawford Seeger, letter to Carl Sandburg, April 7, 1947. SC
26. Ruth Crawford Seeger, letter to Edgard Varèse, May 29, 1948. See Chapter Ten, pp. 212-215, for complete text of this important letter. SC
27. Ruth Crawford Seeger, letter to Miss Prink, September 30, 1940. See Chapter Ten, pp. 208-212, for excerpts from this letter. SC
28. Ruth Crawford, diary entry, August 1, 1929. SC
29. Peggy Seeger, taped recollections, April, 1976.
30. Michael Seeger, letter to the author, August 9, 1984.
31. B.A.B., Book Review of American Folk Songs for Christmas by Ruth Crawford Seeger, in New York Folklore Quarterly (Spring 1954), pp. 73-4.
32. Ruth Crawford Seeger, copy of a letter to Katherine and Carl Crawford, November 14, 1950. SC
33. Peggy Seeger, taped recollections, April 1976.
34. Washington Post (Friday, November 20, 1953), p. 32. SC
35. Sidney Robertson Cowell, "Ruth Crawford Seeger," International Folk Music Journal, vol. VII (1955), pp. 55-56. SC
36. Ruth Crawford, diary entry, March 25, 1928. SC

37. Charles Seeger, taped interview, October 7, 1974.
38. Charles Seeger, letter to the author, London, April 7 1967.

CHAPTER EIGHT--The Art Music

1. Faubion Bowers, Scriabin. Tokyo and Palo Alto, Calif.: Kodansha International Ltd., 1969, vol. 2, p. 187.
2. Ruth Crawford, letter to Charles Seeger, April 20, 1931. SFC
3. Rudhyar D. Chenneviere, "The Rise of the Musical Proletariat," The Musical Quarterly, vol. 6, no. 4 (October 1920), pp. 500-509.
4. Martha Beck Carragan, letter to the author, September 5, 1983.
5. Edward Burlingame Hill, "Young Composers Movement," Modern Music, IV, no. 4 (May-June 1929), pp. 32-34.
6. Ruth Crawford, diary entry, November 12, 1928. SC
7. Ibid., October 28, 1928.
8. A manuscript copy of a Sonata for Violin and Piano, violin part only, dated 1925, is extant. It is practically identical to the full score manuscript which Crawford did not date. Presumably she worked on the sonata during 1925 and 1926. SC
9. Musical Courier (February 13, 1927).
10. Chicago Journal (February 9, 1928).
11. Ruth Crawford, diary entry, February 9, 1928. SC
12. Ruth Crawford, autobiographical material, n.d., probably around 1948. SC
13. Vivian Fine, letters to the author, February 24, 1983, November 21, 1985, and December 9, 1985.
14. Ruth Crawford, letters to Alice, from October 17, 1929, through January 24, 1930. Mrs. Walton was Ruth's patroness during her year in New York. SC
15. Ruth Crawford, diary entry, August 27, 1927. SC
16. Ibid., September 5, 1927.
17. Charles Seeger, taped recollections, London, July 28, 1967.
18. Charles Seeger, taped interview, Santa Monica, California, March 19, 1968.
19. The title of this work implies that Ruth had written a Suite No. 1 for Piano and Strings; however, other than being listed among her compositions in the Music of the Americas, vol. 2, p. 38, as Quintet for Piano and Strings, there is no trace of any such work.
20. The quotation above and the following discussion were taken from a taped interview by the author with Charles Seeger, Santa Monica, California, March 19, 1968. The article, "On Dissonant Counterpoint," written by Seeger and appearing in Modern Music (June-July 1930), p. 25-31, provides a good presentation of the subject, an article which Ruth doubtless read.
21. Charles Seeger, taped interview, Bridgewater, Connecticut, October 6, 1974.
22. Charles Seeger, taped interview, Santa Monica, March 18, 1968.

Chapter Notes   233

23. Ruth Crawford, letter to Charles Seeger, September 20, 1930. SFC
24. Charles Seeger, Tradition and Experiment in Twentieth Century Music, Preface, p. iv. The manuscript for this book in the Music Division of the Library of Congress bears no title page. Seeger referred to it by the title above in taped recollections prepared for the author, London, July, 1967.
25. Charles Seeger, letter to the author, January 6, 1979.
26. Willi Apel, Harvard Dictionary of Music, second edition. Cambridge: Belknap Press of Harvard University Press, 1969, p. 231. The numbering used by the author is that assigned to the four suites by A. Broude when they were published in 1972. In her original manuscript, Ruth numbered them as follows:
    1) bassoon and cello (or two celli)
    2) two B-flat clarinets
    3) solo flute (or oboe)
    4) oboe and cello (or viola and cello)
    A letter from Edward N. Waters, Assistant Chief of the Reference Department, Music Division, Library of Congress, dated November 27, 1967, to the author, states that Crawford herself changed the numbering of the suite for solo flute from No. 3 to No. 1 when it was first published in New Music, April 1953.
27. Charles Seeger, letter to Ruth Crawford, n.d. probably around March 1, 1931. SFC
28. Ruth Crawford, letter to Charles Seeger, April 4, 1931. SFC
29. Edward Ansel Mowrer, "Music in Berlin," Daily News (April 9, 1931). SC
30. "Das Opus einer Dame, 'Diaphonic Suite' für Bratsche und Cello von Ruth Crawford, wirkt deshalb so blutleer, weil eine völlig belanglose musikalische Substanz verarbeitet wird." Translated by Garrett Welch from an article in the Morgen Post by Friedrich Deutsch, Berlin (April 14, 1931). SC
31. Enlightening comments on these works are found in American Composers on American Music, edited by Henry Cowell, in the article on Ruth Crawford by Charles Seeger.
32. Frederick Jacobi, letter to Ruth Crawford, June 18, 1933. SC
33. Nicolas Slonimsky, letter to Ruth Crawford, March 16, 1932. Apparently the singer performed both Rat Riddles and In Tall Grass. SC
34. Musical America (May 25, 1933). SC
35. Henry Beckett, New York City Post (May 8, 1931). SC
36. Edward Cushing, Brooklyn Daily Eagle (May 8, 1931). SC
37. Ruth Crawford, letter to Charles Seeger, n.d., probably October 1930. SFC
38. Ruth Crawford, letter to Gerald Reynolds, n.d., probably late 1930. New York Public Library.
39. Ruth Crawford, letter to Gerald Reynolds, November 10, 1930. NYPL

40. Charles Seeger, letter to Ruth Crawford, November 1, 1930. SFC
41. Record review, signed H. K. in Trend (March 1934). SC
42. George Grossman, "Third Meeting," Dynamics (April 19, 1934). SC
43. Virgil Thomson, New York Herald Tribune (March 16, 1949). SC. This movement has been reprinted in the Norton Scores: An Anthology for Listening, 3rd ed. New York: W. W. Norton Co., 1977, 2:747-50.
44. Charles Seeger, "Ruth Crawford," ACAM, p. 115.
45. Review signed O. H. in the Philadelphia Ledger (March 28, 1933). SC
46. Ruth Crawford Seeger, letter to Edgard Varèse, May 19, 1948. SC

CHAPTER NINE--Folk Music Activities

1. Carl Sandburg, The American Songbag. New York: Harcourt Brace Jovanovich, 1927, 1955, p. ix.
2. Charles Seeger, taped interview, Bridgewater, Connecticut, October 7, 1974.
3. Autobiographical information says 24 American Folk Tunes; the extant manuscript of the title page reads 22 American Folk Tunes; however, only nineteen of these survive in manuscript. SC
4. This set of piano pieces is scheduled for publication by A. Broude in 1986.
5. Charles Seeger, taped interview, October 7, 1974.
6. Alan Lomax, taped telephone interview with the author, December 30, 1985.
7. John Lomax, Adventures of A Ballad Hunter. New York: Macmillan Company, 1947, p. 296.
8. Charles Seeger, taped interview, October 7, 1974.
9. Ruth Crawford Seeger, "Music Preface," in Our Singing Country, John A. and Alan Lomax. New York: Macmillan Company, 1941, p. xix.
10. Ibid., pp. xixff.
11. Unfortunately, copyright difficulties preclude the use of musical examples from Our Singing Country as well as from Folk Song U.S.A. Readers may refer to those works themselves.
12. Ruth Crawford Seeger, letter to Charles Seeger, October 26, 1938. SFC
13. In one of her autobiographical resumes, Ruth gives the complete title of this work as Rissolty, Rossolty: An American Fantasy for Orchestra. SC
14. Alan Lomax, taped telephone interview, December 30, 1985.
15. Charles Seeger, letter to the author, Bridgewater, Connecticut, September 5, 1971.
16. Charles and Ruth Seeger, "Musical Foreword," in Folk Song U.S.A., John A. and Alan Lomax. New York: Duell, Sloan

and Pearce, Inc., 1947, pp. xiv-xviii.
17. In his interview of March 10, 1968, with the author, Charles Seeger stated that Ruth was responsible for the setting of Go Down, Moses.
18. Michael Seeger, letter to the author, August 9, 1984.
19. Ruth Crawford Seeger, letter to Edgard Varèse, May 29, 1948. SC
20. Ibid.
21. Peggy Seeger, taped recollections, July 22, 1977.

CHAPTER TEN--Selected Writings

1. Throughout these jottings Ruth often mentions names not widely known; for example, Alma Wertheim, well-known patroness of music in New York, and the Pro Arte, a prominent string quartet of the time. Jeanne de Mare was a casual friend in both New York and Europe; her name appears in the New Music Edition of the Three Songs (Carl Sandburg) as translator of the words into French. Oscar Ziegler and Teresa Carreño were concert pianists, Joseph Yasser was a theorist and musicologist, probably best known for his book A Theory of Evolving Tonality (1932), and Carl Buchman was a composer whom Ruth had met at the MacDowell Colony. Bernard Wagenaar, Emerson Whithorne, Werner Josten, and Joseph Achron were all well-known composers at the time of Ruth's New York sojourn.
2. Ruth Porter was a name Ruth often used in her fictional writing. Her paternal grandmother's maiden name was Porter.
3. Dio is a family name for Ruth.

CATALOG OF MUSIC

The works are listed in order of composition within each of three groups. Art Music contains the following categories: Small Orchestra, Chamber Music, Piano Solo, Songs with Piano Accompaniment, and Choral Music. Early Works include entries for Chamber Music, Piano Solos, Songs with Piano Accompaniment, and Arrangements of Works by Others. Folk Music publications are listed chronologically and identified as Accompaniments, Arrangements, or Transcriptions.

All extant manuscripts are housed in the Music Division of the Library of Congress, Washington, D.C., and are available for reproduction, if requests are accompanied by any necessary permissions. The entire collection is also available on microfilm. For printed editions, see individual catalog entries. Publishers of art music are noted in the entries by the following abbreviations:

- AB   Alexander Broude, Inc., 575 Eighth Avenue, New York, N.Y. 10018
- CM   Continuo Music Press, New York (A. Broude, Inc., sole agent)
- MM   Merion Music, Inc., Bryn Mawr, Pa. (Theodore Presser, sole representative)
- NM   New Music Edition (available through Theodore Presser)
- SP   Soundings Press, P.O. Box 8319, Santa Fe, N.M. 87504-8317
- TP   Theodore Presser Company, Bryn Mawr, Pa. 19010

Catalog information for each entry (where known) includes the following: 1) Catalog number; 2) Year of composition; 3) Title; 4) Titles of tempi of pieces or movements within the work; 5) In parenthesis: city of publication, name of publisher, date of publication, and repeat for any recent in-print reissue; 6) Premier performances; 7) "R" alerts reader to look under Discography for recordings; 8) One asterisk preceding the title indicates a work well received or much played in the composer's life; 9) Two asterisks indicate its suitability for today's repertoires; 10) A "p" or "s" beside asterisks indicates interest to professionals or students; 11) Durations cited are either for the whole work, and/or for each movement or piece.

Catalog of Music 237

ART MUSIC

Small Orchestra

1. 1926. p-s**Suite for Small Orchestra, 1) Slow, pensive, 2) Tempo indication illegible, but looks like fast; premiers: Canyon, Texas, December 1969, West Texas State University; N.Y.C., February 19, 1975, Ruth Crawford Seeger Retrospective Concert; R; time, 7:42; ms. score only in Wc.

2. 1931. **String Quartet, Third Movement, Andante. The printed editions state "The third movement of this quartet, Andante, can be performed separately by string orchestra, which includes double bass. Parts are available on rental." See Catalog No. 13.

3. probably 1938-1940. p-s**Rissolty, Rossolty: An American Fantasy for Orchestra, based on American folk tunes; premier: probably January 1941, on CBS "School of the Air"; time, 3:45; ms. score and parts R 1, it. 6 in Wc. See Catalog No. 52.

Chamber Music

4. 1925-6. p**Sonata for Violin and Piano, 1) Agitated--vibrant--andante lusingando, 2) Buoyant, 3) Mystic--intense, 4) Fast, with bold energy; (pub. TP, 1985); premiers: Chicago, Ruth Lilien Parker, vln. and Ruth Crawford, piano, May 22, 1926, New York, Joseph Stopak, vln. and Irene Jacobi, piano, 1927, Washington, D.C., Library of Congress, Coolidge Auditorium, November 1982, Ida Kafavian, vln. and Vivian Fine, piano; R; time, 15:28; ms. piano and vln. parts in Wc, R 1, it. 7.

5. 1927; rev. 1929. Suite for Five Wind Instruments and Piano, Intro) Adagio religioso, 1) Giocoso--allegro non troppo, 2) Andante tristo, 3) Allegro con brio--brilliante-andante religioso; premier: New York, January 1930, musicale at home of Blanche Walton, played by the Pan American Ensemble; time, 12:00; ms. score only in Wc.

6. 1929. p**Suite No. 2 for Piano and Strings, 1) Lento, 2) Leggiero, 3) Allegro energico; premier: New York, January 1930, musicale at home of Blanche Walton, played by the New World Quartet and Colin McPhee, piano; R; time, 9:45; ms. score and parts in Wc, R 1.2, it. 11.

7. Feb. 1930. Diaphonic Suite No. 2, bsn. and cello, 1) Freely, 2) Andante cantando, 3) Con brio; (pub. CM, 1972); R; time, 3:57.

8. Mar. 1930. Diaphonic Suite No. 3, 2 B flat clarinets, 1) Tranquillo, 2) Giocoso, 3) Moderato; (pub. CM, 1972); time, 3:20.

9. 1930. p**Diaphonic Suite No. 1, unaccompanied flute (oboe), 1) Scherzando, 2) Andante, 3) Allegro, 4) Moderato, ritmico; (pub. Montevideo, Boletin Latin-Americano de Musica, Vol. 1, Suplemento Musical, 1941); NM, 1954; CM, 1972. premier: N.Y. March 1, 1931, Frances Blaisdell, flute, League of Composers concert; R; time, 5:00.

10. Dec. 1930. Diaphonic Suite No. 4, oboe (viola) and cello, 1) Moderato, 2) Andante cantando, 3) Scherzando ritmico; (pub. CM, 1972); premier: Berlin, April 8, 1931, Hans Wigand, viola, and Hermann Weil, cello; time, 8:00.

11. Mar. 1930. p**Rat Riddles (Three Songs to poems of Carl Sandburg, for contralto, oboe, piano and perc. with optional wind and string ostinati); (pub. NM Orchestra Series, 1933); premier: N.Y. April 21, 1930, Radiana Pazmor, soloist, Pan American Association of Composers, Carnegie Chamber Hall; R; time, 3:25. NM Edition states "a transcription of the ostinati for piano or mixed chorus is available."

12. Jan. 1931. p**In Tall Grass (Three Songs to poems of Carl Sandburg, for contralto, oboe, piano and perc. with optional wind and string ostinati); (pub. NM Orchestra Series, 1933); premier: N.Y. probably 1932, Radiana Pazmor, soloist, Pan American Association of Composers, New School for Social Research; R; time, 4:05.

13. 1931. p**String Quartet, 1) Rubato assai, 2) Leggiero, 3) Andante, 4) Allegro possibile; (pub. NM, Jan. 1941; MM, 1941); premier: N.Y. Nov. 13, 1933, New World String Quartet, Pan American Association of Composers; R; time, 9:47; ms. score and parts in Wc R 1.2, it. 8. See Catalog No. 2 above.

14. Nov. 1932. p**Prayers of Steel (Three Songs to poems of Carl Sandburg, for contralto, oboe, piano and perc. with optional wind and string ostinati); pub. NM Orch. Series, 1933); premier of Prayers of Steel and of the Three Songs as a set: Amsterdam, June 15, 1933, ISCM Festival, Hans Gruys, alto, Jaap Stotijn, oboe, Felix de Nobel, piano, Chr. Smit, perc., Frederick Jacobi, conductor, at the Amsterdam Conservatorium Bachzaal; R; time, 1:50; ms. for the Three Songs in Wc; also scores and parts for Rat Riddles, R 1.4, it. 35a, Prayers of Steel, R 1.4, it. 35h and i, In Tall Grass, R 1.35, it. 35j.

15. 1952. p**Suite for Wind Quintet, 1) Allegretto, 2) Lento rubato, 3) Allegro possibile; score and parts pub. AB, 1969); premier: Wash. D.C., Dec. 2, 1952, National Woodwind Quintet; R; time, 11:00, ms. score and parts in Wc R 1.2, it. 10.

16. n.d. Fragment (1 page); clarinet, bsn. and piano; ms. in Wc.

Piano Solos

17. 1924-1925. p-s**Five Preludes for Piano, 1) Andante, 2) With subtle, sparkling humor, 3) Simply, wistfully, 4) Grave, mesto, 5) Adagio; premier: N.Y., Dec. 12, 1925, Gitta Gradova at Town Hall; R; time, 7:40 (0.50, 1:00, 2:05, 2:20, 1:25); ms. in Wc.

18. 1925. Adventures of Tom Thumb (with narrator) words probably adapted from Grimm Brothers by Ruth Crawford); 1) Tom Sets Out, 2) Tom's First Adventure: Chased by the Angry Tailor's Wife, 3) Tom Steals the King's Dollars, 4) Tom Sleeps, 5) Tom Meets the Mouse: They Gallop Home, 6) Tom Recounts His Adventures; premier: no public performance recorded. The composer probably played parts of this work for musical soirees held at Mme. Herz's studio, Chicago, and at the MacDowell Colony, Regina Watkins Hall; time, 11:00; ms. in Wc.

19. 1927-1928. p-s**Four Preludes for Piano, 1) Andante mystico, 2) Intensivo, 3) Leggiero, 4) Tranquillo; (pub. NM Oct. 1928; Bryn Mawr, TP, 1985); Wc has ms. for No. 6 only; whereabouts of Nos. 7, 8, 9, not known; premier: probably N.Y., May 6, 1928, Richard Buhlig, piano, at a Copland-Sessions concert; R; time, 9:55 (2:01, 1:56, 2:24, 3:08).

20. Dec. 1930. p**Piano Study in Mixed Accents; (pub. NM, Oct. 1932; Bryn Mawr, TP, 1984); location of ms. not known; premier: not known. Played in N.Y., May 5, 1966, by Paul Jacobs on Composers' Showcase program; R; time, 1:05.

Songs with Piano Accompaniment

21. 1929. p**Five Songs (poems of Carl Sandburg), 1) Home Thoughts, 2) White Moon, 3) Joy, 4) Loam, 5) Sunsets; premier: N.Y. Jan. 1930, musicale at home of Blanche Walton, Radiana Pazmor, voice, Ruth Crawford, piano, also N.Y., 1930, for League of Composers concert; time, 9:00 (2:00, 2:00, 1:10, 1:50, 2:00) ms. in Wc.

22. 1932. Two Songs (poems of H. T. Tsiang), 1) Sacco, Vanzetti, 2) Chinaman, Laundryman: (pub. SP Soundings 7-8, OP, 1973: MM 1973); premier: N.Y. 1933, Radiana Pazmor, for Workers Music Olympiad; time, 7:30 (4:30, 3:00), ms. in Wc.

Choral Works

23. 1930. To an Unkind God (Three Chants); text consists of meaningless phonemes by Ruth Crawford; no public performance recorded; time, 2:40; ms. in Wc.

24. 1930. p**Chant, 1930 (To an Angel) (Three Chants); text consists of meaningless phonemes by Ruth Crawford; (pub. AB, 1971); premier: N.Y., May 7, 1931, Women's University Glee Club, cond. Gerald Reynolds in Town Hall; R; time, 2:30.

25. 1930. Untitled (Three Chants); text consists of meaningless phonemes by Ruth Crawford; no public performance recorded; time, 3:25; ms. in Wc.

EARLY WORKS

Chamber Music

26. 1923. Nocturne for Violin and Piano; class assignment?; time, 2:00; ms. in Wc.

27. n.d. Untitled, for Violin and Piano; p. and v. score plus vln. score; class assignment?; time, 2:50; ms. score and parts in Wc R 1.2, it. 12.

28. n.d. Fugue, for four voices; string quartet; class assignment?; time, 1:35; ms. in Wc.

29. n.d. Fugue Theme (same as Catalog No. 28); treated in free style for piano or close-score string quartet; class assignment?; time 1:00; ms. in Wc.

Piano Solos

30. n.d. s**Little Lullaby; teaching piece; time, 1:10; ms. in Wc.

31. n.d. s**Whirligig: Study in Triplets; teaching piece; time, 1:20; ms. in Wc.

32. n.d. s**Jumping the Rope; teaching piece, "to Jane Whitman"; also titled Playtime in another ms.; time, 1:25; ms. in Wc.

33. n.d. s**Mr. Crow and Miss Wren Go for a Walk (A Little Study in Short Trills); teaching piece; time, 1:20; ms. in Wc.

34. n.d. s**Caprice; teaching piece; time, 2:15; ms. in Wc.

35. n.d. s**Playtime; teaching piece; "to Jane Whitman"; also titled Jumping the Rope in another ms.; time, 1:25; ms. in Wc.

36. 1922. s**Little Waltz; teaching piece; time, 1:20; ms. in Wc.

37. 1923. Theme and Variations; class assignment?; time, 11:00; ms. in Wc.

Catalog of Music 241

38. 1923. Sonata, first movement; class assignment?; time, 7:10; ms. in Wc.

39. 1924. Five Canons, 1) Canon in Fifth, 2) Canon in Octave, 3) Canon in Lower Fifth, 4) Canon in Octave, 5) Canon in Lower Sixth; class assignment?; time, 4:30 (1:10, 0:40, 1:25, 0:25, 1:00); ms. in Wc.

40. 1924. p**Kaleidoscopic Changes on an Original Theme, Ending with a Fugue; premier: Chicago, May 31, 1924, Ruth Crawford, piano, Kimball Hall recital of Adolf Weidig's composition students; class assignment?; time, 11:00; ms. in Wc.

41. probably 1926. We Dance Together; teaching piece; "to Dorothy Sinnott"; (pub. Chicago, 1926, self-published?); time, 1:10. copy in Wc.

Songs with Piano Accompaniment

42. 1923. Two Songs (poems of Sara Teasdale), 1) To One Away, 2) Return; class assignment?; time, 2:00 (1:15, 0:45); ms. in Wc.

43. n.d. Joy (poem of Sara Teasdale); class assignment?; time, 1:00; ms. in Wc.

44. n.d. To Night (poem of Louisa C. Moulton); class assignment?; time, 0:55; ms. in Wc.

45. n.d. A Russian Lullaby (poem of Louis Untermeyer); class assignment?; time, 2:00; ms. in Wc.

46. n.d. Lolipop a Papa (words and music by Fred Karlan, pseudonym for Ruth Crawford); popular song; copyright by Ruth Porter Crawford; time, 1:20; ms. in Wc.

47. n.d. Untitled (words and music by Fred Karlan, pseudonym for Ruth Crawford); popular song; time, 1:20; ms. in Wc.

Arrangements of Works by Others

48. 1924. E Minor Fugue from Bach WTC, I, No. 8; arr. for vln., vla., and cello; class assignment?; time, 3:20; ms. in Wc.

49. n.d. Sonata, Op. 2, No. 2, Largo, Beethoven; arr. for str. orch.; class assignment?; time, 5:30; ms. in Wc.

FOLK MUSIC

Accompaniments, Arrangements, Transcriptions

50. 1927. American Songbag (Carl Sandburg); 4 piano accompaniments: 1) Those Gambler's Blues, 2) Lonesome Road, 3) There Was an Old Soldier, 4) Ten Thousand Miles Away from Home; (pub. N.Y. Harcourt Brace and Co.)

51. 1936-1938. s**Twenty-two American Folk Tunes, arr. for piano elem. grades, ms. has only 19 settings; 1) Turtle Dove, 2) The Old Gray Mare, 3) The Babes in the Wood, 4) Charlie's Sweet, 5) Mammy Loves, 6) Lord Thomas, 7) London's Bridge, 8) The Gray Goose, 9) The Boll Weevil, 10) The Higher Up the Cherry Tree, 11) What'll We Do with the Baby?, 12) I Ride an Old Paint, 13) Billy Boy, 14) The Three Ravens, 15) Ground Hog, 16) Sweet Betsy from Pike, 17) Frog Went a Courtin', 18) Cindy, 19) Darby's Ram; (N.Y., AB, in press); ms. contains notes and a foreword by Ruth Crawford Seeger.

52. probably 1938-1940. p-s**Rissolty, Rossolty, See Catalog No. 3 above for details.

53. 1941. Our Singing Country (John A. and Alan Lomax); 205 transcriptions; pub. N.Y. The Macmillan Co.)

54. 1943. Coal Dust on the Fiddle (George Korson); 13 transcriptions; Ruth Crawford Seeger, music editor; (pub. Phila., U. of Pa. Press)

55. 1947. Folk Song U.S.A. (John A. and Alan Lomax); 111 songs; piano arrangements by Charles and Ruth Crawford Seeger, music editors; (pub. Duell, Sloan and Pearce)

56. 1948. American Folk Songs for Children; 96 piano arrangements for school and home use; (pub. Garden City, Doubleday and Co.); R.

57. 1949. Anthology of Pennsylvania Folklore (George Korson); music editor; (pub. Phila., U. of Pa. Press).

58. 1950. Animal Folk Songs for Children; 56 piano arrangements for school and home use; (pub. Garden City, Doubleday and Co.)

59. 1951. Treasury of Western Folklore (B.A. Botkin); 32 transcriptions with suggested chord letters for possible acc.; (pub. N.Y., Crown Publishers, Inc.)

60. 1953. American Folk Songs for Christmas; 65 piano arrange-

Catalog of Music   243

ments for school and home use; (pub. Garden City, Doubleday and Co.)

61. 1954. Let's Build a Railroad; 6 arrangements; (pub. N.Y., Aladdin Books).

62. 1955. Folklore Infantil do Santo Domingo (Edna Garrido Boggs); transcriptions; (pub. Madrid, Ediciones Cultura Hispanica).

63. n.d. 1001 Songs; Ruth and Charles Seeger, with Duncan Emrich; folk songs, melodies and words only; never completed; ms. in Wc.

ADDITIONAL FOLK MUSIC ARTICLES
BY RUTH CRAWFORD SEEGER

Most of Ruth Crawford Seeger's professional writing is concerned with and contained in the introductory materials she wrote for the books of folk songs she compiled or for which she acted as music editor. A few additional titles follow.

1. Rough typescript of a long introduction for Our Singing Country, approx. 60 pages. Lacks about a dozen music examples. ca. 1941. Unpublished. (Wc)

2. Work, John N., comp. and arr. American Negro Songs for Mixed Voices. Philadelphia: Theodore Presser Co., 1948, 259p. Reviewed by Ruth Crawford Seeger in Notes (December 1948), pp. 172-3.

3. Seeger, Ruth Crawford, "Keep the Song Going!" NEA Journal (February 1951), p. 93-95.

4. Transcript of demonstration-lecture titled Pre-School Children and American Folk Songs, given for a group of educators, time and place unknown (probably 1952-1953, in Washington, D.C.) (Wc?) (published?).

5. Thompson, Stith, ed. Four Symposia on Folklore. Westport, Conn.: Greenwood Press, 1976. (Reprint of the edition published by Indiana University Press, Bloomington; issued as No. 8 of Indiana University publications, Folklore series, 1953.) Pages 191-194 contain comments by Ruth Crawford Seeger on Symposium III, Making Folklore Available.

DISCOGRAPHY

American Folk Songs for Children (1948). Somerville, Mass.: Rounder Records, 1977, 8001/8002/8003.

Chant (1930). New York: Vox, 1979, SVBX-5353.

Diaphonic Suite No. 1, with oboe solo. New York: CRI, 1980, S-423.

Diaphonic Suite No. 2, with bassoon and cello. Nashville: Gasparo, 1981, GS 108CX.

Nine Preludes for Piano (1924-28). New York: CRI, 1968, S-247; Columbus, Ohio: Coronet Records, 1983, 3121.

Piano Study in Mixed Accents. New York: CRI, 1968, S-247; Boston: Northeastern Records, 1981, NR 204, cassette SQN 79062; Columbus, Ohio: Coronet Records, 1983, 3121.

Preludes for Piano, nos. 6-9 (1927-28). Boston: Northeastern Records, 1981, NR 204, cassette SQN 79062.

Sonata for Violin and Piano (1925-26). New York: CRI, 1984, SD 508.

String Quartet, Andante only. New York: New Music Quarterly Records, 1934.

String Quartet. New York: Columbia, 1960, ML 5477; New York: Nonesuch, 1973, 71280; Nashville: Gasparo, 1980, 205.

Suite No. 2 for 4 Strings and Piano (1929). New York: New World Records, 1984, NW 319.

Suite for Wind Quintet. New York: CRI, 1970, SD-249.

Three Songs for contralto, oboe, piano, and percussion. New York: New World Records, 1978, NW 285.

Three Songs for mezzo-soprano, oboe, piano and percussion. New York: CRI, 1984, SD-501.

Two Movements for Chamber Orchestra. Pacific Palisades, Calif.: Delos, 1975, 25405.

BIBLIOGRAPHY

BOOKS

Allen, Frederick Lewis. Only Yesterday. New York: Harper and Row, 1931; reprint ed., New York: Perennial Library Edition, 1964.

──────. Since Yesterday. New York: Harper and Row, 1939; reprint ed., New York: Perennial Library Edition, 1972.

Baigell, Matthew. Thomas Hart Benton. New York: Harry N. Abrams, n.d.

Bauer, Marion. Twentieth Century Music. New York: G. P. Putnam's Sons, 1933.

Botkin, Ben A. "Folklore as a Neglected Source of Social History," in The Cultural Approach to History. Edited by Carolyn F. Ware (for the American Historical Association). New York: Columbia University Press, 1940, pp. 308-315.

──────, ed. A Treasury of Western Folklore. New York: Crown, 1951.

Bowers, Faubion. Scriabin. 2 vols. Tokyo and Palo Alto, Calif.: Kodansha International, 1969.

──────. The New Scriabin. New York: St. Martin's Press, 1973.

Brand, Oscar. The Ballad Mongers. New York: Funk and Wagnalls, 1962.

Cage, John. Silence. Middletown, Conn.: Wesleyan University Press, 1961.

Chase, Gilbert. The American Composer Speaks. [Baton Rouge]: Louisiana State University Press, 1966.

──────. America's Music. 2nd ed. New York: McGraw-Hill, 1966.

Cole, Rossetter G. "Adolf Weidig," in Dictionary of American Biography. Edited by Dumas Malone. Vol. X. New York: Charles Scribner's Sons, 1936.

Composers of the Americas. Vol. 2. Washington, D.C.: Pan-American Union, 1956; Ruth Crawford Seeger, pp. 36-40.

Cowell, Henry. American Composers on American Music: A Symposium. Palo Alto, Calif.: Stanford University Press, 1933; reprint ed., New York: Frederick Ungar, 1962.

Dedmon, Emmett. Fabulous Chicago. New York: Random House, 1953.

Denisoff, R. Serge. Great Day Coming: Folk Music and the American Left. Urbana: University of Illinois Press, 1971.

Drinker, Sophie. Music and Women. New York: Coward-McCann, 1948.

Dunaway, David King. How Can I Keep from Singing: Pete Seeger. New York: McGraw-Hill, 1981.

Ekirch, A. A., Jr. Ideologies and Utopias: The Impact of the New Deal on American Thought. Chicago: Quadrangle Books, 1969.

Goldston, Robert. The Great Depression: The United States in the Thirties. Greenwich, Conn.: Fawcett, 1968.

Gornick, Vivian. The Romance of American Communism. New York: Basic Books, 1977.

Hitchcock, H. Wiley. Music in the United States: A Historical Introduction. Englewood Cliffs, N.J.: Prentice-Hall, 1969.

Howard, John Tasker. Our American Music. New York: Thomas Y. Crowell, 1929.

_____. Our Contemporary Composers. New York: Thomas Y. Crowell, 1941.

Hull, A. Eaglefield. Modern Harmony: Its Explanation and Application. London: Augener, 1914.

Jackson, George Pullen. White Spirituals in the Southern Uplands. Chapel Hill: University of North Carolina Press, 1933; reprint ed., New York: Dover, 1965.

Krummel, D. W.; Geil, Jean; Dyer, Doris J.; and Root, Deane L., eds. Resources of American Music History. Urbana: University of Illinois Press, 1981.

Lomax, John A. Adventures of a Ballad Hunter. New York: Macmillan, 1947.

_____, and Lomax, Alan. American Ballads and Folk Songs. New York: Macmillan, 1934.

_____, and _____. Our Singing Country. New York: Macmillan, 1941.

_____, and _____. Folk Song U.S.A. New York: Duell, Sloan and Pearce, 1947; reprint ed., New York: Signet Books, 1966.

Mangione, Jerry. The Dream and the Deal: The Federal Writers' Project, 1935-1943. New York: Little, Brown, 1972.

Mead, Rita. Henry Cowell's New Music 1925-1936. Ann Arbor, Mich.: UMI Research Press, 1981.

Mitgang, Herbert, ed. The Letters of Carl Sandburg. New York: Harcourt Brace and World, 1968.

Neuls-Bates, C., and Block, A. F., comps. and eds. Women in American Music: A Bibliography of Music and Literature. Westport, Conn.: Greenwood Press, 1979.

Neuls-Bates, Carol, ed. Women in Music: An Anthology of Source Readings from the Middle Ages to the Present. New York: Harper and Row, 1982.

Olson, Tillie. Silences. Chicago: Delacorte, 1978.

Perle, George. Serial Composition and Atonality. Berkeley: University of California Press, 1962.

Reis, Claire. Composers in America. New York: Macmillan, 1938.

_____. Composers, Conductors, and Critics. New York: Oxford University Press, 1955.

Rosenfeld, Paul. Musical Portraits. First published in 1920; reprint ed., Freeport, N.Y.: Books for Libraries Press, 1968.

_____. An Hour with American Music. Philadelphia: Lippincott, 1929.

Salzman, Eric. Twentieth Century Music: An Introduction, 2nd ed. Englewood Cliffs, N.J.: Prentice-Hall, 1974.

Saminsky, Lazare. Living Music of the Americas. New York: Jowell, Soskin and Crown Publishers, 1949.

Sandburg, Carl. The American Songbag. New York: Harcourt Brace Jovanovich, 1927.

Seeger, Charles. [Tradition and Experiment in Twentieth Century Music], typescript. Washington, D.C.: Library of Congress, Music Division, Seeger Collection, 1930. (Unpublished)

―――. "Folk Music as a Source of Social History," in The Cultural Approach to History. Edited by Carolyn F. Ware (for the American Historical Association). New York: Columbia University Press, 1940, pp. 316-323.

―――. Studies in Musicology, 1935-1975. Berkeley: University of California Press, 1977.

Slonimsky, Nicolas. Music Since 1900. New York: W. W. Norton, 1938; reprint ed., New York: Charles Scribner's Sons, 1971.

Smith, Cecil. The World of Music. Philadelphia, Lippincott, 1952; reprint ed., Westport, Conn.: Greenwood Press, 1973.

Sundermann, Lloyd F. Historical Foundations of Music Education in the United States: Metuchen, N.J.: Scarecrow Press, 1971.

Terkel, Studs. Hard Times: An Oral History of the Great Depression. New York: Simon and Schuster, Washington Square Press, 1978.

Thomson, Virgil. American Music Since 1910. New York: Holt, Rinehart, Winston, 1971.

Weidig, Adolf. Harmonic Material and Its Uses: A Treatise for Teachers, Students and Music Lovers. Chicago: Clayton F. Summy, 1924.

Wilgus, D. K. Anglo-American Folk Song Scholarship Since 1898. New Brunswick, N.J.: Rutgers University Press, 1959.

Yasser, Joseph. A Theory of Evolving Tonality. New York: American Library of Musicology, 1932.

Zuck, Barbara. A History of Musical Americanism. Ann Arbor, Mich.: UMI Research Press, 1980.

PERIODICALS

"American Songs for American Children." Music Educator's Journal, May-June 1942, p. 29.

"American Youth to Have Its Fling in League Concert." Musical America, XLV/17 (February 12, 1927), p. 27.

Bibliography

Brown, Rollo Walter. "Mrs. MacDowell and Her Colony." The Atlantic Monthly, July 1949, n.p.

Chenneviere, Rudhyar D. "The Two Trends of Modern Music in Stravinsky's Works." The Musical Quarterly, V/1 (January 1919), pp. 169-174.

_____. "The Rise of the Musical Proletariat." The Musical Quarterly, V1/4 (October 1920), pp. 500-509.

Commanday, Robert. "Women Composers: A Place to Stand." High Fidelity-Musical America, January 1975, MA pp. 23, 39.

Copp, Laura Remick. "Whither the Trend of Modern Music?" An Interview with Darius Milhaud. The Etude, April 1928, p. 277.

Cowell, Henry. "Charles Louis Seeger, Jr." The Fortnightly, I/10 (January 15, 1932), pp. 5-7.

Cowell, Sidney Robertson. "Ruth Crawford Seeger, 1901-1953." International Folk Music Journal, VII (1955), pp. 55-56.

Dunaway, David King. "Unsung Songs of Protest: The Composers' Collective of New York." New York Folklore Quarterly, January 19, 1979.

_____. "Charles Seeger and Carl Sands: The Composers' Collective Years." Ethnomusicology, May 1980, pp. 159-168.

Gilbert, Steven E. "The Ultra-Modern Idiom: A Survey of New Music." Perspectives of New Music, 12:1/2 (1973-74), pp. 282-314.

Green, Archie. "Thomas Hart Benton's Folk Musicians." John Edwards Memorial Foundation Quarterly, 12 (Summer 1976), pp. 74-90.

Hull, A. Eaglefield. "Will Quarter-Tones Come?" The Musical Digest, February 1928, p. 20.

Jepson, Barbara. "Ruth Crawford Seeger: A Study in Mixed Accents." Feminist Art Journal, Spring 1977, pp. 13-16, 50.

Kerr, Harrison, "Creative Music and the New School." Trend, III/2 (March-April 1934), pp. 88-89.

Mandel, Alan and Nancy. "Composers to Re-emphasize." Clavier, XIV/4 (April 1975), pp. 14-17.

Montgomery, Merle. "We're on the Air! It's Time to Tune In!" Music Clubs Magazine, LI/5 (Summer 1972), p. 5, 12, 14.

Music Educators Journal. Obituary of Ruth Crawford Seeger. January 1954, p. 54.

Musical America. Obituary of Ruth Crawford Seeger. 73 (December 15, 1953), p. 20.

Musical Courier. Obituary of Ruth Crawford Seeger. 148 (December 15, 1953), p. 30.

New York Times. Obituary of Ruth Crawford Seeger. November 20, 1953, p. 23.

Pan Pipes of Sigma Alpha Iota. Obituary of Ruth Crawford Seeger. 46 (January 1954), p. 59.

Perle, George. "Atonality and the Twelve-tone System in the United States." The Score, July 1960, p. 51ff.

Pettis, Ashley. "The WPA and the American Composer." The Musical Quarterly, XXVI/1 (January, 1940, pp. 101-112.

Pool, Jeannie. "America's Women Composers." The Music Educators Journal, 65:5 (January 1979), pp. 28-41.

Reuss, Richard A. "Folk Music and Social Conscience: The Musical Odyssey of Charles Seeger." Western Folklore, 38:4 (1979), pp. 221-228.

Rev Mus Chilena (Santiago de Chile). Obituary of Ruth Crawford Seeger. 9 (April 1954), p. 47.

Rosen, J., and Rubin-Rabson, G. "Why Haven't Women Become Great Composers?" High Fidelity-Musical America, February 1973, MA pp. 47-50.

Salzman, Eric. "Modern Music in Retrospect." Perspectives of New Music, II/2 (Spring-Summer 1964), pp. 14-20.

_____. "The Tradition of the New in American Music, 1900-1950." Current Musicology, 7 (1968), pp. 10-11.

Seashore, Carl. "Why No Great Women Composers?" Music Educators Journal, January 1979, pp. 42-44-72. (Reprint of a March 1940 article.)

Seeger, Charles. "On Style and Manner in Modern Composition." The Musical Quarterly, IX/3 (July 1923), pp. 423-431.

_____. "On the Principles of Musicology." The Musical Quarterly, X/2 (April 1924), pp. 244-250.

_____. "On Dissonant Counterpoint." Modern Music, VII (June-July 1930), pp. 25-31.

_____. "On Proletarian Music." Modern Music, XI/3 (March-April 1934), pp. 121-127.

_____. [Carl Sands]. "Proletarian Music Is a Historic Necessity." Daily Worker, March 6, 1934, p. 5.

_____. "Grass Roots for American Composers." Modern Music, XVI/3 (March-April 1939), pp. 143-49.

_____. "Contrapuntal Style in the Three-Voice Shape-Note Hymns." The Musical Quarterly, XXVI/4 (October 1940), pp. 483-493.

_____. "Professionalism and Amateurism in the Study of Folk Music." Journal of American Folklore, LXII (1949), pp. 107-113.

_____. "Music and Class Structure in the United States." The American Quarterly, IX/3 (Fall 1957), pp. 281-294.

Spivacke, Harold. "The Archive of American Folk Song." Music Educators Journal, September-October 1942, pp. 29-30.

Upton, William Treat. "Aspects of the Modern Art-Song." The Musical Quarterly, XXIV/1 (January 1938), pp. 11-30.

Waite, Esther. "Are Men Better Musicians Than Women?" Musical Digest, January 1928, pp. 26, 54, 61.

Washington Post. Obituary of Ruth Crawford Seeger. November 20, 1953, p. 32.

Weiss, Adolph. "The Lyceum of Schoenberg." Modern Music, IX/3 (March-April 1932), pp. 99-107.

UNPUBLISHED DISSERTATIONS

Canon, Cornelius B. The Federal Music Project of the Works Progress Administration: Music in a Democracy. Ann Arbor, Mich.: University Microfilms, 1963. (Ph.D. Dissertation, University of Minnesota)

Gaume, M. M. Ruth Crawford Seeger: Her Life and Works. Ann Arbor, Mich.: University Microfilms, 1973. (Ph.D. Dissertation, Indiana University)

Reuss, Richard A. American Folklore and Left-Wing Politics: 1927-1957. Ann Arbor, Mich.: University Microfilms, 1971. (Ph.D. Dissertation, Indiana University)

LINER NOTES

American Folk Songs. Folkways Records, Album FA 2005, 1957. Notes by Charles Seeger.

American Folk Songs for Children. Rounder Records 8001/8002/8003, 1977. Notes by Peggy and Michael Seeger.

American Songs During the Great Depression. New World Records 270, 1977. Extended essay and notes by Charles Hamm.

Courting and Complaining Songs. Signet Records FL 5401, c. 1952. Notes not signed.

Cowell, H., Quartet Romantic; Riegger, W., Wind Quintet; Becker, John, The Abongo; Crawford, Ruth, Three Songs. New World Records, NW 285, 1978. Notes by Alfred Frankenstein.

Saturday Night at the Benton's. Decca A-311, 1942. Notes by Tom Benton.

ORAL HISTORY

Seeger, Charles. Reminiscences of an American Musicologist. Interviewed by Adelaide G. Tusler and Ann Briegleb. Oral history program, University of California, Los Angeles, 1966, 1970, 1971.

NEWSPAPERS

Brooklyn Daily Eagle

Chicago Journal

Chicago Sunday Tribune

Daily News (New York)

Morgen Post (Berlin)

New York City Post

New York Herald-Tribune

New York Times

Philadelphia Ledger

Washington Post

INDEX

Achron, Joseph 198,235n1
Adventures in a Perambulator (Carpenter, John A.) 139
Akademie der Kunste 78
All Around the Kitchen (folk song) 218
Alt Wien (Castelnuovo-Tedesco, M.) 143
American Ballads and Folk Songs (Lomax, John A. and Alan) 101, 175, 207
American Conservatory of Music vx, 33, 34-35, 48, 131; faculty 20
American Library of Musicology 102
American Life (Weiss, A.) 195
American Society for Comparative Musicology 102
American Songbag (Sandburg, Carl) 43, 173-174, 175, 178
Ameriques (Varèse, E.) 51
Antheil, George xvi 51
Anthology of Pennsylvania Folklore (Korson, George) 186
Ara, Ugo 68, 227n18
Arcana (Varèse, E.) 51
Archive of American Folk Song 176
Archive of American Folklore 214
Archive of Folk Culture 176
Arma, Paul (pseud.) see Weisshaus, Imre
art music 114-115, 121, 127, 192; and folk music 186-188
atonality, Haba on 84
Aunt Mollie see Jackson, Aunt Mollie

Bach, J. S. 60, 198; and jazz 109
Bachaus, Wilhelm 20
Barth, Hans 67
Bartók, Béla 19, 50, 75, 77; art music and folk music 84; and Ruth Crawford 81-82; at Blanche Walton's 62
Bauer, Harold 16, 67
Bauer, Marion xvi, 20, 61, 67, 69, 80, 114, 191, 196; in Europe 91; at MacDowell Colony 59-60
Beck, Martha see Carragan, Martha Beck
Becker, John 192, 207
Beethoven, Ludwig van 65, 134, 196, 220

Benton, Tom, and American folk music 99; friendship with the
    Seegers 100-101
Berckman, Evelyn 50
Berg, Alban 75, 80; and Ruth Crawford 82-83, 84; Wozzeck 80,
    83
Berlin 74, 76-79, 86
Bhagavad Gita 46, 135
Blaisdell, Frances 155
Blitzstein, Marc 50
Boggs, Doc 99
Boggs, Edna Garrido (de) 184
Bois, Jules 58
Botkin, Ben A. 186, 187
Boulanger, Nadia 194; and Ruth Crawford 87-88
Brahms, Johannes 65
Brooklyn Daily Eagle 160
Bruch, Max 20
Buchman, Carl 58, 195, 235n1
Buchmanism 206
Budapest 81-82, 84
Buhlig, Richard 51, 55, 61, 63, 138, 226n50
Burrows, Alice Lee: identified 226n44; letters to 144, 191, 227n2
    and Ruth 48, 55, 59, 132
Busoni, Ferruccio 78

CBS "School of the Air" 115, 181, 213
Carpenter, John Alden 19, 139
Carragan, Martha Beck 48, 61
Carreño, Teresa 196, 235n1
Carrillo, Juan 67, 68
Casella, Alfredo 19
Castelnuovo-Tedesco, Mario 50; Alt Wien 143
Chain, Ernest 79
Chaliapin, Feodor 20
Chanler, Theodore 50
Chaplin, Charlie 195, 196
Chavez, Carlos 74-75
Chester Publishing Company 76
Chiapusso, Jan 22
Chicago xv, 16-17, 23, 28, 32, 36, 45-46, 52, 54, 55, 61-62; concert life in the 1920s 19-20; and "new music" 50; see also
    University of Chicago
Chicago Civic Association Orchestra 132, 224n34
Chicago Daily Tribune 86
Chicago Symphony Orchestra 19, 21, 22, 131
Choephores, Les (Milhaud, D.) 165
Chopin, Frédéric 198
Christian Science Monitor 66
Cindy (folk song) 177
Cliff Dwellers Club 144

Index

Coal Dust on the Fiddle (Korson, George) 186
Coal Miner's Child (folk song) 180
Collett, Valborg 15, 16, 31
Columbia Symphony Orchestra 181
Columbia University 212
Communism, Communist xv, xvi, 79, 97, 206
Composers' Collective, and folk music 174; and the Seegers 97-98, 102, 106, 108, 125, 168
Composers' Forum-Laboratory 115, 192, 201-205
Coolidge, Mrs. Sprague 67
Copland, Aaron xvi, 50, 63, 84, 90, 98; and American music 51; on Stravinsky 198
Copland-Sessions Concerts 20, 51, 138
Cotten, Libba 123
Cowell, Henry xvi, 20, 62, 66, 79, 102, 103, 136, 198; in Chicago 36; and Composers' Collective 97; and Ruth Crawford 41-42, 56, 68; and New Music 42; New Musical Resources 42; and Charles Seeger 63, 227n10
Cowell, Sidney 114, 124
Crawford, Carl (Ruth Crawford's brother) xv, 91, 116; in Chicago 49; and family records 223n1; relationship with Ruth 22-23
Crawford, Clara Alletta Graves (Ruth Crawford's mother) 5, 6, 8, 23, 27, 29, 55, 211; in Chicago 32-34; illness and death 49; personality 30
Crawford, Clark (Ruth Crawford's father) 4, 5, 6, 49; illness and death 8
Crawford, Eliza Porter (Ruth Crawford's grandmother) 4
Crawford, Ruth see Seeger, Ruth Crawford
Crawford, Thomas (Ruth Crawford's grandfather) 4
"Creator" (poem) (Crawford, Ruth) 190, 194
Curwen Publishing Company 76

Dadaism 206
Dahlberg, Edward 58
Dallapiccola, Luigi 165
Danville Girl (folk song) 99
Darrow, Clarence 46
Debussy, Claude 19, 83, 137
Depression see Great Depression
Die Mutter see Mutter, Die
d'Indy, Vincent see Indy, Vincent d'
Dio 209, 210, 235n3
dissonant counterpoint 63, 78, 99, 149-150, 152, 153, 227n14
dissonant rhythm 150, 153
Division of Music and Visual Arts, Pan American Union 108, 119
Dohnányi, Ernst von 82
Downes, Olin 51

Eckermann, Johann Peter 46

Eisler, Hanns 97, 115
Elmhurst College 35, 43, 47
Emrich, Duncan 186, 214
Encyclopaedia of Social Sciences 102, 230n37
Eschig Publishing Company 86
Essig, Miss 202
ethnomusicology 81, 102, 108
European sojourn 76, 88, 91; Berlin 76-79; Budapest 81-82, 84; Munich 83-84; Paris 84-88; Vienna 79-80, 82-83, 84

Farm Security Administration 186
Fascism 206
Federal Music Project of the WPA 108, 115
Feinberg, Samuel 79, 134
Ffrench, Florence 20
Fine, Vivian 47-48, 61, 144, 225n13, 226n40; Four Pieces for Violin and Oboe 94
Flaubert, Gustave 46
Fletcher, Mary Unity see Graves, Mary Unity Fletcher
Flonzaley String Quartet 20
Flop-eared Mule (folk song) 180
Flos Campi (Vaughan Williams, Ralph) 165
folk music see Seeger, Ruth Crawford, folk music; see also Bartók, Béla; Benton, Tom; Botkin, Ben A.; Emrich, D.; Jackson, G. P.; Korson, George; Lomax, John A. and Alan; Sandburg, Carl; Seeger, Charles; Seeger, Peggy
Folk Song Archive see Archive of American Folk Song
Folk Song U.S.A. (Lomax, John A. and Alan) 184, 214, 234n11
Folklore Infantil de Santo Domingo (Boggs, Edna Garrido de) 184
Foss, Hubert 80
Foster, Bertha 15, 16, 17
Four Indiscretions (Gruenberg, L.) 143
Four Pieces for Violin and Oboe (Fine, Vivian) 94
Four Preludes (Weiss, A.) 138
Foxhall Nursery School 112
fractional tones 67-68
France, Anatole 46
Frankenstein, Alfred 42-43, 132, 173

Galli-Cursi, Amelita 20
Galsworthy, John 46
Go Down, Moses (folk song) 185, 235n17
Godowsky, Leopold 16, 20, 22
Goethe, Johann Wolfgang 46
Goodbye Old Paint (folk song) 218
Goossens, Eugene 19, 50
Gradova, Gitta 38, 39, 137, 225n11
Graham, Martha 66, 90
Grainger, Percy 15, 20

Graves, Clara Alletta see Crawford, Clara Alletta Graves
Graves, Mary Unity Fletcher (Ruth Crawford's grandmother) 4, 5
Graves, William Plummer (Ruth Crawford's grandfather) 4
Great Depression 95-96, 98, 100, 101
Grimm Brothers 139
Grossman, George 165
Gruenberg, Louis 50, 67, 195; Four Indiscretions 143
Guggenheim Foundation fellowship 15, 42, 46, 71, 72; and Ruth Crawford 73-74, 85, 89, 91, 181; and Rudhyar 41; and Sandburg 45
Gutman, Hans 78

H. K. (Harrison Kerr?) 165
Haba, Alois 83-84; Die Mutter 83
Hager, Mina 61
Hairston, Mamie (Seegers' domestic help) 212
Hanson, Howard 200
Harmonic Material and Its Uses (Weidig, Adolf) 132
Hastings, Nellie 17, 91
Hattstaedt, John 55
Haubiel, Charles 58
Hauer, Josef Matthias 75, 80
Haydn, Joseph 220
Hecht, Ben 46
Heifetz, Jascha 20
Hertzka, Emil 79
Herz, Djane Lavoie 46, 61, 73, 74, 94; and Clara Crawford 49; and Ruth Crawford 36, 38-39, 55, 91; and Vivian Fine 47; musicales 36; personality 38; and Scriabin 35, 133-134
Herz, Siegfried 19, 35-36, 38, 46
Herz, Tristan 38
Hill, Edward Burlingame 139
Hindemith, Paul 38, 43, 50, 78; Let's Build a Town 139
Hirsh, Albert 225n12
Hoffman, Josef 15, 20
Honegger, Arthur 19, 50, 75, 86-87; Judith 86
Howe, Mary 67
Huberman, Bronislaw 22
Huchet, Miss 87-88
Huffaker, Kenneth 10
Hush, Little Baby (folk song) 216, 218
Hutcheson, Ernest 67
Hyperprism (Varèse, E.) 51

ISCM (International Society for Contemporary Music): in Amsterdam 157, 213; in Berlin 77; in Chicago 20, 50; in Liege 76, 199; in New York 68, 194
improvisation 109, 219
incomplete projects (Seeger, Ruth Crawford) 116, 179, 184, 186, 244(1)

Indy, Vincent d' 19
Institute of Musical Art (New York City) 56, 98, 149
Integrales (Varèse, E.) 51
International Folk Music Journal 124
International Gesellschaft für Neue Musik 200
Ives, Charles 63, 84, 194, 195

Jackson, Aunt Mollie 97
Jackson, George Pullen 99-100, 175
Jacksonville, Florida, Crawford family in 6, 8, 17, 18, 23, 131; musical activities in 15
Jacobi, Frederick 157
James, William 46
jazz xv, 51, 109-110
Jim Along Josie (folk song) 218
John Henry (folk song) 184, 185
Josten, Werner 195, 235n1
Judith (Honegger, A.) 86
Judson, Arthur 19, 36
Juilliard School of Music 34
Juilliard Student Club 165
Jungle (Josten, W.) 195

Kadosa, Paul 81
Kafavian, Ida 144
Karlan, Fred (pseud. for Ruth Crawford) see Seeger, Ruth Crawford, art music
Kelen, Hugo 82
Kling, Harry 76
Kober, Georgia 36
Kodály, Zoltán 81, 82
Koechlin, Charles 87
Korson, George 186
Kósa, György 82
Krazy Kat (Carpenter, John Alden) 139
Krenek, Ernest 50
Kreymbourg, Alfred 67

Lajtha, Lázló 81
Landowska, Wanda 19
Lao-tsu 135, 139
Last of Callahan (folk song) 181
League of Composers 20, 50, 62, 144
Le Sacre du Printemps see Sacre du Printemps, Le
Les Choephores see Choephores, Les
"Les Six" 86
Let's Build a Town (Hindemith, P.) 139
Levy, Heniot 20, 21, 27, 28

Index

Lhevinne, Josef 20
Library of Congress 106, 116, 144, 186, 214
L'Oiseau de Feu see Oiseau de Feu, L'
Lomax, Alan 176, 177-178, 181
Lomax, John 176, 178
Lomax, John A. and Alan 175, 179; American Ballads and Folk Songs 101, 175, 207; folk music collectors 176; Folk Song U.S.A. 184, 214, 234n11; Our Singing Country 119, 177-180, 192, 207, 214, 234n11; and Ruth Crawford Seeger 177-180
Lonesome Road (folk song) 174
Lopatnikof, Nicolai 78
Love Lyric (poem) (Crawford, Ruth) 190, 193

MacDowell, Edward 57, 196
MacDowell, Mrs. Edward 15, 58, 61, 196
MacDowell Colony 55-56, 57-61, 69, 125, 148, 190
Macmillan Publishing Company 101
McPhee, Colin 66
Maeterlinck, Maurice 46
Mary Wore Her Red Dress (folk song) 218
Malipiero, Gian Francesco 83; Torneo Notturno 83
Mare, Jeanne de 61, 195, 235n1
Martinot, Maurice 87
Metzger-Latterman, Frau Ottilie 158
Milhaud, Darius 43, 50, 75, 87; Les Choephores 165; Sixth String Quartet 143
"modern music" 63-64
Moe, Henry Allen 41, 190, 198
Molnár, Antal 81
Monteverdi, Claudio 83
Morgen Post (Berlin) 156
Mozart, W. A. 220
Munich 83, 84
Music in American Life (music selected by Ruth Crawford Seeger for radio broadcasts) 186, 214
Music Teachers' National Association Convention 114
Musical America 159
Musical Courier 226n51, 229n1
Musical Leader 15, 20, 61
Musicological Congress (New York) 207
musicology 101-102, 108, 126, 197
Mutter, Die (Haba, Alois) 83
Mysterium (Scriabin, A.) 135

National Association for American Composers and Conductors 115
National Woodwind Quintet 115
neo-classicism 135, 198
New Music 42, 87-88, 115, 165, 192, 201
New Music Orchestra Series 92

New Music Quarterly Recordings 42, 165
New Music Quartet 166
New Music Society 20, 42, 199, 201
New Musical Resources (Cowell, H.) 42
New School for Social Research 68, 92, 98-99, 100, 102, 165, 175, 200, 230n37
New World String Quartet 66, 99
New York City 16, 17, 38, 41, 48, 55, 56, 58, 72; Ruth Crawford moves to 61-63; musical activities 67-68
New York City Post 160
New York Jottings (diary) 191, 194-198
New York Musicological Society 102
New York Times 51
Ney, Elly 22
Nietzsche (class) 46
Nono, Luigi 165
Novembergruppe 77, 200
nursery school 111-114, 183, 192, 214

Octandre (Varèse, E.) 51
Oedipus Rex (Stravinsky) 198
Offrandes (Varèse, E.) 51
Oiseau de Feu, L' (Stravinsky) 38
Old Joe Clarke (folk song) 218
Opus 11, Drei Klavierstücke (Schoenberg) 65
Opus 19, Sechs kleine Klavierstücke (Schoenberg) 65
Opus 25, Suite for Piano (Schoenberg) 65, 82
Oracle, The 13, 190
Otto, Max 46
Our Singing Country (Lomax, John A. and Alan) 119, 177-180, 192, 207, 214, 234n11, 244(1); Ruth Crawford Seeger's unpublished introduction 179, 244(1)
Oxford Press 80

Paderewski, Ignace Jan 15
Palmer, John 20, 22, 23, 131
Pan American Association of Composers 67, 84, 165, 200; and Cowell 42; premiere of Ruth Crawford's String Quartet 99
Pan American Ensemble 66, 144
Pan American Union 108, 119
Paris 74, 84-88
Pauline (folk song) 180
Pavlova, Anna 20
Pazmor, Radiana 66, 67, 98, 114, 197
Penderecki, Krzysztof 165
Peter and the Wolf (Prokofiev) 139
Petit, Raymond 76
Pettis, Ashley 61, 115
Philadelphia Ledger 168

Phoebe (folk song) 181
Picasso 195
Pictorial Review 46
Pierre Degeyter Club 97
Plato 46
Portals (Ruggles, Carl) 88
Porter, Eliza see Crawford, Eliza Porter
Porter, Ruth 207, 235n2; see also Seeger, Ruth Crawford
Potomac School 112
Poulenc, Francis 50
Pre-School Children and American Folk Songs 193, 216-220, 244(4)
Pretty Polly (folk song) 99
Prink, Miss 119, 192, 208-212
Pro Arte 194, 235n1
Pro Musica Society 20, 41, 50, 62
Prokofiev, Serge 19, 50, 75; Peter and the Wolf 139
Prunières, Henri 87

quarter-tone music 67, 83-84
Quebec (City) 71, 85
Quintet for Winds, Op. 26 (Schoenberg) 65

Rachmaninoff, Serge 20
Ravel, Maurice 19, 50, 75, 87
Regina Watkins Hall 58
Resettlement Administration 104, 106, 108, 214
Respighi, Ottorino 50
Reynolds, Gerald 159, 199, 200; letter from Ruth Crawford 161-162
Rheinberger, Josef 20
Riegger, Wallingford xvi, 63, 68, 74, 98, 114
Riemann, Hugo 20
Rieti, Vittorio 50
Roberts, Stella 34
Robyn, Louise 20; and Ruth Crawford 22, 25, 28-29, 32, 55
Roosevelt, Eleanor 108
Rosenfeld, Paul 41, 67
Roussel, Albert 87
Rubenstein, Artur 20
Rubenstein, Beryl 15
Rudhyar 19, 38, 50, 61, 84; and Ruth Crawford 41, 49, 135-137; and Madame Herz 40
Rufer, Josef 78-79
Ruggles, Carl xvi, 62, 68, 71, 74, 76, 88, 100, 195; Portals 88
Ruggles, Charlotte 71
Russia, Ruth Crawford's proposed trip to 79

Sacre du Printemps, Le (Stravinsky) 38

Salzedo, Carlos 67, 195
Salzman, Eric xvii, 96
Saminsky, Lazare 67
Sandburg, Carl 46; and <u>American Songbag</u> 43, 173, 178; and Ruth Crawford 43-45, 116, 173-174, 183-184, 192-193; poems of 58, 60, 148, 157, 202
Sandburg, Margaret 215
Sands, Carl (pseud.) <u>see</u> Seeger, Charles Louis
Satie, Eric 87
<u>Saturday's Child</u> (Whithorne, Emerson) 195
Schillinger, Joseph 102
Schmitz, E. Robert 50
Schmolke, Frau 159
Schoenberg, Arnold 19, 36, 75, 80, 83, 97; and Ruth Crawford 38, 65, 78, 82, 136, 139, 145-148; Opp. 11 and 19 65; Quintet for Winds, Op. 26 65; Suite for Piano, Op. 25 65, 82
Schnabel, Artur 20, 35
School of Musical Art, Jacksonville, Florida 15, 16, 17, 131
"School of the Air" (CBS) 115
Schubert, Franz 215
Schumann, Robert 46
Schwerke, Irving 86
Scriabin, Alexander 78, 195; and Ruth Crawford 41, 63, 64, 133-135, 137, 139, 170; and Djane Lavoie Herz 35; and Rudhyar 40
Seeger, Barbara 109, 113, 208-211, 214
Seeger, Charles Louis xv, 16, 45, 56, 76, 78; Andante (String Quartet) 166; and Tom Benton 100-101; Carl Sands and Composers' Collective 97; concerts for underprivileged 95; and Cowell 227n10; description 68; and Diaphonic Suite No. 1 155; and dissonant counterpoint 227n14, 228n25; and family 69, 209-212; Federal Music Project, WPA 108; and folk music 174-178, 181, 184-185, 186; influence on Ruth and influence of Ruth 125-127; at Institute of Musical Art 56, 98, 149; marriage to Ruth Crawford 92, 229n5; at New School for Social Research 98; Pan-American Union 108; in Paris 85-86; personal relationship with Ruth Crawford 71-72, 75, 96, 103, 109, 128, 191, 196, 197; professional relationship with Ruth Crawford 63-64, 73, 74, 134, 145, 150-152, 156, 165, 169, 201, 214; at Resettlement Administration 106-108; theories of dissonance treatment 149-150
_____, works: <u>John Hardy</u> 213; <u>Not If, But When</u> 98; <u>Queen's Masque</u> 151; <u>Tradition and Experiment in Twentieth Century Music</u> 71, 86, 96, 127, 152, 227n22, 233n24
Seeger, Charles, Jr. 69, 71
Seeger, Constance Edson 69, 88, 92
Seeger, John 69, 71
Seeger, Margaret <u>see</u> Seeger, Peggy
Seeger, Michael 94, 102, 123, 124, 169, 209-211, 214
Seeger, Peggy 102, 123, 124, 169, 208-210, 214; and folk music 187-188; mother's piano teaching 110
Seeger, Penelope 109, 169, 214
Seeger, Peter 69, 71

Index

Seeger, Ruth Crawford: diaries 3, 13, 46, 57, 58, 112, 190; early works 133; and feminism 54, 58, 79-80, 119-120, 125; health problems 13, 25, 52, 123-124, 131; incomplete projects 116, 179, 184, 186, 244(1); influence on Charles and influence of Charles 125-127; at MacDowell Colony 55-61; marriage 92; self-analysis 10, 19, 28, 29, 31, 54-55
─────, art music: Adventures of Tom Thumb 51, 52, 139; Andante see String Quartet; Chant, 1930 see Chant No. 2 below; Chinaman, Laundryman 98, 168, 169; Diaphonic Suites 65, 76, 86, 153, 157, 233n26; Diaphonic Suite No. 1 114, 153-154, 155, 233n26; Diaphonic Suite No. 2 153; Diaphonic Suite No. 3 153; Diaphonic Suite No. 4 77, 86, 94, 153, 155, 156; Elf Dance 16, 23; Five Preludes for Piano see Piano Preludes below; Five Songs 66, 67; 148; (Home Thoughts 148; Joy 58, 59, 148, Loam 58, 148, 149, Sunsets 58, 148, White Moon 148); Four Preludes for Piano see Piano Preludes below; Kaleidoscopic Changes on an Original Theme, Ending with a Fugue 32, 133; Lolipop a Papa (Fred Karlan) 52; Piano Preludes 66, 82; Piano Preludes, Nos. 1-5 52, 115, 136; Piano Prelude No. 2 137; Piano Prelude No. 3 137; Piano Preludes Nos. 6-9 42, 52, 87, 137, 202; Piano Prelude No. 6 35; Piano Prelude No. 8 137, 139; Piano Prelude No. 9 135, 137, 138, 139; Piano Study in Mixed Accents 65, 115, 153, 156, 167, 202; Rissolty, Rossolty 115, 181-183, 213; Sacco, Vanzetti 98, 168, 169; Sonata for Violin and Piano 50, 52, 140-143, 144, 232n8; String Quartet 25, 60, 76, 82, 84, 86, 94, 115, 157, 165-167, 202, 204, premier performance of 99, and Varèse 116, 213, 214, Andante movement 166, 234n43; Suite for Five Wind Instruments and Piano 52, 65, 66, 73, 144, 145, 148, 153; Suite for Small Orchestra 52, 139, 140; Suite No. 2 for Strings and Piano 52, 66, 67, 73, 145-148, 232n19; Suite for Wind Quintet 115, 170, 171; Three Chants 76, 157 (Chant No. 1 159, Chant No. 2 76, 160, Chant No. 3 160, 161-162, 163-165); Three Songs 60, 61, 84, 92, 94 (Berlin and Amsterdam) 115, 153, 156, 157, 159, 168, 202, 204, 213 (In Tall Grass 84, 156, 157, 158, 159, 205, Prayers of Steel 92, 156, 159, 168, 205, Rat Riddles 65, 67, 84, 87, 153, 156, 158, 159, 160, 165, 205); To an Angel see Chant No. 2 above; To an Unkind God see Chant No. 1 above; Untitled popular song (Fred Karlan) 52; Variations 16; Violin and Piano Sonata see above; We Dance Together 52; When, Not If 98; Whirligig 16
─────, European sojourn: 76, 88, 91; Berlin 76-79; Budapest 81-82, 84; Munich 83-84; Paris 84-88; Vienna 79-80, 82-83, 84
─────, folk music: xvi, 124, 173-174, 213, 217, 218; accompaniments 174; activities 186; arrangements and transcriptions 177-180, 185, 186, 214; and art music 115, 121, 127, 170, 181, 186, 187, 188; and Bartók 84; and Composers' Collective 98; and the Lomaxes 175-178, 184-185; and nursery school 113, 183; and Carl Sandburg 43, 45, 174; and Charles Seeger 101, 102, 106, 108, 125, 214; treatise on 179, 214

_____, folk music collections: American Folk Songs for Children
43, 183, 184, 193, 214; American Folk Songs for Christmas 120,
183-184, 185; Animal Folk Songs for Children 92, 183-184; Let's
Build a Railroad 184; Nineteen American Folk Tunes 176, 177,
234n3
_____, Guggenheim Foundation fellowship: 15, 42, 46, 71, 72,
73-74, 85, 89, 91, 181; and Rudhyar 41; and Sandburg 45
_____, letters: to John Becker 192, 207-208; to Henry Allen
Moe 190, 198-201; to Mis Prink 192, 208-212; to Carl Sandburg
192-193, 215; to Edgard Varèse 170, 173, 189, 192, 212-215
_____, literary activities: 3, 13, 46, 69, 244; humorous writings
192, 205-207; poems 144, 190, 193, 194
_____, music study: American Conservatory 20-23, 27-35; with
Madame Herz 35-39; School of Musical Art 15-17, 131; with
Charles Seeger 63-65, 71
_____, teaching: Chicago 27, 28, 31, 35, 43, 47, 51; Jackson-
ville 16, 17, 223n13; Washington, D.C. 109-114, 121, 174, 176
Seeger Collection 223n1 (Chapter One)
Seeger Family Collection 224n20 (Chapter One)
Senart Publishing Company 86
Serenade in A (Stravinsky) 143
Sessions, Roger 63
shape notes 99
Shaw, George Bernard 46
Shenandoah (folk song) 186, 187
Shostac, Mrs. 25
Siegmeister, Elie 98
Sigma Alpha Iota 51, 226n51
Silver Spring, Maryland 104, 112
Sixth String Quartet (Milhaud, D.) 143
Slonimsky, Nicolas xvi, 84; letter to Ruth Crawford 158; letter
from Ruth Crawford Seeger 191
Smallens, Alexander 195, 196
Society for Contemporary Music (Philadelphia) 168
Sonata 1924 (Stravinsky) 198
Sowerby, Leo 19
Special Skills Division, Resettlement Administration 104, 214
Stock, Frederick 19, 144
Stokowsky, Leopold 195
Strauss, Richard 19, 20
Stravinsky, Igor 19, 43, 50, 75; Le Sacre du Printemps 38;
L'Oiseau de Feu 38; and neo-classicism 198; Oedipus Rex 198;
Serenade in A 143; Sonata 1924 198
Stuckenschmidt, Hans H. 78
Suite for Piano, Op. 25 (Schoenberg) 65, 82

Tao (Lao-tsu) 135, 139
Ten Thousand Miles Away from Home (folk song) 174
Theory of Evolving Tonality (Yasser, Joseph) 235n1
There Was a Man and He Was Mad (folk song) 218

Index   267

There Was an Old Soldier (folk song) 174
Theremin, Leon 66, 77
Thompson, Randall 50
Thomson, Virgil 63, 166
Thoreau, Henry 46, 54
Those Gambler's Blues (folk song) 174
Tinayre, Yves 76
Toccata (Vogel, W.) 78
Torneo Notturno (Malipiero, G. F.) 83
Toscanini, Arturo 67
transcription techniques 179-180
Traubel, Helen 114
Trautonium 77
Trautwein, Frederick 77
Treasury of Western Folklore (Botkin, Ben A.) 186-187
Treatise on Modern Composition and Manual of Dissonant Counterpoint 201; see also Seeger, Charles: Tradition and Experiment in Twentieth Century Music
Trend, J. B. 76
Trend (journal) 165
Tryon, Winthrop 66, 69
Tsiang, H. T. 168
Tugwell, Rex 108
twelve-tone music 65, 80

Universal Edition 79
University of Chicago 46

Valiant, Margaret 91, 94-95, 100, 101; and Resettlement Music Project 106-107
Varèse, Edgard xvi, 51, 62, 74, 136; at Herz musicales 36; in Paris 84-85; Ruth Crawford Seeger letter to 170, 173, 189, 192, 212-215; and twentieth-century music 116
Vaughan Williams, Ralph 19, 165
Vienna 79-80, 82-83, 84
Vogel, Wladimir 78

WPA, Federal Music Project 108, 115
Wagadu (Vogel, W.) 78
Wagenaar, Bernard 58, 194, 235n1
Walton, Mrs. Blanche 57, 102, 103, 144, 191; art patron 56, 62, 63; and Ruth Crawford 64, 66-67, 68, 69, 71, 197
Washington, D.C. 104, 175
Washington Post 124
Weidig, Adolf 48, 55, 65, 73, 131; at American Conservatory 20-21; compared with Charles Seeger 152, and Harmonic Material and Its Uses 132; as teacher of Ruth Crawford 22, 23, 29-35, 132, 133, 134

Weiss, Adolph xvi, 62, 132, 136, 138, 195; <u>American Life</u> 195; in Europe 84-85; Four Preludes 138; at Herz musicales 36; student of Schoenberg 36
Weisshaus, Imre 77, 84, 159
Wellesz, Egon 80
Wells, H. G. 46
Wertheim, Alma 194, 235n1
<u>White Spirituals in the Southern Uplands</u> (Jackson, G. P.) 99, 175
Whitehall Country School 112
Whithorne, Emerson 195, 235n1
Whitman, Walt 45, 46
"Why Don't They Eat Cake?" (humorous piece) (Seeger, Ruth Crawford) 192, 205-207
Wiener, Jean 78
Wilder, Thornton 58
Williams, Ralph Vaughan <u>see</u> Vaughan Williams, Ralph
Women's University Glee Club (New York City) 159, 160, 199
Workers' Music League 97
Workers' Music Olympiad 98
<u>Workers' Songbooks I and II</u> 97
<u>Wozzeck</u> (Berg, A.) 80, 83

Yasser, Joseph 102, 196, 197, 235n1; <u>Theory of Evolving Tonality</u> 235n1
Yost, Edna 69

Ziegler, Oscar 200, 235n1